(19)

THE
CIVIL
SERVANTS

THE
CIVIL
SERVANTS

An Inquiry into Britain's Ruling Class

Peter Kellner and Lord Crowther-Hunt

A Raven Book
MACDONALD GENERAL BOOKS
Macdonald and Jane's · London and Sydney

A Raven Book

This is a joint project of Macdonald General Books, Macdonald and Jane's Publishers Limited, and Futura Publications Limited

First published in Great Britain in 1980 by
Macdonald General Books, Paulton House,
8 Shepherdess Walk, London N1 7LW

ISBN 0 354 04487 7

Printed in Great Britain by
Richard Clay (The Chaucer Press) Ltd, Bungay, Suffolk

CONTENTS

PREFACE

THIS BOOK IS THE PRODUCT of first-hand experience and of journalistic inquiry. One of us (Lord Crowther-Hunt) served in the 1960s on the Fulton Committee of Inquiry into the Civil Service (the committee's membership is given in full in Appendix One); between 1974 and 1976 he worked in Whitehall, first as Constitutional Adviser to the Prime Minister (mainly on devolution), then as a Minister of State at the Department of Education and later in the Privy Council Office, maintaining throughout a special responsibility for devolution.

The other author (Peter Kellner) is a journalist on the *Sunday Times*, where a vigorous scepticism towards all bureaucrats and most politicians is encouraged by its editor, Harold Evans.

Although the two authors worked in tandem throughout, we felt that it would be more honest to indicate to the reader the principal author of each chapter, rather than strive for a somewhat artificial uniformity. Lord Crowther-Hunt's chapters (2, 3, 9) are based largely on events in which he was directly involved, whereas Peter Kellner's (1, 4, 5, 6, 7, 8, 10, 11, 12) are the result of an outsider's explorations.

Many present and past civil servants gave their time generously to help us prepare this book, even when they must have suspected that our conclusions were likely to differ from their views. Even though most, for obvious reasons, insisted on anonymity in our interviews, they were usually more helpful than they probably realised and – sometimes – possibly intended. We do, however, owe two particular debts of gratitude. One is to Mike Finn of the Civil Service Department

vii

Press Office who – though he won't thank us for saying this – acted at times like an unpaid researcher, guiding us through the maze of Civil Service structures and towards some of the more arcane facts and figures that the Civil Service is capable of providing.

The other debt of gratitude is to Clarence Tuck and his staff at the Civil Service Selection Board. The opportunity to observe at first hand the selection process for future administrators is a chance to enter a necessarily intimate world that outsiders cannot reasonably be expected to invade too often.

It goes without saying that the civil servants, and others, we spoke to bear no responsibility for any errors of fact in this book.

Extracts and statistics from official publications are reproduced with the permission of the Controller of Her Majesty's Stationery Office. We should also like to thank Messrs Hamish Hamilton and Jonathan Cape for permission to quote from Richard Crossman's *The Diaries of a Cabinet Minister*.

Finally, the stimulus and understanding of our families was not only welcome but absolutely invaluable. We hope we did not take them too much for granted.

Peter Kellner and Norman Crowther-Hunt
London and Oxford, January 1980

INTRODUCTION

THERE IS A SPECIAL SENSE in which the Civil Service reflects the British constitution. Neither is clearly defined in writing: both evolve and change with mood and circumstance. The only legal definitions of 'civil servant' appear in Superannuation Acts; and even there the term is less than watertight. A civil servant 'means a person serving in an established capacity in the permanent Civil Service'.[1] So what is the Civil Service? 'In this Act "Civil Service" means the civil service of the State.'[2] So what is the State? It has no legal existence – for most normal purposes the legal equivalent of the everyday idea of the State is the Crown.

A Royal Commission fifty years ago suggested that civil servants should be defined as

> Servants of the Crown, other than holders of political or judicial offices, who are employed in a civil capacity and whose remuneration is paid wholly and directly out of moneys voted by Parliament.[3]

It sounds good but it does not work. Members of the royal household, for example, would have a greater claim to count as civil servants under this definition than (say) the staff of the Science Museum.

In 1977 a committee of MPs drew attention to the problem:

> The full difficulties of defining 'civil servant' are perhaps best realised by considering who in the working population is primarily paid for his employment directly or indirectly from the Exchequer.

That includes all local government employees and indeed in many countries, eg France, such employees – even including teachers – are regarded as civil servants, though they are not so regarded in Britain. Such a definition, if adopted in the UK, would add another 3 million people.[4]

Almost four million more people work for 'subsidiaries' of the State – nationalized industries, the National Health Service, and so on. They do not count as civil servants. Who says they do not? The Government says. In the mid-1960s there were one million officially certified civil servants. Today there are three-quarters of a million. What happened was that the General Post Office – in Victorian times the principal employer of civil servants – became a separately run corporation. One morning your local postman was a civil servant; the next morning he was not.

The statistical conjuring trick keeps happening. In 1974 18,000 'civil servants' were hived off from the Department of Employment to the Manpower Services Commission, and ceased to count as civil servants. Two years later the Commission regained its Civil Service status, and back trundled its staff into the figures.[5]

Looking at how the numbers of civil servants have changed through time is, then, a hazardous exercise. Even looking at individual departments has its pitfalls. In 1968 the staff of the National Economic Development Office were logged as a separate group of civil servants. In 1969 they counted as officials of the Department of Economic Affairs. In 1970 they counted as officials of the Cabinet Office. In 1971 they were on their own again. In 1972 they were deemed to be hived off and stopped counting as civil servants altogether.[6]

The MPs of the 1977 committee wanted an agreed definition of a civil servant to be drawn up with the Government. The Government declined. It regarded the position as perfectly acceptable:

The most important distinguishing characteristic is service on behalf of the Crown. The employees of bodies which do not in law have Crown status (eg local authorities; nationalized industries) are not civil servants. Political, judicial and other Crown office holders whose terms and conditions of service are separately provided for are distinguished from civil servants, as are the Armed Forces and the Royal Household. . . . It is the Home Civil Service, together with the Diplomatic Service, which the published Civil Service manpower count covers.[7]

Reduced to essentials, the Civil Service remains a concept governed by administrative convenience rather than by legal authority. To the ordinary citizen there may appear little difference between the civil servant in the local Social Security office who calculates his or her state benefits, and the non-civil servant behind the Post Office counter who pays them out. But to the Government the difference is considerable.

If civil servants cannot readily be defined, they can very easily be stereotyped. The standard images invoked by newspaper and television artists whenever civil servants are discussed are the bowler hat and the furled umbrella. The casual reader may receive the impression that three-quarters of a million uniformly dressed men swarm daily into central London to regulate our lives. The image, of course, is false even on its own terms: hardly any civil servants today wear bowler hats, and there is no empirical evidence that the use of umbrellas is any greater than among other commuters. Yet as a symbol of the Civil Service, the bowler and the brolly retain their potency. Flash them on a television screen a moment before the newsreader speaks, and the viewer knows instantly the subject about to come up. They are the symbols of *Them* – the people who wield power and who are different from *Us*.

It is well known that images cannot be dislodged by mere facts; nevertheless it is worth sketching in the reality that lurks behind the symbols.

There are 730,000 civil servants (April 1979 figures), according to the Government's present definition.[8]
– Of these 170,000 are not male Whitehall bureaucrats because they are industrial civil servants: blue-collar workers, mostly working for the Ministry of Defence on the upkeep of military establishments, or for the Department of the Environment on the maintenance of Government buildings. That leaves 560,000 non-industrial civil servants.

– Of these, 250,000 are not male Whitehall bureaucrats because they are women. Most women in the Civil Service have clerical or secretarial posts. That leaves 310,000 non-industrial male civil servants.

– Of these, 90,000 are not Whitehall bureaucrats because they are specialists: scientists, engineers, statisticians and so on. That leaves 220,000 non-specialist, non-industrial, male civil servants.

– Of these, 110,000 are not Whitehall bureaucrats because they perform particular tasks for the community: tax collectors, prison officers, local social security officers, customs officials etc. That leaves 110,000 male 'bureaucrats' – members óf the Administration Group of civil servants.

– Of these, 60,000 are not *Whitehall* bureaucrats because they work outside London, in the regional and local offices of Government departments. That leaves 50,000 London bureaucrats.

– Of these, 46,000 are 'support' staff in executive and clerical grades.

That leaves *just 4,000 'policy-makers'*: London-based Principals and above. (That includes 400 women. There are some policy-makers outside London, notably in the Scottish and Welsh Offices, but not many.) In terms of numbers a bowler and a brolly are infinitely less accurate symbols of Britain's present civil servants than a donkey jacket, a pair of jeans or a brassière.

When Sir Ian Bancroft was appointed Head of the Home Civil Service in December 1977, a leading article in *The Times* judged that he had made a 'poor start. His first act as Head of the Civil Service-elect was to refuse to talk to the newspapers.' The leading article argued that:

> The Civil Service needs somebody to speak in its defence. It is no good officials expecting their ministers to protect them. Many ministers share the popular prejudices against their servants, often superimposing a self-serving one of their own which imagines civil servants as engaged in a kind of continuous *coup d'état* against the manifesto pledges of elected governments . . . Sir Ian must therefore overcome his longstanding dislike of personal publicity

and do the job himself. If he does not publicly protect his people as often as he can, nobody will . . .

Sir Ian's profession is vital to the country's fortunes. It is a sheet anchor of the constitution and a great bulwark against change of the worst kind. It is currently undervalued on all sides. Sir Ian's first task should be to raise its self-esteem and the regard in which it is held by others. Above all, he must speak for Whitehall.[9]

The Times was to be disappointed. Bancroft continued to shy away from publicity. Occasionally he would meet journalists for off-the-record interviews, insisting that 'this is a notebooks away chat, so we can speak more freely'. Even then he would be scarcely more informative than in his – even rarer – on-the-record interviews. His instinctive technique is to invite the interviewer into a conspiracy of discreet evasion. He applies it not only to journalists. These are some of the ways he began answers to MPs when he gave evidence in 1976 to the 'English Committee' – the General Subcommittee of the House of Commons Expenditure Committee, meeting under the chairmanship of the Labour MP Michael English.

'May I answer that in rather general terms and then come to more particular issues about it?'[10]
'Obviously you would not want to draw me too much in this.'[11]
'May I come straight to your question in just a second?'[12]

One of the few points of substance Bancroft does willingly make is that the Civil Service is much maligned, and often unfairly so, as he told me* when I interviewed him in September 1978. After the last question Bancroft added a postscript:

When I agreed to this interview I didn't think, what's in it for me, but what's in it for the Civil Service. I am genuinely proud to be a civil servant, and I would like to see a greater mutual understanding with the public and with Parliament. I think we need to be more responsive and more open; but I think the public needs to be aware that there are 730,000 of us, including industrial civil servants, and most people work very hard, with very little waste.

*PK.

> We and our families get angry and hurt by some of the ill-informed criticism about brollies and bowler hats. People don't realise that nearly a half of non-industrial civil servants are women; a third are under 30; and four-fifths work outside London.

Otherwise, Bancroft has said little to stem the tide of criticism.

There are four broad types of criticism that the Civil Service has to contend with: first, that it seeks to usurp the political power of ministers and Parliament; second, that it has failed to respond to the need for internal reform; third, that civil servants live in a protected world of total job security and index-linked pensions, unlike the rest of the population; fourth, that civil servants waste public money. The substance of these criticisms is discussed elsewhere in this book. The point here is their impact on Whitehall – and Whitehall's response.

The first criticism – usurping political power – is the hardest for civil servants to reply to publicly. *The Times'* leading article unwittingly indicates why, for while it contemptuously dismisses the idea of Whitehall mounting a 'continuous *coup d'état*' against manifesto pledges, it also describes the Civil Service as 'a great bulwark against change of the worst kind'. The argument is pregnant with contradiction: one man's solemn manifesto pledge is another man's worst kind of change. If it is wrong to resist the first, you cannot logically be a bulwark against the second. Most senior civil servants take the prudent course and avoid public discussion of this issue until they retire.

The second criticism – resistance to reform – has increasingly involved civil servants in public debate. This is especially so since the days of the Fulton Committee; and the responses of a substantial number of senior officials to the details of reform (though seldom to the principles) are recorded in the evidence to the English Committee when it met to review the progress of reform. The arguments on both sides have begun to percolate through to the media – notably *The Times,* the *Guardian,* the *Economist* and the *Sunday Times* – but it would be something of an exaggeration to say they have seized the public imagination.

It is the third criticism – the protected lives of civil servants – that starts to excite visible criticism. Within the Civil Service Department, the date when the service was last forced onto the defensive – a posture it has since failed to break out of – is marked down as 14 September, 1975. That day the *Sunday Express* led its front page with a story headed 'Top Pensions Rock the £6 Policy'. At the time the Labour Government was embarking on the first stage of a rigid incomes policy, which was in detail devised by civil servants in the Treasury, and subsequently monitored by civil servants in the Department of Employment. The *Sunday Express* story began:

> A damaging threat to the Government's whole strategy for curbing wages has erupted with a revelation that former top civil servants – some of whom have switched to lucrative commercial jobs – are to get increases of more than £40 a week in their publicly financed pensions from next December.

The *Sunday Express* specifically cited the example of Lord Armstrong as one of those destined for a large pensions increase. The following July, the *Sunday Express*'s editor, John Junor, returned to the point in his weekly column. Again he cited Armstrong, due for a further £1500 pension rise in 1976:

> Isn't it almost beyond belief the way public servants have managed to get their greedy snouts into the public trough? Why should they, any more than the rest of us, be protected from rising prices? It was an Act of Parliament in 1971 which made their pensions inflation-proof. I say it is time for another Act – this time to make sure that they are treated in exactly the same way as the rest of us poor peasants who have to provide every penny of their pensions.[13]

A few months later Whitehall was forced further back into its bunker by the emergence of an improbable public hero in the form of Leslie Chapman, himself a retired civil servant. An article in the *Sunday Times* in December 1976 recounted Chapman's attempts – thwarted by other civil servants who defied the wishes of successive ministers – to save money in the maintenance of government buildings.[14] (For five years before his retirement in 1973 this had been Chapman's responsibility in Southern England.) Waste – like pensions – strikes a sensitive public nerve. Following the *Sunday Times* story, Chapman was interviewed by a score of newspapers, magazines, radio stations and television current affairs programmes; he wrote a best-selling book about his efforts to cut

15

waste;[15] two major television documentaries were made about him; and the House of Commons Public Accounts Committee was forced to re-open an inquiry into waste when a Granada TV researcher demonstrated that it had been given false information by Sir Robert Cox, the civil servant in charge of the Property Services Agency.

By 1978 it was scarcely surprising that some senior civil servants felt under siege. Added to the persistent public rumblings over pensions and waste came strictures from the English Committee on the Civil Service's excessive political influence and its inadequate progress over internal reform. Indeed, the Committee only narrowly defeated a proposal by the then Labour MP Brian Sedgemore – himself a former Principal in the Ministry of Housing and Local Government – to rewrite the opening chapter. Sedgemore wanted to accuse civil servants of 'frustrating democracy. They are arrogating to themselves power that properly belongs to the people and their representatives.' According to the Sedgemore draft:

> Civil servants at the Department of Industry have been culpable in frustrating the interventionist industrial policies of the current government. In this case political bias may have played a part. The result is that instead of an industrial strategy we have a series of industrial problems. The Department of Trade contains civil servants who are steeped in nineteenth-century Board of Trade attitudes, totally out of sympathy with any ideas of a positive trade policy, and gullible in the extreme when it comes to understanding and taking appropriate counter action over the way in which other countries take the United Kingdom for a ride over trading rules and practices . . . The Home Office, the graveyard of free thinking since the days of Lord Sidmouth early in the nineteenth century, is stuffed with reactionaries ruthlessly pursuing their own reactionary policies, which is not so bad when reactionary governments are in power but less good otherwise. So far as the EEC is concerned officials have on more than one occasion badly advised ministers and some Foreign Office officials interpret being a good European as being synonymous with selling out British interests. The Vichy mentality which undoubtedly exists in some parts of our Foreign Office establishment does not to the best of our knowledge and belief reflect the views of Her Majesty's ministers. And so we could go on.[16]

In the face of these assaults – whether ferocious like Junor and Sedgemore, or forensic, like much of the English Committee's final report – Bancroft's reticence has had its critics, from other civil servants as well as from journalists. Lacking a robust public defence from their chief, officials in the Civil Service Department have had to prepare an internal document, called 'The Quarry', which from its slightly rough appearance (it was originally run off on a duplicating machine) has something of the air of a Russian underground news-sheet. It is up-dated from time to time and circulated among senior civil servants as a handy guide for answering Civil Service critics. An issue distributed in August 1979 is printed in full as Appendix 2.

'The Quarry' is interesting at several levels. It is highly defensive in tone – on everything from index-linked pensions to the granting of honours to senior civil servants. (On honours, 'The Quarry' suggests that the awards are less a mark of observed service to the community – wherever it is to be found – than the product of a mathematical formula; civil servants' proportion of honours 'has deliberately been reduced from over thirty-five per cent in the late 1950s and early 1960s to about twenty per cent in the last few years.' Somewhere in some Whitehall files must be the records of civil servants debating the correct proportion of honours that civil servants should receive. They would make fascinating reading.)

By adopting a defensive stance, 'The Quarry' presents a number of virtues of civil servants – how some of them have 'thankless but necessary jobs'; that 'there is no equivalent in the Civil Service of "the company car" '; that 'the inflation-proofing (of pensions) is not unique to the Civil Service'; and so on. While these points counter some of the more extravagant blasts, like that of John Junor – and at the same time provide in economical form some basic information about the Civil Service, which is why we publish it in full – 'The Quarry' is careful to sidestep many of the more specific and fundamental criticisms made (for example) by the English Committee. It does not touch the arguments raging around Sir Ian Bancroft's in-tray on efficiency controls, the use of specialists, and the political influence of senior administrators. The central Fulton criticism of generalist mandarins is ignored, as it was in the CSD's memorandum to the English Committee.

Instead, recipients of 'The Quarry' are advised to emphasise 'what the Civil Service *is* and *does*.' Its points include:

> – not a mysterious mass of bureaucrats but real people doing real jobs because the country wants them done;
> – providing services to firms (export credit guarantees), to farmers (drainage engineers), above all to the public generally (social security benefits, finding new jobs for the unemployed);
> – thankless but necessary jobs (tax collectors; prison officers; driving test examiners; Customs Officers; Immigration Officers) . . .

It is, of course, all true. Not only is it all true: it is explicitly acknowledged by all serious critics. Fulton spoke of the Civil Service's 'unquestioned' integrity and impartiality: 'We believe that the country does not recognise enough how impressively conscientious many civil servants are in the personal service they give to the public.' The English Committee decided 'to put on record that we have a high opinion of the Civil Service. It has served the country well.' Even Brian Sedgemore, in a Commons debate in January 1979, said:

> There are 750,000 civil servants who, in my view, are doing an excellent job, to the best of their ability. Many of them deserve far better rewards than they are getting. They do not deserve the barbed comments and stings which are directed at them.[17]

Such recognition of 'real people doing real jobs' does not weaken the CSD's case for issuing reminders. But on its own it is not enough. Indeed, there is a sense in which 'The Quarry' aids the critics' case: if an army is doing badly, and a general says his troops are wonderful, then the logical thing is to look at the army's leadership. So it is with the Civil Service. 'The Quarry', by defending the Civil Service's infantry, leaves the general staff – occupying administrative jobs in Whitehall – badly exposed.

When *The Times* called on Sir Ian Bancroft to 'speak for Whitehall', it did not have in the forefront of its mind drainage engineers or driving test examiners. (Perhaps it should have done: but that is a separate point.) What *The Times* – and, privately, a number of senior civil servants – wanted was a defence of the way Whitehall is run: its power, its policy-making expertise, its constitutional role, its willingness to reform. To mount such a defence, however, means overcoming two problems. The first is that – as we shall see – the Civil Service does *not* like reforming itself. The second problem is more fundamental. An important component of the power of the executive as a whole, taking ministers and civil servants together, lies in the mystery of its operation. At a formal level, the membership and existence of ministerial and official committees is kept secret; at an informal level, arguments and debates during the formation of government decisions generally remain private. (With few exceptions press 'leaks' of Whitehall debates are either planned exercises to test public attitudes before a formal announcement, or come from ministers in the final stages of a cabinet battle where the options have already been crystallised.) The mystery of the executive prevents proper scrutiny of decision-making. But by the same token, when the executive *as such* becomes a target for criticism, ministers and civil servants must either engage in the debate and surrender some of the mystery; or they can preserve the mystery and avoid the debate. In 'The Quarry' the Civil Service Department has chosen the safer second option.

There are, in fact, two Civil Services. One is small, and helps to make Government policy. The other is large and helps to carry Government policy out. The division is not total, especially at the more senior levels: civil servants who run substantial regional offices, for example, can be (and arguably should be more often) useful sources of advice about the practicability of planned policy changes. Richard Crossman, for a fleeting moment, even considered holding regular meetings with *junior* local officials in the Department of Health and Social Security 'so that this kind of person can come up and talk in an open and fresh way to the people who make policy'.[18] But his idea came to nothing.

A comprehensive book about the Civil Service would describe both sides to its character; it would also describe the various institutions that huddle under the common name of

Civil Service – from the Cabinet Office in London to the Driver and Vehicle Licensing Centre at Swansea. This book does not set out to be about institutions (hence the title, *The Civil Servants*, rather than *The Civil Service*). Nor does it attempt to be comprehensive. Instead it seeks to inform a debate – or, rather, a series of debates – that has enveloped the Civil Service for more than a decade, since the establishment of the Fulton Committee in 1966. The criticisms and the replies, the reforms and the resistance to reform, involve a minority of civil servants. In particular they involve the administrators – the people who advise ministers and who ultimately manage the execution of Government policy. This book, therefore, does not address itself to the competence of driving test examiners or customs officials. If the essence of the Civil Service could be divined from the sum total of its rank-and-file activity, then the departure of almost a quarter of all civil servants with the hiving off of the Post Office would have had a profound effect. It did not. So we do not analyse the efficiency or honesty of the vast majority of civil servants, for that is not the essence of the debate.

What is at issue is the competence of senior civil servants – and also their power: their power to influence governments and parliaments, their power to select their own successors, and their power to resist change. This power directly shapes the Civil Service itself. Less directly, but more potently, it affects almost every aspect of Britain's national life. One of the first casualties of the debate has been the constitutional myth that Civil Service advice and ministerial decision live in separate watertight compartments. It will not be the last casualty.

PART ONE
A FAILURE TO REFORM

'THE CULT OF THE GENERALIST'

IN A STIRRING SPEECH at the 1963 Labour Party Conference in Scarborough, Harold Wilson outlined the sort of Britain his Government would seek to create if, as he confidently expected, he became Prime Minister within the next twelve months. It was a lofty vision. Linking socialism with science, his Government would create the new Jerusalem founded on the twin pillars of technological revolution and social justice. So, when he scraped into Downing Street in October 1964, he brought with him a collection of radical policies for transforming Britain.

The reform of the Civil Service was not on the original list. But when it was added in 1966, Wilson's Government made the most determined effort this century to produce root and branch change. It failed. The failure was not caused by the economy or by financial stringency, which put paid to many Wilsonian hopes. It was not due to the absence of careful preparation or of opposition in Parliament, which proved fatal or near fatal to others. Nor was it due to ministerial opposition. In fact, reform was successfully blocked by the civil servants themselves. The very men whose job it is to administer government policy to the rest of the public failed to administer it to themselves.

Britain's Civil Service, like all our institutions, is a product of its history and, in particular, of a damning report in 1854 by Sir Stafford Northcote and Lord Trevelyan on the Victorian Civil Service. This established many of the principles on which today's Service is based. Traditions may die hard but a great deal has changed since then. So to lay bare the nature of the Civil Service today, it is not particularly profitable to hark back to the mid-nineteenth century – particularly when more recent events provide us with a much more penetrating insight.

This new insight comes specifically from the last decade of battle between the civil servants and the would-be reformers. It was a battle that started in earnest in 1968 with the publication of the Fulton Report. It ended in 1978 when a Government White Paper apparently conceded victory to Fulton with the assertion that the 'acceptance' of the Fulton Committee's Report had 'resulted in a number of radical changes in the organisation and management of the Civil Service'.[1] This was a brilliant Civil Service ploy to close the Fulton saga. Fulton had now been implemented; no need, therefore, to hark back to that ancient document. In fact this was the reverse of the truth; by then the main Fulton attacks had actually been defeated. The story of that fight tells us not only about what kind of Civil Service we have now, and why; it also provides a remarkable case study of Civil Service power in action.

This ten-year battle was preceded by a certain amount of guerrilla activity. In 1959, for example, Thomas Balogh, an economist who subsequently became an adviser to Wilson in Downing Street, wrote a seminal essay entitled 'The Apotheosis of the Dilettante: the Establishment of Mandarins'. Balogh argued

> that the image of a smoothly and efficiently working parliamentary democracy is one of the most extravagant of all British myths. Its rise has to a large extent been due to the vanity of the politicians and the genius at public relations of the heads of our bureaucracy . . . They do not have to hire expensive copywriters, they do the job themselves ably helped by their own victims – the politicians. Effective power without responsibility, the complete freedom from all criticism, and last but not least, the attainment of higher salaries than their ministerial chiefs – such are the rich rewards of their skilful efforts.[2]

Balogh attacked the way recruitment favoured 'the smooth, extrovert conformist with good connexions and no knowledge of modern problems'[3] who would spend his career flitting from subject to subject, never becoming an expert in any of them.

> No one would be mad enough to advocate the periodic interchange of dentists and surgeons, solicitors and barristers, engineers and musicians. Yet surely the problems which most of these professions encounter are simple in comparison with the complexities of the social and economic system in a modern state.[4]

Balogh's broadside was augmented in 1964 by a Fabian tract, *The Administrators*, which described the Administrative Class as closed as a monastic order, isolated from industry, local government and the rest of society. The wrong people – too many Oxbridge arts graduates – were making the wrong policies the wrong way. Instead the Civil Service should 'assess costs, risks, interractions' in quantitative terms; and this would require greater professionalism, with more influence for people with special expertise.

The following year the Estimates Committee of the House of Commons added its voice to the calls for reform. Under the chairmanship of Jeremy Bray, a Labour MP with a background in mathematics and ICI, the Committee produced damning evidence that recruitment to the Administrative Class was actually becoming *more* biased towards – in Bray's words – 'its hard core of public school, Oxbridge, upper-class classicists with second-class honours degrees'.[5] The Committee said: 'We find it hard to accept that the task of Government justifies the unique significance attaching to the Administrative Class, and that only a select few are fitted to undertake this work.'[6]

The Committee called for a full-scale Government inquiry into the structure, recruitment and management of the Civil Service. Wilson was happy to oblige. It gave him the opportunity he was looking for still further to characterise his government as one of radical reform. He had set up a Royal Commission on Local Government, another on the Public Schools, one on the Trade Unions. An inquiry into the Civil Service fitted admirably into this pattern.

What Bray's Committee had actually recommended, though, was a two-stage operation. The first stage was to be the appointment of 'a committee of officials, aided by members from outside the Civil Service . . . to initiate research upon, to examine, and to report upon the structure and management of the Civil Service.'[7] Mostly this was to be an inside job – and the Committee would report to the Government. The Government would report to Parliament the action they proposed to take; and if necessary a Royal Commission would then be appointed.[8]

The Wilson Government decided it would be a single stage operation, and set up a Committee of Inquiry – not, be it noted, a Royal Commission. To some this seemed to be a downgrading of the inquiry even before it got underway; and the suspicious at once smelled a Civil Service plot. After all, a Committee of Inquiry does not have the same status as a Royal Commission. This is partly indicated by the fact that its chairman does not receive the traditional silver ink-stand which marks the conclusion of the work of a Royal Commission. More important, though, a Committee of Inquiry is not given the power that a Royal Commission has 'to send for persons and papers'. But if this was a Civil Service plot, it made no difference. The Committee never had any difficulty in getting anything it wanted.

The suspicious also saw a Civil Service plot in the fact that one quarter of the Committee's membership (i.e. three out of twelve) were high-level and powerful civil servants. Certainly this was the first time civil servants had been given such a substantial role in an inquiry into themselves; and did not this mean, therefore, that the Committee would be able to produce only a 'safe' report? But if this was a Civil Service plot it, too, misfired. The Committee could not have produced the report it did but for the contribution these three members made to the Committee's work.

Wilson's choice for the chairmanship of the Committee on the Civil Service seemed reasonably safe and suitably non-controversial: Lord Fulton, the Vice-Chancellor of Sussex University. He had, of course, no published views about the Civil Service. His record in *Who's Who* made him a one-man definition of the post-war establishment: he had been a temporary civil servant during the war, at various times Oxford philosophy and also politics tutor, BBC Governor and Vice-

Chairman, Chairman of the British Council, and a member of a host of government inquiries. Indeed, he was doing so many jobs when he was made Chairman of the Committee on the Civil Service that it must have seemed to anyone who took the trouble to think about it that he simply would not have the time to spearhead any serious probe into the operations of the Whitehall machine.

What few people knew, though, was that as early as 1942 he and Wilson had formed similar views about the defects of the Civil Service. For a while they had worked together in the Mines Department of the Board of Trade – Fulton as one of the battalion of academics who moved into Whitehall while the war lasted, Wilson as a young professional economist. Occasionally, their night-time fire-watching rotas overlapped, and in the rambling discussions penetrated by German bombs they discovered they had similar grudges against the old entrenched Administrative Class – Wilson primarily because it failed to give enough weight to specialists and professionals like himself, Fulton primarily because of what he believed to be its lack of drive, originality, inventiveness and the will to innovate.

Before Fulton's Committee started work in 1966, the Civil Service managed to chalk up a couple of victories. It was made clear by the Prime Minister in the terms of reference that the Fulton Committee would not be concerned with 'machinery of government questions'.[9] This exclusion, which was badly wanted by the mandarins, enabled Sir William Armstrong, when he subsequently became head of the Civil Service, to argue that the Committee's work was thus unduly circumscribed and, as a consequence, that there were considerable doubts about most, if not all, of its recommendations. His view was that until 'machinery of government'. questions had been settled, you could not really know what sort of civil servants you needed and how they should be organised. Of course, this was nonsense. The tasks of government were going to be pretty much the same (i.e. dealing with education, pensions, trade, finance, etc.) however many departments you had, or whatever their size and however they were organised, and irrespective of whether or not, for example, the Prime Minister needed a department of his own. So the Committee's main recommendations were concerned with the type of civil servant you needed to undertake the tasks of modern government irrespective of the precise way Whitehall might organise itself to carry out those tasks. So this was a sterile controversy; but it is a nice illustration of the way the Civil Service helped to narrow the Committee's terms of reference – and later was able to argue that this restriction invalidated much of what the Committee said!

The second victory the Civil Service achieved before the Committee got under way was to keep the Committee from any examination of the crucial relationships and balance of power between civil servants and ministers. The Prime Minister made this crystal clear in the Commons when he said on 8 February 1966 that the Government's willingness to consider changes in the Civil Service 'does not imply any intention on their part to alter the basic relationship between ministers and civil servants. Civil servants, however eminent, remain the confidential advisors of ministers, who alone are answerable to Parliament for policy; and we do not envisage any change in this fundamental feature of our parliamentary system of democracy'.[10]

The Fulton Committee then could not directly concern itself with the power of the Civil Service. It could not consider, for example, whether the twentieth-century expansion in the role and functions of Government was affecting the traditional power balance between ministers and civil servants. It had to accept as axiomatic that civil servants were advising ministers, not dominating them – and that they were also giving full effect to ministerial decisions. Though the Committee's terms of reference were circumscribed it had a major investigation on its hands. It was to 'examine the structure, recruitment and management, including training, of the Home Civil Service and to make recommendations'.[11] This detailed investigation led it to conclude that the Civil Service 'is in need of fundamental change. It is inadequate in six main respects for the most efficient discharge of the present and prospective responsibilities of Government.'[12]

By far the most important of these inadequacies – and the Fulton Committee gave this pride of place in its analysis – was that the Service was still based on a belief in the supreme virtue of the 'generalist' or 'all-rounder'. Most of the rest of the Committee's damning criticisms of the Service were, in the Committee's view, secondary to, or derivative from, this prevailing and all-embracing generalist concept which the Committee believed was 'obsolete at all levels and in all parts of the Service.'[13]

Before the Committee reached that conclusion Fulton became more and more determined that, to oppose the cult of the generalist, the main thrust of his Report would emphasise the virtues of professionalism. This very much reflected the ethos of the time. Sir Alec Douglas-Home had been found wanting as Prime Minister because he dealt with economic problems by counting match-sticks; he was replaced by economist Harold Wilson, a Fellow of the Royal Statistical Society. So with professionalism now the vogue, little wonder that Fulton should seek to capture this mood in his Report. 'We must fly the flag of professionalism', he would say. Only when the drafting of the Report got under way did anyone realise that to be *for* professionalism, you had to be against, and contrast it with – well, what? To preserve the symmetry of the argument, the use of the word 'amateur' virtually became irresistible, and the Committee gave the clear impression that the words 'amateur', 'all-rounder' and 'generalist' were synonymous. The Report (in para. 3) talked of the emergence of 'the tradition of the "all-rounder" as he has been called by his champions, or "amateur" as he has been called by his critics.'[14] And then, a few pages further on, the Report gives priority to the word 'amateur' when it first criticises the Civil Service for its principal failings:

> First, the Service is essentially based on the philosophy of the amateur (or 'generalist' or 'all-rounder'). This is most evident in the Administrative Class which holds the dominant position in the Service.[15]

And a few pages later the word 'amateur' is used for the third and last time when the Report said *not* that amateurs were actually to be found in the Service but that: 'The Civil Service is no place for amateurs.'[16]

29

The subsequent public debate tended very much to become a slanging match based on the 'amateurs' versus the 'professionals' dichotomy – whereas it should have been a sober debate about the relative virtues of *professional* generalists in contrast to *professional* specialists. And the fact that the debate was obscured and confused in this way was one main reason why this fundamental finding of the Fulton Committee has never been implemented. The cult of the generalist still rules supreme in today's Civil Service – and is just as much a major obstacle to the efficiency of the Service today as it was ten years ago.

Fulton's conclusion was not merely the product of the twelve members of the Committee sitting around a table cogitating on the evidence of the witnesses appearing before them. Unlike any previous consideration of the Civil Service since the Northcote-Trevelyan Report the Fulton Committee decided to carry out its own basic investigation of what civil servants were actually doing. Accordingly it set up a Management Consultancy Group – and it was the work of this group that was decisive in the Committee's condemnation of the generalist.

Initially, my* idea was to hand the investigation to a firm of management consultants, and tell them to examine the work of the Civil Service and compare it with the jobs done in industry, local government and the public corporations. We would then expect the consultants to make an appropriate report back to the Committee on how the organization of Civil Service work compared with the best practices in business and local government etc. and whether the civil servants had the right qualifications and experience for the jobs they were doing. Put in this way the idea did not much commend itself to my colleagues. For one thing there were distinguished civil servants on the Committee who felt they knew all that was worth knowing about the work that civil servants did and how they were organized. For another, there were experienced businessmen on the Committee who knew at first hand what happened in industry.

However, the idea gradually got refined until the concept of a

---

*Lord Crowther-Hunt.

Management Consultancy Group emerged. It was a team of four. One came from the Organization and Methods Division of the Treasury, S. D. Walker – a man of hard practical common sense and with an immense knowledge of civil service work. He had spent thirty years climbing the clerical and executive ladders, in contrast with high-flying administrators from public schools and Oxbridge. Before he joined the team, he got the Treasury to agree that he could behave completely independently of the Service and that he was not necessarily representing official attitudes; he had the freedom to sign whatever he thought was right. Then there was John Garrett, now a Labour MP, but then working for a firm of management consultants; he had wide experience of management in industry, and the drive and intelligence to get to the heart of the problems that confronted us. The third member of our Group was Kim Ferguson, an executive loaned to us by British Petroleum; he had special experience of their personnel, organization and training problems. Finally, there was myself. The Fulton Committee made the whole project conditional on my being given leave of absence from my College to take daily charge of the work of the group. Presumably, this was to give the Committee some control over what was happening – and, also, perhaps to help ensure that the problems the group was dealing with should be seen through the eyes of a political scientist as well as the eyes of a management consultant, a business executive and a civil servant.

The Management Consultancy Group started its work in the different departments in October 1966. Between then and April 1967 we examined twenty-three blocks of Civil Service work in twelve departments. Primarily we investigated the actual tasks civil servants were performing and whether they had the necessary qualities, qualifications, skills and experience needed for the jobs they were doing. The Group also investigated the relationship between administrators (including members of the Executive Class) and specialists (e.g. architects, engineers, scientists, etc.) – and whether the pattern of responsibilities and deployment of expertise were well designed to secure the efficient achievement of the block's objectives.

The twelve departments were most helpful and cooperative

as we sought to probe below the surface. They usually provided us in advance with an initial detailed description of the block of work we were going to investigate; and during the investigation of each block we were normally able to study any of the files we wanted to see – and this was not limited to the files of the current government. So we did not have to rely on what the departments and civil servants told us. We could, from the files, see the advice given to ministers on particular problems and how that advice was formulated; and, of course, from the minutes we could also see the communications that civil servants had with each other.

Never before had any committee or commission on the Civil Service sought to base its work on such a detailed consideration of the wide range of different jobs civil servants were actually performing. Moreover, in setting up the Management Consultancy Group, the Fulton Committee, inadvertently perhaps, ensured that its work had a bigger impact on its own thinking than is normally the case when a Royal Commission or investigating committee commissions 'research'. This was because the Fulton Committee was able to keep in constant, if informal, touch with the day-to-day investigations of the Management Group. At each weekly meeting of the Committee the members – and particularly the Permanent Secretaries – were anxious to hear about the progress of the Management Group's investigations. So I gave them a weekly informal progress report during lunch – and no doubt the Permanent Secretaries had similarly informal reports from the departments about what the Management Consultancy Group had been up to. Nor was this a one-way process. There was a regular feedback to the Management Consultancy Group of the reactions and developing interests of the members of the Fulton Committee. All this was crucial in a number of ways. It enhanced the quality of the work of the Group. It kept the Committee and the Group working on similar wave-lengths. It enabled the Group to have a constant and continuous impact on the thinking of the Committee whilst this was still in a relatively formative and fluid state. Indeed, much of the Group's findings had been incorporated into the thinking of the Fulton Committee before the Group's final report was available to the

Committee. This was partly because of the regular and informal weekly discussions – and also because the Group produced a hard-hitting interim report which bluntly set out our probable conclusions. Very different, all this, from the more normal state of affairs in which a Royal Commission or a Committee of Inquiry commissions a research project and then goes on with its own evidence-taking oblivious of the work of the researchers, which often emerges too late, or too out of tune with the development of the Commission's ideas, to have much, if any, influence on them.

What was the evidence, then, that the management Consultancy Group found which was so decisive in the Fulton Committee's condemnation of the generalist?

Perhaps this question is best answered by being clear, first of all, what is meant by the concept of the 'generalist' and the way this concept is fundamental to the recruitment, organization, and deployment of staff in government departments. The concept of the generalist was, and is, most evident in the pre-Fulton Administrative Class. At the time of the Fulton Committee the members of this class numbered just 2,500: almost all the direct entrants were graduates; their job was to examine policy options and prepare advice for ministers; they were responsible for the administration and control of government departments. Despite their small numbers they wielded enormous influence.

After much discussion with civil servants and consideration of their career patterns, Fulton and its Management Group built up a clear picture of the Service's ideal administrator. He is a man (or woman) of good education and high intelligence who can take an overall view of any problem, irrespective of its subject matter, in the light of his knowledge and experience of the government machine. The 'generalist' is an expert in the *processes* of government – a craft to be picked up mostly by experience on the job. The role of the administrator is that of the intelligent layman whose unique and vital contribution is an intimate knowledge of the government machine. This background enables him to synthesize the views of specialists both within and without the government machine and to evaluate them in terms of what is feasible.

33

The same broad definition of the generalist was given by the First Division Association (the Staff Association of the Administrative Class) in its published evidence to the Fulton Committee:

> The essential function of this group of staff [i.e. the generalist administrators] is to bring together the disparate issues involved in taking major decisions of policy, to advise on what these decisions should be and subsequently put them into effect. The Administrative Class is uniquely able to perform this function because of its broad background, intellectual capacity and experience of operating in government. Administrators *become conversant* with the special subjects with which individual departments are concerned; collectively they know about the whole range of governmental and parliamentary affairs; they know how to cope with the complexities of the government machine; finally, they are politically aware in the sense of regarding politics as the art of the possible.[17]

The First Division Association was anxious to justify the state of affairs in which administrators, as non-specialists (except in the operation of the governent machine), dominated the work of departments. The Association argued that this sprang 'from the generally accepted principle in this country that non-specialists should take major policy decisions on behalf of the community as a whole.'[18]

In a recent spirited defence of the generalist, the former Permanent Secretary of the Department of Agriculture, Sir Basil Engholm, said it was the job of the administrator 'to take and understand the advice of experts in the different disciplines on any particular problem, to analyse and assess that advice, and to reach a balanced view on the pros and cons of different possible courses of action'. Generalist administrators are 'general managers who have, through experience,˙ acquired a considerable skill as professional administrators'. For good measure, Sir Basil emphasized the dangers of a man with a specialist discipline (e.g. in agriculture or engineering) filling such a role; he may be so prejudiced or blinded by his specialism that he may not be able to take a broader or impartial view which will carry conviction with the different experts involved.[19] It is the familiar argument that the experts should be on tap but not on top.

So why did the Fulton Committee conclude that this concept 'has the most damaging consequences'? Quite simply, the evidence produced by the Management Consultancy Group left it no alternative. The Group had documented two main groups of reasons which led inexorably to the condemnation of the generalist and all his work. The first was concerned with the sort of men and women it produced as administrators, and the way they operated. The second was the effect of this generalist concept on the organization and staffing of the Service as a whole.

As far as the Administrative Class itself was concerned, the Management Consultancy Group was very surprised indeed to discover how short a time each administrator spent in one job before being moved to another job dealing with an entirely different area of activity. And it soon became clear that one of the main reasons for this extraordinary frequency of movement between jobs was the Service's concept of the generalist administrator.

The statistics the Management Group produced on this showed that the administrators we interviewed (about one-tenth of the total membership of the Class) had averaged 2.8 years in a job before being moved to something completely different; and the modal (most frequently occurring) period in completed jobs was two years.[20] The main reason for this 'turbulence' – as the Service charmingly called it – was the need to make an administrator into a true generalist. Only by regular moves between different jobs can an administrator 'become conversant' (to use a phrase from the First Division Association's evidence to Fulton) with the wide range of often very different specialist activities that fall under the umbrella of a particular department. Frequency of movement is crucial, too, if the administrator is to develop what is regarded as his real specialism – his knowledge and experience of the working of the government machine; you can develop this only if you can serve in as many different parts of the machine as is humanly possible during your career.

The detailed investigations of the Management Consultancy Group were able to document conclusively the extent to which this frequency of movement between jobs, so crucial to the proper development of the generalist, had, in fact, seriously adverse consequences for the overall efficiency of the Service. Its main conclusions were:

● Many administrators have so short a tenure in any job that even the most able of them rarely have time thoroughly to grasp the complex subjects with which they are dealing.
● Without a deep understanding of these subjects, either by experience, or training, few of them are in a position to evaluate in any fundamental way the extent to which the policies they are administering are successful. This must inhibit the drive for innovation.
● [High mobility] produces inefficiency and slows down the administrative process, since an administrator has to spend so much time familiarizing himself with problems his predecessor may just have mastered . . .
● Short tenure and frequent hand-overs produce administrative instability and inconsistency . . .
● Many administrators are neither able, nor concerned, to establish adequate contact with sources of expert advice inside or outside the Service or to develop a fruitful relationship with such sources. One officer in a highly technical area said that there was no point in making a great effort to find out what other countries were doing in his particular area of activity – or even to get to know as many British experts on the subject as possible – since he would be in that particular job for only three years at the most . . .
● It prevents an administrator from handling the complete cycle of the policy-making process: analysing the problem, conducting or supervising or contributing to research into it, recommending a course of action and modifying policy in the light of results.[21]

The Management Consultancy Group then gave some of the specific evidence on which these generalizations were based:

● It takes the sponsoring department of a nationalized industry several months to process the industry's annual investment programme. A great deal of the work is done at Principal level. We found in a division dealing with one industry that it took a Principal six months to familiarize himself with the job and that he therefore could make little positive contribution to the first annual cycle. He could deal more confidently with the second annual review – by which time he would have been in the job up to two years. At this time he may be under consideration for a move. His removal to another division would occur at the very point when he would have acquired sufficient familiarity with the routine to

permit him to enquire more deeply into such factors as the
structure of the industry, its standards of operating efficiency, its
management – all of which have a bearing on the efficiency of
investment – and to apply analytical techniques to the data
provided by the industry . . .
● Because of legal complexities and public enquiry procedures, it
takes about five years for the appropriate ministry to process
county or town development plans . . . Two or three different
Assistant Secretaries or Principals may be primarily responsible for
a plan during the time it is being processed. Each new administrator has to spend a long time familiarizing himself with the main
problems associated with the plan, and has to establish afresh the
personal contacts with the local authorities concerned . . .
Continuity has to be supplied by the specialist planning officers
who find themselves briefing new administrators at frequent
intervals.

The full Fulton Committee had little choice but to concur.
Many administrators, they concluded,

do not develop adequate knowledge in any aspect of the department's work . . . Often they are required to give advice on subjects
they do not sufficiently understand or take decisions whose
significance they do not fully grasp. This has serious consequences.
It can lead to bad policy-making; it prevents a fundamental
evaluation of the policies being administered; it often leads to the
adoption of inefficient methods for implementing those policies . . .
and it obstructs the establishment of fruitful contacts with sources
of expert advice.[22]

Significantly, this damning verdict on the generalists was
accepted by the two traditional generalist Permanent Secretaries who were members of the Fulton Committee. They made
no reservations whatever about this judgement. Their own
experience did not enable them to fault the detailed findings of
the Management Consultancy Group.

This condemnation of the role and function of the generalist
was, in the view of the majority of the Fulton Committee,
strengthened by the sort of people who were recruited to fill the
role. It was not just that the graduates recruited direct from our
universities to become generalist administrators were predominantly Oxbridge *and* public school. What was much more
important was that the recruitment of generalist administrators

was not linked to any vocational educational requirement. Degrees in classics, English and ancient history were deemed to be just as likely to fit a man to be a generalist administrator as degrees in economics, public administration, the pure and applied sciences, and modern social and economic history. Indeed, probably more so – because 'relevant' degrees carry dangerous connotations of specialization.

In this respect our recruitment practices contrasted strongly with those of other Civil Services. In France, Western Germany, Australia, Sweden and the United States, for example, higher civil servants were generally recruited on the basis of their qualifications and experience for the actual tasks they would be involved in while running the modern state. These countries differed only in whether they defined these requirements broadly or narrowly. Some recruited into specific posts evaluating candidates' education, skills and experience in terms of the job specification; others recruited into broad classes for which relevant educational qualifications were prescribed. Only in Britain were educational qualifications (apart from the possession of, and class of, a degree) irrelevant.

The fact that direct entrants recruited to our higher Civil Service did not need to have any relevant vocational educational background could be seen as the logical corollary of the fact that they were being recruited to be generalists. If our administrative civil servants were to be generalists in function, then it could be argued that all that was relevant to this role was natural ability and a trained mind. Thus it was beside the point to consider whether the mind had been trained and exercised in, for example, ancient history or modern science and the social sciences – since the true generalist will never be specializing in a particular subject area of government.

On the other hand it could certainly be argued that even a generalist would be a better generalist if his educational background had at least made him familiar with some of the broad economic, social or scientific problems which modern government have to deal with. This was why the majority of the Fulton Committee were so disturbed to find that the great majority of graduate recruits to the Administrative Class had taken their degrees in arts or humanities (71 per cent – and mainly in history or classics); there were only just over 25 per cent from the social sciences, only about one in ten had studied natural science and only a negligible proportion had graduated in applied science. This, of course, was in sharp contrast to the United States and France. In the USA only a small proportion were arts graduates – the rest coming from social sciences, natural and applied sciences. In France the counterparts of our Administrative Class were graduates of the École Nationale where they had a two-and-a-half year general education in social sciences (e.g. economics, law, public administration and statistics etc.) – preceded by three to five years in one of the Instituts d'Études Politiques.

Against this background, the Fulton Committee was particularly disturbed that the British recruitment process seemed to discriminate in favour of those who had read arts and humanities degrees as opposed to those seeking entry with a more 'vocationally' oriented educational background (e.g. with degrees in social, natural and applied sciences). This recruitment pattern, it was believed, made generalists even less efficient than might otherwise have been the case.

But Fulton was not just concerned that the cult of the generalist produced a breed of men and women whose educational background and subsequent rotation between jobs seriously weakened the efficiency of the Service. We were also concerned with the effect the cult of the generalist had on the organization and staffing of the Service as a whole.

The essential point here is that, at the time of Fulton, generalist administrators had a monopoly of virtually all the top posts in the Service. Thus a large block of jobs was exclusively and specifically reserved for members of the Administrative Class and their supporting grades in the Executive Class. And these jobs formed the main chain of command posts in a department beneath the generalist Permanent Secretary. This had damaging consequences.

It had the effect of relegating scientists and other specialists in the Service – like accountants and economists – to a mainly subordinate role. It was their job to tender advice – and that advice normally went to the administrators in the departmental command structure – and it was the administrators who took the decisions on it themselves or, when necessary, submitted it to ministers with their own recommendations. And since administrators formed the departmental financial chain of command as well as the main policy chain of command this had the effect of relegating specialists to a still more subordinate position.

The Management Consultancy Group, on the basis of its own detailed investigation, had concluded that:

● on the question of financial control, administrators did not have the technical competence properly to challenge the specialists except on obvious or relatively trivial points . . .

● under present circumstances there is a waste of specialists' time since administrators change jobs more frequently than specialists. Thus specialists find themselves having to explain the technical background to newly-arrived administrators . . .

● in industry, managers with specialist backgrounds are very often entrusted with the expenditure of funds without having their decisions under continuous scrutiny by laymen . . .

● there is no evidence that specialists are unsuited to the role of policy-makers in their own specialist field . . . they were prevented from exercising the full range of responsibilities normally associated with their professionalism and exercised by their counterparts in industry.[23]

Plenty of reason here, then, to condemn the concept of the generalist for its impact on the rest of the Service. It has the inevitable consequence of tarring specialists with an inferior status and of producing organizational forms in the Service which promote inefficiency and impede the development of accountable units and accountable management which are so crucial to the promotion of efficiency. It also deterred able specialists from wanting to join, or remain in, the Service – a Service where their career prospects (in terms of salary and ultimate rank) were markedly inferior to those similarly qualified generalists.

The concept of the generalist, the Fulton Committee also believed, acted as a major obstacle to the more flexible deployment of staff and the best use of individual talent in the service as a whole. Clearly, in the division between generalist administrators and specialists, with each group operating within its own specifically reserved spheres, these highly desirable objectives could be achieved only if transfer from one sphere to another was relatively easy. But this was not the case. Where a specialist sought to move to a job with greater administrative content, he had to transfer from his own specialist class to the quite separate Administrative or Executive Class. And in such a move, there was no guarantee that the man concerned would become an administrator in the area of his own specialism. Indeed, quite the contrary; since the transfer involved becoming a generalist administrator, the normal practice was to employ the transferee in a post as far removed from his specialism as was humanly possible. Only in that way had he a chance of becoming the true generalist administrator. It was an effective deterrent to a specialist whose main aim, for a start at any rate, was to administer in the area of his specialism.

As leader of the Management Consultancy Group I was particularly shocked to discover the waste of talent among able young men and women who had entered the Service straight from school with their A-levels. I sat with many of these young Executive Officers working in contracts divisions, establishment divisions, and in accounts and town and country planning. I saw what they were doing and discussed their work with them. Almost all of them believed they would do their work better, and find it more stimulating, if they took relevant courses in, say, contract law or accounts. Many would have been eager to attend College courses in the evenings, in their own time.

Yet none of the ones I spoke to did so. They felt there was no point, for they would almost certainly be moved to quite different work before their course was completed. More seriously, they recognised that a fresh qualification could actually jeopardise their promotion prospects – for they would then start looking like narrow specialists, when the crucial consideration in getting promoted to Higher Executive Officer was the ability not to do a *particular* job in the higher grade, but to do any of the *full range* of different departmental jobs. The Service was wasting the very enthusiasms and human assets it should have been nurturing.

It is the cult of the generalist, too, which has been a major factor in the failure of the Service to recognize early enough the need for new kinds of specialism. Fulton quoted two examples of this; in 1963 there were only nineteen economists in the whole of the Home Civil Service (less than in most major companies at that time) and by 1967 still only 106. The Service's failure to recognize the need for, and importance of, accountants was even more marked – and this after lamentable financial experience with such projects as Blue Streak and TSR2, for example, and when government expenditure amounted to over £19,000 million pounds a year.[24] Thus, when Fulton reported in 1968, the Service employed only 309 accountants; and, at a time when a permanent Secretary was paid £9,200 p.a., there was no accountant post in the whole of the Civil Service which carried a salary of more than £4,500 p.a. and there were only six accountants' posts with salaries above £3,650. Moreover, as the Fulton Report pointed out, the Civil Service which organized accountants into a separate Accountants' Class specifically 'excluded its members from financial control. They are limited to the relatively narrow field in which departments themselves keep commercial accounts or are concerned with the financial operations of commercial organizations.'[25]

Fulton also condemned the very limited degree of late entry into the Service after experience in outside jobs. Career civil servants tended to join soon after school or university and stay in the Service until they retired. If you wanted to join after experience in private business, local government, nationalized industry or the professions, the opportunities were very limited. You could try for appointment as an Executive Officer (with your starting salary limited to that then fixed for a 25-year-old), but few posts were available even at that modest level. Or you could try for one of the 20 to 30 late-entry Principal posts a year offered in the mid-1960s. Or you could apply to enter as an Assistant Secretary – but only five of these had been recruited externally in three years. And that was it.

The power of the civil service unions was the main reason for these restrictions, since any significant amount of late entry would jeopardize their members' promotion prospects. But the

generalist ideology played its part, too. A traditional administrator would have difficulty appreciating that a Director of
Education from local government might have a useful policy-
making role in the upper reaches of the Department of
Education. He might know about schools, but what did he
know about *government*?

The final respect in which the concept of the generalist stood
in the way of much-needed Civil Service reform was the way it
perpetuated the class divisions in the Service. The Fulton
Committee considered that the then system of classes seriously
impeded the work of the Service. As the Fulton Report pointed
out:

> The Service is divided into classes both horizontally (between
> higher and lower in the same broad area of work) and vertically
> (between different skills, professions or disciplines). There are
> 47 general classes whose members work in most government
> departments and over 1,400 departmental classes. Each civil
> servant is recruited to a particular class: his membership of
> that class determines his prospects (most classes have their
> own career structures) and the range of jobs on which he may
> be employed.

In Fulton's view the particular fault here was the reservation of
a particular block of jobs for the members of a particular class.
And here it was not so much concerned with the horizontal line
dividing classes as with the vertical line separating classes.
True, it considered that the horizontal line (which was based on
the concept that there were clear divisions of work ranging from
the simple and mechanical kind at the bottom end of the scale
(e.g. Clerical Class Officers), through intermediate level work
(e.g. Executive Class Officers), to work concerned with the
formation of policy at the top of the scale (e.g. Administrative
Class), and that each sort of work should be the preserve of the
class of those recruited to undertake it) no longer made sense
given the very wide range of different kinds of job in a
particular area of work – and given, too, the way individuals
develop. But of greater significance was the vertical line
between classes, between, for example, the Administrative
Class and the Scientific Officer Class with the reservation of

major blocks of jobs to the members of each class. And the basis of Fulton's criticism here was not that this precluded administrators from doing scientific block jobs but that it kept scientists out of the whole range of Administrative Class jobs (jobs in the command structure of a department) in which they could have made a major contribution to the work of the department. Moreover, this rigid and vertical line dividing Administrative Class jobs from the specialist class jobs no longer corresponded with the real nature of an increasing proportion of jobs at all levels in the Service. As Fulton put it:

> A growing proportion of jobs in the Service requires both technical and managerial knowledge and ability, and cannot now be properly classified as either technical (and therefore reserved for the appropriate specialist class) or managerial (and therefore normally reserved for the Administrative or Executive Class).

But though this vertical line between classes was the very focal point of all the criticisms Fulton levelled at the Class system, the two groups who had most to lose by obliterating this particular class line were the generalist Administrators and similar members of the Executive Class. To them it seemed that their preserved area of jobs (and particularly those in the command hierarchy in the departments and the Service as a whole) could be defended only on the basis of maintaining that these were the jobs which required above all the virtues of the generalist – the unique quality they alone could claim to possess. So they had a vested interest in maintaining the cult of the generalist and the vertical lines dividing classes which were an essential part of it. It was the *sine qua non* of their predominant position of power in the Service. In this way, as Fulton believed, the concept of the generalist was a fundamental obstacle to the total abolition of the system of classes which the Committee considered was so essential to the efficient management of our affairs.

With the cult and concept of the generalist then producing, in Fulton's view, the wrong sort of men and women to administer our affairs – and with this cult, too, having such unhappy consequences for the organization, running and staffing of the

Service as a whole – no wonder Fulton directed his main fire at this particular enemy. Hardly surprising, too, that from their command positions in the Service the mandarins were able to deflect Fulton's fire.

3

WHAT FULTON
RECOMMENDED

SINCE FULTON'S MAIN CONCLUSION was that the cult of the
generalist 'is obsolete at all levels and in all parts of the Service'[1]
it naturally followed that the Committee's main objective was
to eradicate this basic ideology and the faults which flowed
from it. To this end the Committee adopted a multi-pronged
approach. It recognized that so all-pervasive and all-powerful
was this ideology that no single recommendation could hope to
eradicate it. So the Committee sought to strike at many points
with a whole series of proposed changes.

Fulton's main proposal here seems relatively modest. It was
in fact fundamental. It rested on Fulton's conviction that it was
no longer enough 'for the administrator to be expert in running
the government machine'. Administrators had to become more
specialist. Gone was the time when they should be thought of as
people who could handle anything from nuclear power to
comprehensive education. So, Fulton identified two broad
areas for administrative specialization – while recognizing that
there was immense variety in the jobs administrators were
called on to perform.

First there was a broad group of administrative jobs in
different departments concerned with 'a subject matter that is
primarily economic and financial'.[2] This covered areas dealing
with general economic planning and control, international
trade or particular industries. It also included jobs involving
the control of major programmes of capital and current
expenditure. And it included the economic and financial aspects
of large technological and scientific projects. These jobs were

not to be found only in the obvious economic and financial departments like the Treasury, the Board of Trade and the Department of Employment. They were also to be found in the more 'social' departments like Education, Health and Social Security – for example, the Accountant General's Branch in the Department of Education. So this broad group of administrative jobs whose content was primarily economic and financial was spread across all departments – though clearly in departments like the Treasury and the Board of Trade they would form a higher proportion of the overall total administrative jobs than they would in, say, the Home Office.

Secondly, there was in Fulton's view another broad group of administrative jobs whose basis was essentially social. These, too, were spread across a large number of departments and included administrative jobs concerned with housing, town and country planning, education, race relations, social security, industrial relations, personnel management and crime and delinquency. Again, these jobs were not to be found only in the obviously 'social' departments like the Home Office or Education. They were to be found, too, in the personnel sections of Establishment divisions in all departments and in those parts of the Treasury and other primarily economic departments where administrators needed to be aware of the 'social' dimensions involved in their work.[3]

Given these two broad categories of administrative work, Fulton recommended that, particularly in their early years in the Service, administrators should specialize in one or other of them. Both these specialized groups of administrators, Fulton believed, would probably find it necessary to add to the basic knowledge of their specialist fields any further degrees of specialization that their particular areas of government work required (e.g. some social administrators in the Home Office might specialize further in, say, crime and delinquency problems, while those in the Department of Education would obviously top themselves up with special concentration on work that had been done in the field of education). With these degrees of specialization these two groups of administrators would move between different jobs in the service appropriate to their knowledge and experience. A typical career pattern would, of course, involve a steady broadening of an individual's responsibility as he moved upwards – but, equally important, it would normally involve moves between posts reserved for members of his group. So, with this degree of specialization among administrators, the concept of the generalist, the Fulton Committee hoped, would be dealt a substantial blow.

It was not intended, of course, that these two groups of specialist administrators would replace specialist economists, accountants, engineers, social scientists, etc. It was, rather, that the administrator, trained and experienced in his subject matter, would cease to be a generalist and would thus not only be better at his job but would also be able to enjoy a more fruitful relationship with specialists than was otherwise possible. In this way, the Service would harness the best contribution from each and the quality of government and administration would be greatly enhanced. It was also believed that this more fruitful relationship would be a force for dynamism and innovation.

It followed logically that this change should be reflected in the Service's recruitment policies, particularly in the direct recruitment of graduates, post-graduates and their equivalents for administrative work. This meant in the Committee's view that:

> In future men and women should *not* be recruited for employment as generalist administrators and intelligent all-rounders – to do any of, and a succession of, the widely different jobs covered by the 'generalist' concept. Instead, they should be recruited to do a specified range of jobs in a particular area of work.[4]

In short, they should be recruited to be either economic and financial administrators or social administrators. The majority of the Committee thought that in recruiting for these two groups 'the relevance to their future work of the subject matter of their university or other pre-Service studies should be an important qualification for appointment'.[5] Instead of the majority of administrators coming into the Service with their degrees in classics or history, in future the balance would tip in favour of those who had chosen to study the political, social, economic, scientific or technological problems of our time.

Those recruited for the Service without a 'relevant' qualification would either have to take a special training course at the Civil Service College in addition to that provided for the 'relevant' entrants, or, alternatively, take a relevant post-graduate degree or course of study (at the Service's expense) at some university or other appropriate institution.

Basic as all this was, it formed only one part of the Fulton strategy. The rest was a mixture of direct assault together with recommendations that, while chiefly designed to eradicate other civil service faults, would also undermine the old mandarin mentality.

Perhaps the most important proposal in this latter category was that each department should have a Planning Unit. Departments were so involved with the urgent issues of the moment that few civil servants found, or made, the time to look ahead. So a newly created Planning Unit in each major department was to become responsible for 'long-term policy planning and research'.[6] It would also be the job of the Planning Unit to see that the department's day-to-day policy decisions were consistent with long-term strategies.

To be successful in both roles each unit had to be staffed mainly by specialists. The head of each Planning Unit – who would become the department's Senior Policy Adviser – would certainly have to be a specialist. And he would have direct access to the minister. As a consequence he would break the grip of the Permanent Secretary and his fellow generalists on the policy-making process.[7]

Fulton's proposal for a sharp increase in the number of late entrants, especially into the administrative ranks, had the same indirect objective. Its main purpose was to inject fresh blood from business, the professions, nationalized industries, local government and the universities. But in time a significant inflow of such people would transform the character of the Service's top echelons.

Another recommendation of the Fulton Committee was designed to have a similar effect even though its main objective was rather different. This was the blessing the Committee gave to the then developing practice of some ministers bringing into their departments one or two political appointees. The

Committee said:

> We think it important that ministers should be free to arrange for
> the holders of such appointments to be closely associated with the
> work of the many 'official' committees (i.e. committees of civil
> servants without ministerial membership) which make an essential
> contribution to policy-making; the work of these committees places
> a heavy responsibility on civil servants to ensure that the choices
> subsequently presented to ministers are not unduly circumscribed.[8]

Clearly the main purpose of this particular recommendation
was to strengthen the hand of the minister in controlling his
department. But by providing an alternative source of policy
advice for the Minister – and, moreover, an expert source of
advice from people who had professional standing and stature
in the policy areas concerned – it was also designed to have the
effect of breaking the grip of the generalist administrator on the
policy-making process.

The Fulton Committee recognized, of course, that in seeking
to eradicate the philosophy of the generalist it would have to do
more than concentrate its fire on the generalists themselves. It
had to concern itself, too, with the specialists in the Service –
the scientists, the economists, accountants and so on.

Here the worry was that so many of the specialists in the
Service were 'equipped only to practise their own specialism; a
body of men with the qualities of the French *polytechnicien* –
skilled in his craft, but skilled, too, as an administrator – has so
far not been developed in Britain'.[9] So, just as the Committee
sought to add a new dimension to administrators – giving them
specialist qualifications and experience in the areas they were
administering – it sought also to add a new dimension of
management and administration to the specialists. One of the
main jobs of the new Civil Service College would be to run
'courses for specialists (e.g. scientists, engineers, architects) who
need training in administration and management both early in
their careers and later'.[10] The addition of this new dimension
would, in the Committee's view, enable specialists to take on
fuller responsibilities and authority within the Service than they
had previously been able to shoulder.

It naturally followed from this that organizational structures

within the Service which were specifically designed to subordinate specialists to the control and supervision of generalist
administrators should be abolished. As Fulton put it:

> We consider the best organization for this kind of work is a single
> integrated structure under a single head. *The head of the structure
> should be the man with the most appropriate qualifications for the
> job.* Beneath the single head administrators and specialists should
> be integrated in teams or unified hierarchies where individual posts
> are filled by administrators or specialists according to the require-
> ments of the task.[11]

So far we have been concerned with indicating the different
means Fulton advocated to get rid of the cult of the generalist
and the dominant control generalists exercised within departments and within the Service as a whole. Hence the recommendations for administrative specialization, for a more specialized
form of administrative recruitment, for planning units headed
by Senior Policy Advisers, for personal appointments by
ministers, for adding a new dimension to the training and
experience of specialists and for abolishing organizational forms
which kept specialists subordinate to administrators. In the last
analysis, though, the Fulton Committee believed one further
major reform was needed to produce the means and climate of
opinion by which the dominance of the generalist could be
ended. This was to abolish the large number of separate civil
service classes.

As we showed in Chapter Two,[12] the Service contained two
quite separate types of class. Horizontal lines marked the
division between higher and lower classes in each particular
area of civil service work (there was even an upper and a lower
Reproduction Class!). Then there was the different type of
classes formed by the vertical lines which separated the
territory of each chain of higher and lower classes from the
other chains. For example, alongside the two Reproduction
Classes, and alongside each other, were the Photoprinters
Class, the Duplicator Operating Class and the Cartographic
and Recording Draughtsmen and Surveyor Classes.[13] But, of
course, what Fulton was primarily concerned with here were
the vertical lines separating the Administrative and Executive

Class chain from the similar chain formed by the Scientific Officer and Experimental Officer Classes and so on.

To replace this complex and restrictive system of classes Fulton proposed that there should be a new open structure based on the following principles:

> (a) Both the grading of a post and the selection of the man to fill it *should be based first and foremost on an evaluation of the job.*
> (b) Management should appoint to each post the person it considers best fitted by his qualifications and experience to fill it.
> (c) No posts should be the preserve of any group except in so far as the individuals comprising the group may be uniquely qualified for them (e.g. doctors for medical posts).[14]

The abolition of the existing class structure of the Service meant, then, two different but parallel operations which in the Committee's view had to be carried out simultaneously. The first was the removal of the 'horizontal' barriers which impeded progress up the various career ladders. More important, though, was the removal of the 'vertical' barriers that, for example, divided Administrators from scientists and engineers. It was these vertical barriers which, by confining the specialists to the relatively narrow range of posts within their specialist fields, kept them out of the departmental command structures – the preserve of the generalists.

With both types of class barriers thus removed there would instead be an open or single grading structure in which there would be an appropriate number of different pay levels matching different levels of skill, responsibility and authority – the correct grading for each post to be determined by an analysis of the job.

The Fulton Committee envisaged that there might be some twenty grades which would contain all the jobs from the top to the bottom of the non-industrial part of the Civil Service; so that all the jobs now performed by the many different classes would be fitted into the appropriate grades. This, the Committee emphasised, 'will require careful job evaluation. This should be based on such factors as the "end-results" required, the degree of personal responsibility involved, the importance attaching to the work and the qualifications and experience needed in the holder to achieve the prescribed results'. [15] So with no block of posts regarded as the preserve of any group or class of staff (except in as far as the individuals comprising the group were uniquely qualified for them) every job in the Service would be an 'open post' to be filled by the person with the best qualifications and experience for it, whether the individuals were one of the new specialist type of administrators or one of the more broadly trained specialists. No longer would there be blocks of posts reserved for members of a particular class or group – and no longer would individuals have to move between different classes to be able to secure jobs in the departmental command structure. An individual progressing up the Service would be able to move vertically, horizontally or diagonally between different jobs. It was to be rather like the structure of the United States Civil Service and, in the Committee's view, this 'open structure' should not be applied only to the higher levels of the Service: 'it is equally, if not more, important lower down'. [16]

The Fulton Committee saw a whole series of advantages flowing from the adoption of this unified grading or open structure; it would promote more efficient and more account-able management and more economical use of manpower (this in part being due to the job-evaluation system needed to set it up and run it); it would lay the foundations for a better promotion system; it was the only practicable way of dealing with the fragmentation of over 1,400 departmental classes each with its own separate pay and career structure; it would help in getting rid of separate and parallel hierarchies; it would make for a reduction in the number of organization levels in a particular block of work; and it would provide for the more flexible use of staff. Above all, it would 'enable the Service to gain the full contribution which scientists, engineers and other specialist staff could, but do not now, make to policy manage-ment and administration.' [17] The Committee concluded that:

> a radical change in the structure of the Service is needed to give real effect to many of the other proposals we have made. The operation of the present structure has bred over a long period of years attitudes and practices that are deeply ingrained. Therefore we do not believe that it is sufficient to leave the structure basically

as it is – incorporate in it some modifications – and then expect the service to operate it in a fundamentally new way. This is the essence of what the Treasury have proposed. They have recommended the merger of the Administrative, Executive and Clerical Classes and a form of open structure at the top of the Service only; the remainder would continue in their existing classes. In our view this partial reform is inadequate. We intend no criticism of the future managers of the Service when we say that, with the best intentions, they could not carry it through to success. As long as a structure based on classes persists the attitudes and practices associated with it will hinder the efforts of management to open up careers to all the talents and to make fully effective all the changes in practice and organization we recommend.[18]

Prophetic words which turned out to be only too true; except that there can be serious doubts about whether it all happened with 'the best intentions'.

To make possible all these collective changes which were to have the effect of ending the concept of the generalist and his monopoly of the departmental command structure, Fulton believed there must be two further organizational changes.

First, the Committee believed it necessary to set up a Civil Service College. This was to help to equip administrators in the subject matter of their field of administration (i.e. to train some as social administrators and others as financial and economic administrators) and also to provide appropriate training in administration and management for specialists. Thus, in the Committee's view the College should provide major training courses which would include courses for specialists (e.g. scientists, engineers, architects) who needed training in administration and management both early in their careers and later; and post-entry training for graduates directly recruited for administrative work in the economic and financial or social areas of government.[19] So the newly created Civil Service College would be committed to a training and research programme which was designed both to undermine the dominance of the traditional generalist and also provide the men and women needed for the more specialist and professional Civil Service Fulton sought to create.

The Fulton Committee also recognized that another crucial

change was necessary if its main objectives were to be achieved. There had to be a force within the Service itself which would be the spearhead or battering-ram of change. So the Committee recommended the setting up of a new department – the Civil Service Department. It would be the job of this new department to implement the Fulton Committee's recommendations and thereafter run the Service in such a way that it would always keep pace with the changing tasks of government. This was such a crucial job that the Committee believed that the new department should be under the control of the Prime Minister. 'No other minister,' the Report said, 'can assert the needs of the government service as a whole over the sectional needs of powerful departmental ministers.' At the same time the Committee recognized that the Prime Minister would require ministerial support. So the Committee recommended that the Prime Minister should 'delegate day-to-day responsibility to a non-departmental minister of appropriate seniority who is also a member of the Cabinet.'[20]

But besides being under the control of the Prime Minister and another senior minister committed to the Fulton programme it was crucial in the Committee's view that the department should be properly staffed. If it were simply to be the old Pay and Management side of the Treasury (which had hitherto been running the Service) under a new guise, that would be disastrous. So the Committee said that the new department 'should not in our view be predominantly staffed by officers who have spent most of their careers in the Treasury.' In particular, the Committee recommended that 'a number of appointments at senior levels within the new department should be made from outside the Service of people with appropriate knowledge and experience of managing large organizations both at home and abroad.'[21]

The Committee recognized that the problems of getting the Report's recommendations fully implemented would be immense. There would be massive civil service resistance to the proposals – which would be more significant than the normal resistance of any organization faced with proposals for fundamental reform. The Civil Service was special. Its powerful role in the running of the state inevitably meant that it would have to be the engine of reform as well as the subject. This was particularly so as far as the recommendations affecting the old Administrative Class were concerned. The class Fulton was trying to transform was the very class which would have to advise ministers on the reforms – and then implement them. As if this were not enough, the Committee expected most of the Civil Service Unions to be up in arms as well. So the Committee sought to counter this in a number of ways.

First and foremost it tried to get the government of the day committed to its proposals before the Civil Service had time to launch a major counter-offensive. Accordingly, the Committee engaged in a great deal of high-level ministerial lobbying before the Report was published. As a result of lengthy discussions with the Prime Minister and the Prime Minister's Principal Private Secretary, Michael Halls, the view gradually crystallized that while one could not expect the Government to commit itself to all the recommendations in the Report on or before the day of publication, nevertheless there was a chance of securing such a commitment to two or three of the Committee's major proposals. This is what in fact happened. We got the Cabinet's agreement the day before publication day to what a cabal of the Committee considered to be our key recommendations – that all civil service classes should be abolished and replaced by a unified grading structure, that a separate and new Civil Service Department should be set up to take over the management of the Service from the Treasury, and that a Civil Service College should be created. And all this the Prime Minister announced in the Commons on the day the Report was published.

But it was a pretty close-run thing, as Richard Crossman's Diaries show. The Prime Minister had circulated a paper to the Cabinet recommending 'that we immediately accept the main recommendations of the Fulton Report'. Roy Jenkins, the Chancellor of the Exchequor, was furious, Crossman says, because the Prime Minister had not consulted him first; after all he was the ministerial head of the department which then had the responsibility of running the Civil Service; and what, of course, made it worse, was that among the recommendations the Prime Minister wanted to accept at once was the setting-up of a new Civil Service Department and thus the complete removal of the Service from the Chancellor of the Exchequer's jurisdiction. No wonder, then, Roy Jenkins was furious. Moreover, the Chancellor had been specifically excluded from our pre-publication lobbying campaign, so clearly he had every right to feel aggrieved.

At this point Crossman's Diaries record that he and Jenkins did a deal; Crossman would support Jenkins in his opposition to any immediate acceptance of Fulton – and in return Jenkins would agree with Crossman's views on House of Lords reform and on his proposal to postpone social service cuts by a week.

As a result when the Cabinet first discussed the Prime Minister's proposals on Fulton, there seemed a majority feeling against what Roy Jenkins described as 'precipitate action'. Crossman recorded that 'all the support Harold got was from Wedgey Benn and Peter Shore, his two hirelings. He was so upset that at this point he stopped the meeting and asked that it should be resumed later'. And when it was next discussed at a special Cabinet meeting on 25 June the Prime Minister began by exploding about a weekend leak on the Cabinet's split over House of Lords reform – pointing out that it must have come from one or two of the Ministers round the table. Then, according to Crossman, 'he glared at us and stopped. There was no discussion and Harold started on the Fulton Report where we gave him a very easy time . . . Harold needed a success for himself and the Cabinet consented to his getting it with a statement tomorrow.'[22] All this is a fascinating insight on the way personal moods and personal antagonisms plus irrelevant rows affect decisions on quite separate issues.

Besides the high-level ministerial lobbying, members of the Committee were also active in seeking to sell the recommendations to the top civil servants most likely to be involved in the implementations of the report. Thus many discussions were held with Sir William Armstrong long before it was publicly announced that he was to head the new Civil Service Department. Discussions were also held with top civil servants in the Pay and Management side of the Treasury about a 'hypothetical' unified grading system if the Committee eventually recommended it. These discussions, of course, were intended to convert them to the idea. Similar discussions were held with at least some of the Civil Service unions.

In the event, these confidential and informal discussions with top civil servants and Civil Service unions were probably counter-productive. They led to a secret meeting of Permanent Secretaries at Sunningdale to discuss among themselves the Fulton Committee's recommendations. So the Civil Service counter-attack was probably launched more quickly and with greater initial weight than might otherwise have been the case. Certainly it ensured that for the two Cabinet meetings ministers were handsomely briefed against the Report.

Still, to the Fulton Committee optimists it did seem on the day of the Report's publication that there was a real chance now of ending the cult of the generalist. Or, as the controversial opening words of the Report put it:

> The Home Civil Service today is still fundamentally the product of the nineteenth-century philosophy of the Northcote-Trevelyan Report. The tasks it faces are those of the second half of the twentieth century. This is what we have found; it is what we seek to remedy.

On publication day the omens seemed reasonably encouraging.

HOW ARMSTRONG DEFEATED FULTON

THE DECISIVE TACTICAL MISTAKE that the Fulton Committee made was to describe administrative civil servants as 'amateurs'. The use of this emotive word may not have altered the eventual outcome of the battles over reform, but it so dominated the early months of public debate that the reformers found themselves unnecessarily on the defensive.

We have seen how the word 'amateur' came to appear in the Fulton report – to bounce against 'professional' rather than to stand on its own as the product of profound contemplation. Yet apart from providing newspaper sub-editors with easy head-lines ('Civil Service amateurs blasted by Fulton' – *Evening Standard*), the word encouraged both the supporters and the opponents of radical change to present Fulton in simple and dramatic terms. 'Ah yes', the radicals said, '"amateurs"'. Fulton's got the heart of the matter – the out-of-touch, old-world mandarins who have been ruining Britain. Off with their heads!' 'Ah yes', the opponents said, '"amateurs". That shows that Fulton doesn't *understand*. We're as much professionals as anyone else – professionals in *government*. How can you take seriously people who make a simple mistake like that?'

There is no doubt that the word 'amateur' did upset a number of people. Although it was used just three times in the whole report, it danced under the eyes of the critics: 'again and again the epithet of amateurism is hurled at the Service', wrote one[1]. When the first full parliamentary debate on Fulton took place – in the House of Lords, one month after publication – it was the dominant issue. 'It is just not fair to refer to the bulk of the present administrative classes as inspired by the philosophy of the amateur,' said Lord Gladwyn, the Liberal peer.[2] 'I much regret that this absurd stereotype was not criticized out of existence during the process of drafting,' said Lord Snow,[3] who in his prebaronial existence as C. P. Snow had invented the phrase, 'corridors of power', to describe the ambience of government decision-making. Lord Redcliffe-Maud, himself a former civil servant, described the 'great profession' as comprising men and women who were 'able, of course; disinterested; with fire in many of their bellies; many of them imaginative, dynamic and creative; all of them humane and honourable.'[4] Baroness Sharp – 'the Dame' in the Crossman Diaries – said 'amateur . . . was the wrong word', but significantly she went on to say:

> I see what the Committee meant, and although I wish they had chosen their language more precisely, I think there was a great deal in it. I believe it is true that in the Service we have overdone what they call the 'cult of the generalist', and the higher one goes in the Service the truer this has been. Far too often, to my way of thinking, Permanent Secretaries have been appointed to take charge of Departments who have come from some quite different area of government.[5]

The Lords debate was important for it defined the terms in which Fulton was publicly discussed. It aired the grievances of senior civil servants at the language of the report (very few *junior* civil servants ever reach the Lords), causing Lord Redcliffe-Maud to quote Shakespeare's Shylock: 'If you prick us, do we not bleed? If you tickle us, do we not laugh? . . . and if you wrong us shall we not revenge?'[6] Above all, the Lords debate forced the supporters on to the defensive, with the albatross of 'amateur' tied firmly round their necks. Four months later Sir Edward (now Lord) Boyle, a member of the Fulton Committee and at the time a Conservative MP, admitted in the House of Commons that:

> On reflection the drafting of Chapter 1 might have been different. I think that many of us on the Committee will have noticed the criticisms which have been made, and I think, looking back, that it would clearly have been better if the tribute to the Civil Service in paragraph 22 of Chapter 1 had been placed before the rather sharp criticisms made in paragraph 14.[7]

Nobody has ever suggested that the great 'amateur' debate was in any way orchestrated. But it served the Civil Service machine well for this diversion to occupy the public stage, for it deflected attention from the detailed substance of Fulton. Threatened with reform, the Civil Service shouted 'revolution!' and set about preventing either.

Recommendation 102 of the Fulton Committee was the touchstone: 'To give full effect to our proposals, the present multitude of classes and their separate career structures should be replaced by a classless, uniformly graded structure.'

On the day of Fulton's publication, 26 June 1968, Harold Wilson told the Commons:

> The government accept the abolition of classes within the Civil Service and will enter immediately into consultations with the Staff Associations with a view to carrying out the throughgoing study proposed by the Committee, so that a practicable system can be prepared for the implementation of the unified grading structure in accordance with the timetable proposed by the Committee.[8]

(Fulton had said: 'Our consultations have led us to believe that it will take from three to five years to produce a detailed scheme and implement it throughout the Service.')

The Prime Minister spelled out what this meant:

> Movement throughout the Service . . . for all civil servants at all levels will be unimpeded. This will mean that for everyone in the Civil Service, whether from a college of technology or from a university, whether he or she comes in from industry or from a profession – all in future, the school-leaver, the graduate, the accountant, the engineer, the scientist, the lawyer – for all of them there will be an open road to the top which, up to now, has been, in the main, through the Administrative Class.[9]

Edward Heath, then the Conservative leader, endorsed Fulton and Wilson on this point. Yet ten years later the 'open road to the top' remained unbuilt. 'Classes' were replaced by 'groups', and some of the lower hurdles to career progress were removed. But only for the 800 or so most senior civil servants was a unified grading system created – the 'open structure' for all people of under-secretary rank and above. Otherwise the Civil Service has remained a jumble of different categories of people with different pay structures, different career prospects, and few chances to escape from the group each one belongs to. More fundamentally, the philosophy of a classless Civil Service has been rejected. The Civil Service Department's defence is that 'encouragement is given to transfers of staff to work outside their normal sphere, enabling specialists to move into the generalist area and vice versa'. This presupposes the survival of a 'generalist area' of work. Fulton's point was that Civil Service work should not be organized like this; the last thing Fulton had in mind was that specialists should be turned into generalists. Instead Fulton wanted, for example, 'integrated hierarchies and teams that embody different skills at appropriate levels under the single command of the officer in charge'. In other words, civil servants with a certain expertise and experience should have greater career opportunities to use their skills – not, as the CSD implies, merely the occasional chance to do something completely different.

Sir William (later Lord) Armstrong remembers clearly the occasion when Wilson revealed his passion for a classless Civil Service. It took place in the spring of 1968 when the finishing touches had been put to the Fulton report.

> There was a little ceremony with four of us – Harold and myself for the Government, and Fulton and Hunt for the Committee – when the report was handed over. Harold and Fulton started reminiscing about the early years of the war. I never knew this, but they both worked as temporary civil servants in the Board of Trade.[10]

It was only then that Armstrong discovered the firewatching bond between Wilson and Fulton on the character of Whitehall.

Wilson evidently liked the conclusions of his wartime colleague, and, as we have seen, obtained cabinet acceptance of the report's main conclusions on the day of publication. This was exactly what some members of the committee most wanted. They felt that if the Government delayed its verdict, the mandarins would mobilize their resources to prevent or qualify the report's acceptance. After the arguments described in the previous chapter, the cabinet agreed to Wilson's proposal on 25 June.

While the cabinet was discussing whether immediate acceptance of the report would be bold and courageous or hasty and precipitate, Sir William Armstrong was operating on an altogether different level. Apart from informing ministers of the Service's mood ('He told me it was very unpopular in Whitehall' – Crossman), he spent his time constructing a loophole in Wilson's announcement large enough to let through Whitehall's slow but determined steam-roller.

Armstrong had no objection to two of the three points Wilson planned to make – the establishment of the Civil Service Department and a Civil Service College. What Armstrong did not like was the third, but most crucial, proposal – the unification of the classes. Yet this was what Wilson most keenly wanted to announce. Armstrong recalls trying to persuade Wilson to postpone a decision on this:

> They [Wilson, Fulton and Hunt] wanted a timetable for common grading announced in the Commons. I told Harold, 'no, no, you'd regret that; it isn't practicable and if you give me a chance I would hope to be able to demonstrate it. I'm with you on getting rid of unnecessary obstacles from bottom to top. But it isn't on for doctors, lawyers or engineers to become administrators. The traffic would be all one way. I think you want to think about this.'[11]

Armstrong was thus arguing against the removal of the 'vertical' barriers whose existence Fulton believed so harmful. Wilson, however, expressed his support for Fulton, and Armstrong was despatched to draft the Prime Minister's statement to Parliament. Obediently Armstrong prepared a draft. It spoke of the absurdity of 1400 different classes and the need for 'an open road to the top' – words which implied acceptance of a unified class structure, but stopped carefully short of a watertight commitment.

Wilson's response revealed an even wider chasm between his thinking and Armstrong's than Armstrong had imagined. Wilson struck out the phrase about 1400 different classes and said: 'Everyone knows what we mean by classes.' The penny dropped in Armstrong's nimble mind. 'What Harold was thinking about,' he recalls realizing, 'was nothing to do with different Civil Service classes, but class with a capital C – upper class, middle class, and lower class. He wanted the abolition of *those* classes.'[12] Thus Wilson's firewatching reminiscences were not so much about personnel management as a *cri de coeur* about the way working class lads became undervalued professionals or executive or clerical officers, while the nobs became administrators and acquired the power. It was an uncomplicated reality that bold reform would change.

To Armstrong, on the other hand, it was an intricate and sensitive issue that required the wisdom of mature, unhurried contemplation. Patiently Armstrong explained the problems: the different pay scales, opposition from the unions, the task of dismantling a baroque structure that had grown up over more than a century. Such details did not interest Wilson. 'I know what you're getting at,' Wilson told Armstrong, suggesting that Sir William was merely casting around for an excuse not to implement a reform he fundamentally disliked.

Armstrong admits that the issue was settled with weaselwords: the two men agreed that Wilson would announce 'consultations with the Staff Associations . . . so that a practicable system can be prepared for the implementation of the unified grading structure . . .'[13] To all the world it sounded like unqualified acceptance of Fulton – to all the world, that is, except Armstrong and (perhaps) Wilson. Wilson meant the idea *was* practicable, and therefore *would* be implemented. Armstrong took it to mean that the scheme would *not* be implemented *unless* it was practicable. 'We both knew what the other would make of it,' says Armstrong. 'It was push and shove.'[14]

The critical point about unified grading was that it required two *simultaneous* operations: the removal of the 'vertical' barriers *at the same time* as the 'horizontal' barriers. The importance of removing the barriers together lay in the interests that had to be reconciled: the staff associations representing executive and clerical civil servants would welcome the removal of horizontal barriers, for this would give their members better career opportunities. But the removal of the vertical barriers would be unwelcome, for their members would then be exposed to competition from specialists for a whole range of jobs; a scientist, for example, might become private secretary to the Secretary for Energy, and engineers might seek policy posts in the Department of Transport. Equally, specialists would favour the removal of the vertical barriers more than the removal of the horizontal barriers. In other words, it might be possible to sell complete unification, as a package, to all the staff associations; each half of the reform would be a bargaining counter for the other half. But if only one set of barriers were removed in the first round of reform, then the bargaining counter would be lost, and powerful interests would come into play to prevent any further reform.

That, in essence, is part of what happened. The horizontal barriers were formally removed, and the administrative, executive and clerical classes were merged into a new Administration Group. But the vertical barriers, except for a few hundred people at the top of the service, were not removed. Ever since, the two largest staff associations, the Society of Civil and Public Servants, and the Civil and Public Servants' Association, have joined with the mandarins in resisting any further unification. The specialists' union, the Institution of Professional Civil Servants, is an isolated minority voice, wanting more reform.

The mechanics of following up Fulton indicate why the approach of the various staff associations mattered. Using the forum of the National Whitley Council, a joint committee was established under the chairmanship of Sir William Armstrong. The official side consisted of eleven generalists (including, of course, Sir William himself), and just two specialists (Sir Robert Cockburn, a scientist, and Roger Walters, an architect). As civil servants their job was to carry out government policy. But as generalists they would apply to Fulton their own special culture and philosophy, amateur or otherwise. They were, according to Fulton, part of the problem to which they now found themselves in charge of finding the detailed solutions – the agents of change, as well as the objects of change.

Facing them across the Whitley table were the representatives of the staff side. If the union leaders had been keenly and overwhelmingly in favour of Fulton, then the official side would have found it difficult to resist them. But on unified grading, they were not. Of the twenty-four people on the joint committee, two or three at most could be counted as Fulton enthusiasts. By finding a formula to satisfy the SCPS and CPSA, the overwhelming majority of the committee could unite behind a form of words that pretended to apply Fulton, but in fact ditched some of its main ideas.

The mandarins' greatest ally – as so often – was time. Politicians are, often, stimulated by brief enthusiasms, while civil servants are motivated by the need to survive the longer term. This divergence helps to explain why civil servants recoil from outright confrontation with politicians. Confrontations reduce the largest thoughts and the subtlest debates to the here and now; they define alternatives and demand action; they require ministerial attention. But if you can defer action and blur choices, then ministers can often be fobbed off when they are interested and (more usually) ignored when they are not. Civil servants win by the cumulative advance of small steps – each one, on its own, a barely perceptible (and presented, therefore, as non-controversial) move, but in aggregate causing a decisive shift of direction. So it was with Fulton.

The first small moves are recorded in an apparently innocuous paragraph in the first report of the Joint Committee on the Fulton Report, in February 1969:

> Tackling the structure of the Service involves difficult problems of timing and order. It would hardly be practicable to concentrate all our efforts over the next few years on working out a complete blueprint for a new structure, and then turn over to it in a gigantic single operation. The present structure of the Service cannot be frozen for five years without damage; there are pressing problems to be dealt with. And the introduction of a new structure is far too great an undertaking to be completed in a single heave. It will therefore be necessary to approach the task in stages . . .[15]

What could be more reasonable? On the face of it, here was the sound of men (not men and women, as it happens: just men) dedicated to Government policy after Fulton, explaining how they were going to smooth the path to reform.

In the light of how things actually worked out, there is another interpretation – that by rejecting the 'single heave', the way was open to precisely the partial reform that Fulton had rejected: the 'stages' Sir William Armstrong had in mind consisted of stage one – what was 'practicable', to recall his conversation with Harold Wilson, and could therefore be implemented fairly quickly; and stage two – what was not 'practicable', which would be postponed, regretfully but indefinitely. The removal, or at least lowering, of the horizontal barriers would be presented as the first part of a long-term reform: but the long-term would never be reached. If the committee's report went unchallenged, it could be used to justify the modesty of subsequent measures: but if it was to be challenged, then where, exactly, was Fulton or Government policy actually being defied?

The committee's report went unchallenged.

What the report left unsaid was the extent to which both the official side and the staff side had already – for their differing reasons – abandoned the Government's commitment to the total abolition of classes. An internal report in December 1968 by the Institution of Professional Civil Servants, speaking for the specialists, recounted discussions on the staff side:

> In our discussions on the National Staff Side Co-ordinating Committee we have reached agreement in principle on the removal of horizontal barriers, i.e. those which impose restrictions on promotion within a hierarchy of classes in addition to a test of merit. We have not yet been able to reach agreement on vertical barriers, i.e. the restrictions which impede movement horizontally or diagonally between classes in different hierarchies. . . . This is understandable. The removal of such barriers largely involves a step into the unknown with no clear view of the consequences. There is, however, a great deal of apprehension about the possible effects on career prospects especially for the generalist classes. That is why a decision on removal of these vertical barriers cannot be taken in isolation. It requires a clear view of career prospects and career structure whatever is done about pay structures. As Sir William Armstrong said at the first Joint Meeting, 'It should also be the task of the Joint Committee to keep the Civil Service in good heart . . . present staff would want to know where they stood.'[16]

Thus the prospect of *simultaneously* removing the horizontal and vertical barriers had already receded. The hope or threat, depending on your point of view, of professional civil servants competing for the policy-advising jobs previously reserved for generalists, was quietly being set aside.

At the core of this development was a new alliance between two groups of people who traditionally keep their distance from each other: the mandarins, and the executive and clerical staff. They combined forces to keep out the specialists. Sir William Armstrong cultivated the unfamiliar role of pal of the workers, and toured union conferences.

On the official side, the generalist-dominated steering committee spawned four subcommittees. The subcommittee on structure – the one charged with handling the issue of class unification – contained, in retrospect, an unusual mixture. Though again mainly generalists, it turned out to include a disenchanted high-flyer, Alex Jarratt, who later resigned from the Civil Service to become managing director of Reed International; and a Scottish Office official, William Pottinger, who was later jailed for his part in the Poulson scandal.

Jarratt and John Heath, an economist at the Board of Trade, were keen to implement the Fulton principles on a unified class structure. They also thought that was the subcommittee's function – a view they subsequently realized was fearfully naive. They found that the subcommittee was serviced by traditional Treasury men with traditional Treasury ideas. One of them, Richard Wilding, had been the Secretary to the Fulton Committee: he was, and is, an unreconstructed generalist, as he revealed in a speech to the London branch of the Institute of Management Consultants in December 1975:

> I come from the ranks of the general administrators who move about in the Civil Service from one kind of job to another. I have had no formal training in management sciences or management itself, and I had had no experience of taking part in management services or consultancy assignments until I was put in this job where I have to supervise them. So, if any of what I have to say seems to you to betray a lack of basic professional knowledge, you will know why.[17]

The Treasury people, Heath and Jarratt felt, set about

implementing the proposals they thought Fulton should have made, not those Fulton actually did make. It was, Heath would complain, 'a funny committee, funny peculiar, that is'. He put in papers using modern management tools such as network diagrams, on how the subcommittee might set about implementing Fulton. The condescending response was that his effort was worthy for an economist but, well, that was not how things were done in the *real* Civil Service.

Heath and Jarratt found that odd things began to happen. Subjects which had nothing to do with Fulton were introduced into the discussion. Decisions they thought had been reached at one meeting were not referred to at the next. Heath started subscribing to the view articulated by Richard Crossman—that he who controls the agenda and the minutes has his hands on the levers of power. The arguments Heath and Jarratt advanced were not so much countered as ignored. Whenever they attacked the enemy, it disappeared into the mist, only to reappear later in different clothes. As disconcerting, the generalists who faced them across the table in the Treasury offices did not even have to discuss their own assumptions in front of Heath and Jarratt: they had their own culture, their own language, which often didn't need words. Instinctively, they *knew* how to wear down the two reformers. According to Heath, 'One of the problems of breaking into this culture was that the discussions were often governed by assumptions which seemed obvious to everyone else. I kept wanting to say, "*Why* is that so obvious?", but you can only do that so often before the system starts breaking down. Jarratt was much tougher than I was.'[18]

The result of this subcommittee's strange deliberations was an internal Civil Service Department paper in April 1969 which set out the 'official side' (i.e., mandarin) attitude to reforming Civil Service structure. This was a masterpiece of Civil Service technique: re-defining Government policy with a subtlety that would confound all but the most expert reader, but with a determination that made the subsequent retreats from Fulton all but inevitable.

It began with an apparently faithful summary of Fulton's criticisms of the Civil Service's structure. One of the weaknesses, it paraphrased Fulton as saying, was the

> under-use of talent and restriction of personal opportunity, because both management and individuals are discouraged from thinking in terms of movement of people across class 'boundaries' except with change of class. In particular, professionals need greater opportunity than they now have to manage *within their own sphere,* to *assist* in the formulation of policy and to enter general management.[19] (emphasis added.)

This version of Fulton was dishonest, not because it was the opposite of what Fulton said, but because it reduced a full-dress condemnation of the class divisions between generalists and specialists to a problem of modest managerial technique. Fulton's own words were:

> The formal and relatively rigid procedures involved in moving from one class to another place unnecessary barriers in the way of the movement of individuals. . . . [The present structure] is a major obstacle to the ability of the Service to adapt itself to new tasks. . . . This rigidity . . . is particularly serious at a time when the tasks are changing rapidly and new techniques are being developed to meet them. . . . The separation of functions has a particularly damaging effect in blurring responsibility and authority in command. . . . The principle of the best man for the job should apply between civil servants of different occupations. . . . This calls for another radical structural change. It means bringing to an end the system in which an individual can normally move between jobs now reserved for different occupational groups only if he himself moves into a different class.[20]

The philosophy of Fulton was to *integrate* the work of specialists and administrators. The philosophy of the official-side paraphrase was to preserve the domain of the generalists, while giving specialists greater freedom 'within their own sphere', and the right merely to 'assist' in policy formulation.

There follows in the official-side paper a sentence which at first seems too trivial to notice, then jars fractionally in the mind, then grabs the reader by the throat and refuses to let go. 'We agree with much of Fulton's diagnosis.'[21] For one thing, the 'diagnosis' reported in the document was sufficiently diluted from the original to render it palatable to the feeblest mandarin.

But who are these people to 'agree' or otherwise? Suppose they did not agree: is their job to implement policy or to make it? Moreover, to agree with 'much' of Fulton is short of agreeing with *all* of Fulton: what does the subcommittee not agree with? And does it see its job as implementing the whole of Government policy regardless, or has it granted itself a mandate to ditch the bits – the undefined gap between 'much' and 'all' – it does not like?

The mystery is partly resolved later in the paper. As we have seen, the Treasury, in evidence to Fulton, had proposed a unified structure for civil servants of Under-Secretary rank and above. Fulton said this would be totally inadequate, and the Government publicly supported Fulton's call for the unification of *all* classes. It is worth quoting extensively from the official side's paper, when it describes its 'approach' to its task of implementing Fulton:

> . . . We would propose to start at the top of the Service, where it is already proposed to introduce a common grading structure, and to see how far down it can and *should* [emphasis added] be extended. We would expect to find – though detailed investigation will be needed to confirm or refute this – that the problems involved in setting up a practicable scheme for a unified grading structure vary in character and in difficulty at the different levels in the organization. We have already proposed in our paper about an open structure at senior levels that the top posts are capable of being organized within a common structure in which occupational groups lose most of their significance and people are selected for posts by reference to their individual skills, experience, and personal qualities on a Service-wide basis. We have agreed that, as an interim measure, this group of posts should have its lower boundary at the Under Secretary level, and it will be for examination whether this boundary should be at a lower level of responsibility in the final structure.
>
> It is important to realize that if it were found . . . desirable to devise different structural patterns at different levels or in different areas of the Service, this would not imply, where this was so, the continued existence of classes in *the present sense*.[22] ·[emphasis added]

Had this paper been published it would have been possible for the advocates of Fulton's reforms to detect, and hence combat, the clear line of retreat that the paper signalled. The mandarins were assuming the responsibility for saying how far unified grading 'should' extend: they were admitting, in advance of 'detailed investigation', that they believed it best to confine it to the 600 or so people at Under Secretary level and above: and the justification they would later use for partial reform was that they had abolished classes 'in the present sense'. It is as if a government, committed to the abolition of capital punishment, were to decide to switch from the rope to the electric chair, and then justify its proposal by saying it would abolish capital punishment 'in the present sense'.

Throughout 1969, the steering committee and its subcommittees worked diligently at re-defining Civil Service reform to suit their own tastes. At no point was Fulton condemned as wrong, or even blatantly ignored: but many of its ideas were subtly yet steadily eroded. Public interest – in terms of press coverage and parliamentary debates – had been substantial while Fulton was sitting, and for a few months after the publication of its report. But as time passed, interest diminished. The Government had announced its policy: Fulton, in the ephemeral world of Westminster and Fleet Street passions, had 'been done'. The mandarins had sheltered from the storm, but now found they could once again wander where they wished.

By November 1969, the new Civil Service Department had prepared for Harold Wilson a memorandum explaining how it proposed to approach unified grading. First, it would implement the 'open structure' at the top. Then it would merge the Administrative, Executive and Clerical classes, to take effect from 1 January 1971 – hence appearing to remove the main horizontal barriers and ending classes 'in their present sense'. The various scientific classes would be merged into one occupation group; and equivalent groupings would take place for other professional civil servants. After that, 'preparatory work' would be done to merge all these groups to provide, eventually, a fully unified grading structure.

Was this really what Fulton had proposed? Through Michael Halls, Wilson's private secretary, the Prime Minister asked Norman Hunt (later Lord Crowther-Hunt) to assess the CSD's proposals. On 21 November Hunt replied. His minute said:

. . . This seems to me an entirely wrong approach. It postpones indefinitely the introduction of a unified grading structure covering all levels of the Service below Under Secretary and it will almost certainly add to the cost. I might add that in my lunch-time conversation my host [Lord Shackleton, then Lord Privy Seal, and minister in charge of the Civil Service Department] hinted that the extra cost of a unified grading structure could well hold it up indefinitely. . . . If the real concern is to do something for the lower echelons of the Service . . . the right approach might now be to start at the bottom of the Service – say CA and Scientific Assistant, etc. level – produce a real open (i.e. merged) structure at these levels and work up.

In a background paper to expand on the minute, Hunt warned No. 10 of the likely consequences of the CSD's partial reform:

The Society of Civil Servants will fundamentally oppose the abolition of vertical barriers between classes. This is because EOs, HEOs, etc. will feel their positions threatened by their Experimental Officer, etc. counterparts. At the same time the Society of Civil Servants want to abolish the horizontal barrier between the Administrative and Executive classes. To concede the latter demand (as the [CSD] Paper on structure does) before the Society has been forced to accept the abolition of the vertical barrier is to abandon an important bargaining counter; this could mean that the Society of Civil Servants will be able successfully to resist the further and more vital merger (i.e. ending vertical barriers) needed to produce a unified grading structure.

Hunt concluded that the CSD scheme

should *not* be proceeded with even though it has been accepted in principle. Excuses are, therefore, needed which will impose such delay as will result in the abandonment of the scheme in its present form. The following ploys might produce this amount of delay . . .

Hunt then listed six ways the Prime Minister might hold things up – asking for extra information, challenging cost estimates, revising the plans for promoting clerical staff to executive rank, and so on.

Wilson could not easily ignore Hunt's sharp critique, for here was the authentic voice from the Fulton Committee saying that their intentions were being thwarted. Wilson asked Halls and Armstrong to continue consulting Hunt. This, Lord Crowther-Hunt recalls, 'was a good ploy. It gave me the impression that I might achieve something; it canalized my energies. But it hardly ever produced any results.' The Hunt-Halls-Armstrong group became known as the 'inner circle': 'a good description, this. We certainly went round in circles. And Michael Halls and myself were mostly taken for a ride!'

On 23 December, 1969, Armstrong proposed to No. 10 his detailed plans for structural reform, including the open structure and the creation of occupational groups. His strategy was also enshrined in the draft of the second National Whitley Council Joint Committee report, due to be published the following spring. Ten days later Hunt wrote to Halls:

The proposed strategy . . . is not the way the Fulton Committee expected the unified grading structure to be introduced into the Service. The Fulton strategy envisaged that the *whole* operation would be based on job evaluation. [Armstrong was proposing only very limited job evaluation.] The first stage would be to determine the optimum number of grades in the Service (the Committee envisaged that some 20 grades could contain all the jobs from the top to the bottom of the non-industrial part of the Service) and then the different jobs would be slotted into the appropriate grades. On this strategy no structural or class changes would be introduced into the Service until a decision had been taken about the optimum number of grades and until the necessary job evaluation and analysis had shown which jobs or groups of jobs should be slotted into particular grades. The Fulton Committee believed it would take from three to five years to produce a detailed scheme and implement it throughout the Service.

A few paragraphs later Hunt voiced his worst fears.

I have serious doubts whether the CSD is any longer actually pursuing the objective of a unified grading structure for the whole of the Service. . . . There is no need at all to give any priority to the abolition of the Class barriers between the Clerical, Executive and Administrative Classes. There is already a great deal of upward mobility. . . . The priority need of the Service is to make possible more sideways movement from the Scientific and other Specialist Classes into adjacent areas of administration/management and to give these Specialists some experience of administration/management *at lower levels* of the Service. This means having a real unified grading structure throughout the Service below the level of Under Secretary and is the only means of equipping these various Specialists with the necessary experience to enable them to take full advantage of the open structure. . . . This, however, is now put off to some indeterminate future with vague warnings that it may never be a practical proposition.

Hunt, then an academic with little experience of Whitehall in-fighting, found himself engaged in an unequal struggle against the arch-mandarin, Sir William Armstrong. Hunt told Armstrong that succeeding drafts of the Joint Committee report represented further retreats from Fulton, and complained, in a note on 13 January, 1970, that

> the new draft talks about going ahead during 1970 to develop and refine a satisfactory job evaluation system for the Assistant Secretary level: 'the aim would be to complete this study . . . with a view to being able to put forward definite proposals about a year from now on *whether there should be a unified grade at this level,* and if so what form it should take.' (Hunt's emphasis.)

Armstrong's feline response, on 19 January, was:

> I quite see why you should think that the new draft represents a retreat. . . . In reality, however, at the cost of saying rather less we are going to do rather more. . . . I feel sure that the programme of work is what counts – and what we have now got is one that enables the study of unified grading to go forward without interruption. I myself am quite content to accept the more qualified statements to which you refer in order to get the substance of the programme.

If that ingenious formulation – reminiscent of BBC wartime news accounts of heavy defeats as 'tactical withdrawals to prepared positions' – left the water more than a little muddied, Armstrong went on to unveil his own version of Government policy, the version he had privately constructed when arguing with Wilson in the weeks before Fulton's publication:

> 'A practicable scheme' for a unified grading structure can mean two things. In one sense, of course, unified grading is practicable right across the Service at all levels – the sense in which we could

have a unified grading structure tomorrow if we threw all the grades together on the nearest approximation of their present pay-scales. But in the other sense of an economical and durable scheme which would help rather than hinder the efficient organization and manning of the work, there are some real questions to be resolved before the Government can decide whether unified grading is practicable over the whole Service.

Thus, finally, the Armstrong gambit was out: his idea of Government policy was not that unified grading *was* practicable and *would* be carried out; but that unified grading would *only* occur *if* it was deemed practicable.

Hunt replied on 12 February by requoting Wilson's original statement to the Commons, that 'the Government accept the abolition of classes . . . and will enter immediately into consultations . . . so that a practicable scheme can be prepared. . . .' Hunt commented:

It is quite clear from this that the remit to the Civil Service Department is to devise a practicable scheme for the implementation of a unified grading structure to replace all the different Civil Service Classes. The remit is NOT to see whether such a practicable scheme can be devised. This being so there are a number of sentences or phrases in the rest of the document [the draft Joint Committee report] which are clearly incompatible with the Government's policy.

Armstrong responded on 25 February:

Perhaps I can say quite simply that the programme proposed represents in our view the best method of carrying out the Government's policy. If that is common ground between us, the question is one of presentation. On that, I do not see any substantial difference between devising a practicable scheme and seeing whether a practicable scheme can be devised, unless one is prepared to say that a unified grading structure is practicable by definition – i.e. regardless of its cost, stability and management consequences. But that is not what you or I mean by 'practicable'. I understand and sympathise with your desire to see the report more positively worded. But we do not yet know, and shall not know until the further work has been done, whether unified grading at all levels is really practicable in the full sense . . .

That the future of Civil Service reform should be reduced to a semantic quibble over the word 'practicable' is, perhaps, something that could only happen amid the rarefied idiosyncrasies of British bureaucracy. But in reality, it served to channel Hunt's energies into a bothersome but, to Armstrong, ultimately harmless debate, while the CSD pursued the mandarins' wishes unhindered.

Hunt was even offered the consolation prize – on Wilson's instructions – of seeing a restoration of the Government's formal commitment to unified grading in the published version of the Joint Committee report when it was published in March 1970. But, to recall the phraseology of one of Armstrong's earlier letters, if it was possible to 'say rather less and do rather more', it was, presumably, equally possible to say rather more and do rather less.

Hunt continued to chip away at Armstrong's defences. He prepared a critique of the Joint Committee report, and spoke to Halls over the telephone on the evening of Easter Monday, 30 March, to arrange to discuss it with him and Armstrong. On 2 April Halls suffered a heart attack, and died a few days later. The 'inner circle' came to a halt. Plans were laid to revive it with Halls's successor, Sandy Isserlis, but within a few weeks Wilson dissolved Parliament and called a General Election. Following Labour's defeat Hunt attempted to pursue the cause of Fulton through the Conservative junior minister in the CSD, David Howell. But the Conservatives had their own priorities, and the contest fizzled out. Armstrong and the CSD had seen off the one man capable of challenging their actions.

Hunt's parting shot was an *aide memoire* for Wilson three months after the 1970 election, after Labour had gone into opposition. Hunt recorded that

I am becoming more and more convinced that the Civil Service Department has no intention of abolishing classes, even though your Government committed itself to this.

5

THE LOST REFORMS

IN MARCH 1978 A GOVERNMENT White Paper on the Civil Service said of the Fulton Committee: 'The acceptance of that Committee's Report in 1968 resulted in a number of radical changes in the organization and management of the Civil Service.'[1] The basis for this bold statement was a checklist prepared by the Civil Service Department for the General Sub-Committee of the House of Commons Expenditure Committee – the 'English Committee', chaired by the Labour MP Michael English. The 20,000-word checklist, 'Response to the Fulton Report', presented the record with evident pride. The CSD's very existence, it said, was designed 'to ensure that [Fulton's] wide-ranging proposals could become fully effective.[2]

On the face of it, much had been done. With the establishment of the CSD, the role of running the Civil Service had been hived off from the Treasury. A Civil Service College had been set up to improve training facilities. A scheme was established 'to promote secondments between the Civil Service and industry and other organizations for periods of about two years.'[3] Internal management methods were updated to improve efficiency. The Civil Service had acted to expand the role of accountants in policy-making and management. And so on. The picture painted by the CSD was of willing public servants actively implementing Government policy.

Fulton had made 158 recommendations. The fact that the vast majority had been, or were being, implemented, was cited by the CSD in support of its case. But Fulton's reforms cannot be reduced to such arithmetical tests. The proposals were, as we have seen, constructed round a central criticism of the dominance of the generalists. The 158 recommendations addressed themselves to changing this: they were detailed means to a precisely identified end. For all its detail, the CSD checklist dwelt solely on the means and studiously ignored the end. The most significant illustration of this involves the central Fulton thesis that the cult of the 'generalist is obsolete at all levels in the Service'. 'The Response to the Fulton Report' makes no reference to this fundamental point. *Indeed in the CSD's checklist the word 'generalist' does not appear at all.*

We have already recounted how the most important battle of all – for a unified class structure – was lost. Although the byzantine complexities of the old class structures were replaced by 1972 with new, simpler, groupings, the essential 'vertical' barriers remained: below Under Secretary level, the Administration Group retained its hold on all policy-making jobs. Other important reforms were also fudged, however. Because much of today's Civil Service is a product of that process, it is worth exploring what happened.

The creation of the Civil Service Department is, perhaps, the best example of a key Fulton proposal which at least *appears* to have been implemented. After all, this change was specifically accepted by the Prime Minister in his statement in the Commons on the day the Report was published. And the CSD has been beavering away ever since. Yet from the beginning it lacked the one crucial ingredient that Fulton considered was vital to its success.

As we have seen this new department was, among other things, to be the main driving force for implementing the rest of the Fulton recommendations. So the Committee particularly emphasized that this new department must not simply be the existing Pay and Management side of the Treasury (which then ran the Service) hived off and somewhat expanded so it could then masquerade as the new Civil Service Department. If that were to happen the change would have been a change in nomenclature only. So the Report emphasized that 'the staffing of this new department must be of critical importance'. In particular the Committee said it was 'important that a number of appointments at *senior level* within the new department should be made from outside the Service of people with appropriate knowledge and experience of managing large organizations both at home and abroad.' Only in this way, the Committee believed, would it be possible for the new Department to develop the 'radical spirit' which, in the Committee's view, was the *sine qua non* for any successful and proper implementation of the rest of its proposals.[4]

In fact, the new department has turned out to be very much the old 'Pay and Management side of the Treasury' writ large. But that is successfully camouflaged in 'The Response to the Fulton Report'. First of all the CSD misquotes Fulton as wanting 'able people from other government departments and from outside the Service.'[5] Nothing there to indicate that what Fulton had really recommended was a number of appointments at *senior levels* from outside the Service. Secondly, in the wealth of detail which then follows about how, in establishing the Civil Service Department, the Fulton recommendations about functions and staffing have been so faithfully followed, it manages to avoid any further reference to outsiders, and therefore makes no mention whatsoever of the crucial Fulton recommendation about outsiders at senior levels in the new CSD itself.

This misleading watering-down process actually started in one of the Appendices to the Fulton Report itself – the one which lists the Committee's 158 recommendations. Here this key recommendation is summarized as: 'Departments should release some of their best men for a period of service in it (i.e. the new Civil Service Department) and some should be appointed from outside the Service.'[6] This summary list of recommendations was drafted by the Civil Service secretary, Richard Wilding – unlike the bulk of the Report which was based on a first draft done by Hunt and subsequently redrafted by Wilding and Hunt jointly. When the list was put before the committee as a whole, neither Hunt nor the other members of the Committee spotted the watering-down. It is a disturbing illustration of Civil Service sleight of hand and of the crucial importance of careful drafting and of being in detailed charge of the process. In addition it provides an example of the Civil

Service claiming to have implemented one of the most important of Fulton's recommendations – the setting-up of a new Civil Service Department – yet omitting from the outset the one ingredient the Fulton Committee believed was vital if the new Department was to mount the necessary effort to implement the rest of the proposals.

The defeat of Fulton's crucial recommendation of the abolition of classes and their replacement by a unified grading structure has been detailed in the previous chapter. The Committee's other recommendations directed at similar objectives met a similar fate.

The proposal that administrators in the future should specialize either as social administrators or financial and economic administrators was very cleverly dealt with. The CSD mounted a special study to consider this. Departments were asked what their requirements were for particular types of expertise and skills in administrative work. The CSD checklist gives the results in general terms:

> The survey showed that the needs of the work did not accord with the proposal to develop administrators in two broad streams: a greater variety of expertise was required and staff would be needed with sufficient breadth of experience to respond to the changing demands of the work.

This was an astute way to justify the maintenance of the generalist tradition. And, of course, there was no publication of the findings that justified this decision. Moreover, the survey had been in the hands of Departmental Establishment Officers – a group of men whom Fulton considered formed much of the dead traditionalist wood in the Service.

But even before Fulton's proposals for some administrative specialization had been rejected, its advocacy of 'preference for relevance' had been summarily dismissed. Five months after Fulton reported the Prime Minister announced in the Commons on 21 November 1968 that the Government had decided not to give any preference in selecting graduates for administrative posts to those who had their degrees in subjects closely relevant

to Civil Service work. Instead, as the Prime Minister put it, the
Service was concerned with getting the relevant individual
rather than the man with a relevant education. Since the Head
of the Civil Service at that time had read Greats at Oxford –
and so had some of his closest advisers – perhaps no other
decision could have been expected.

Another important group of Fulton proposals was expected,
indirectly at any rate, to undermine the generalists. Apart from
unified grading, Fulton proposed various specific ways of in-
jecting greater expertise and experience into the senior ranks of
administrative civil servants. Behind the CSD's bland account
of their implementation, the reality is that little has changed.

First, Fulton wanted late entry to be 'considerably expanded;
there should be no restriction on the levels to which suitably
qualified and experienced people from outside the Service can
be directly appointed.' The CSD's checklist said 'Fulton's
recommendations have been accepted in principle'.[7] The interesting words there are 'in principle'. Could it be that *in practice*
something has gone wrong? Fulton had observed that in the
mid-1960s around thirty Principals were directly recruited a
year, with provision for the direct recruitment of up to three
Assistant Secretaries: 'This is very far from enough.'[8] Ten years
later the numbers were even fewer: around fifteen direct-entry
Principals appointed, and no Assistant Secretaries at all.[9] After
a trial period the Assistant Secretary scheme was terminated by
the CSD as 'a dismal failure'[10] – something that the checklist
omits to mention.

Second, Fulton wanted more secondments to and from the
Civil Service: 'At 1 December 1967 only thirty civil servants
were away on secondment to industry, commerce and local
government. We cannot believe that this is the most that can be
managed.'[11] In the House of Commons in June 1968, Wilson
underlined the point:

> It is envisaged that not only would there be a regular flow of
> recruits on a temporary basis from private and public industry, the
> industries, the professions, local government, finance and com-
> merce, but also that established career members of the Civil
> Service would be encouraged to work in industry and in local

government, with appropriate safeguards of course, so that there would be a two-way flow of experience in these matters.[12]

The CSD's checklist proudly recorded that

a scheme for the interchange of administrators was launched in 1968, after consultation with the CBI, to promote secondments between the Civil Service and industry and other organizations for periods of about two years.[13]

But the CSD then gives the results of that scheme: 'There are currently (October 1975) twenty-three civil servants seconded into industry, local authorities and other UK organizations, and some fifty-six people from industry and other organizations on secondment into the Civil Service.'[14] In addition, a smaller number were involved in exchanges under a special scheme for scientists and engineers.

Those figures do suggest a rise, if only a modest one, in the number of secondments into and out of the Civil Service since Fulton. But other evidence given later to MPs by the CSD suggests that even this picture of slight improvement must be regarded with caution. In an appendix on the annual number of administrative civil servants seconded to industry, universities and local government, the number appears to double from 12 in 1968 to 25 in 1975. But a statistical footnote adds: 'The rise in the figures . . . indicates an improvement in the data flow from departments rather than a real increase in activity.'[15]

Third, Fulton wanted more people with specialist background to have access to the top policy-making posts. The previous chapter recounted how Fulton's plan for unified grading was undermined. But even the one reform that was introduced – the 'open structure' for posts at Under Secretary level and above – has had little effect. The CSD's checklist appears to say the opposite, however:

Appointment to the most senior posts at the top of the Service is open to all, irrespective of their background, who are qualified to fill them. Of some 860 posts at Under Secretary level and above, nearly forty per cent are now occupied by people whose earlier service was wholly or mainly in specialist grades.[16]

What the CSD omitted to mention was that this proportion has changed little since the open structure was introduced in 1972. On 1 January 1970 there were 648 civil servants in the relevant grades: 405, or 62.5 per cent, had administrative backgrounds, while 243, or 37.5 per cent, had specialist backgrounds. On 1 January 1978, the total number in the open structure was 802; they were divided into 471, or 58.7 per cent with administrative backgrounds, to 331, or 41.3 per cent with specialist backgrounds.[17]

In its evidence to the English Committee, the Institution of Professional Civil Servants indicated how the reform was more cosmetic than real:

> The specialists are normally only posted or promoted to specialist posts in their own discipline or profession. There is very little cross posting. This is illustrated by an examination of the top structure of the Department of the Environment in September 1976 . . . Of the four Permanent Secretaries none came from the specialist grades. Seven of the sixteen Deputy Secretaries did. The Committee may not, however, think it particularly revolutionary to find:
> – an economist as Director General, Economics and Resources;
> – a lawyer as Solicitor;
> – an engineer as Deputy Secretary (Environmental Pollution) and Chief Water Engineer;
> – a planner as Deputy Secretary and Chief Planner;
> – a scientist as Director General Research; and
> – an architect as Director General of Design Services.
>
> The remaining specialist – an engineer – is Deputy Chief Executive III in the Property Services Agency. The Director General, Highways, on the other hand, is an administrator economist.[18]

In principle, the open structure abolished the vertical barrier that kept specialists away from the policy-making posts. In practice an invisible barrier has remained: the running of policy divisions is still almost exclusively the preserve of civil servants who have climbed the administrative, and therefore generalist, ladder.

Fulton strongly criticized the failure of the Civil Service to use accountants properly, and called for 'a strong force of highly-qualified professional accountants within the Service . . . at present the Service employs only 309 accountants of whom 64 are temporary.'[19]

The CSD checklist admits that progress has been slow. An internal Civil Service working party studied how to implement Fulton, and came up with a number of ideas; but 'many of these initiatives could not be sustained in practice.' The CSD goes on:

> It was clear that a deeper and more detailed diagnosis was required, and Sir Anthony Burney, a distinguished professional accountant in private practice, and Sir Ronald Melville, then Permanent Secretary at the Ministry of Aviation Supply, were accordingly invited to undertake a thorough inquiry. This was started in 1971 and their report, 'The Use of Accountants in the Civil Service', was published in 1973.[20]

The CSD does not add that publication of this report was delayed almost a year from the time it was completed. Neither Melville nor Burney knew why.[21]

The Melville-Burney report recommended the creation of a strong accountancy service, with the appointment of an eminent accountant to be the head of the profession inside the Civil Service. For more than a year the Civil Service Department hunted for one who would come for a Deputy Secretary's pay; but eventually the post had to be promoted to Permanent Secretary pay and status to attract a man of sufficient calibre. The man they picked was Kenneth Sharp, who took up the post in November 1975 – more than two years after Melville-Burney, and seven years after Fulton. Sharp had been a partner in a private firm of accountants, Armstrong Watson, and was a past President of the Institute of Chartered Accountants.

When the English Committee started interviewing witnesses in May 1976, therefore, Sharp had not been in his new job long enough to make great changes. Even so, the snail's pace of change since Fulton, and even since Melville-Burney, came as a surprise. Six accountancy institutions submitted joint evidence to the English Committee. They said: 'There has been no significant increase in the numbers of qualified accountants in the Service since 1968 when Fulton reported.'[22] A writer on the *Observer,* Michael Davie, read this sentence out to Sir Anthony Burney. 'Good God!' Burney said. 'Unbelievable.'[23]

Fulton had reported that there were 309 members of the Accountancy Service in 1967;[24] at the beginning of 1979 there were 364[25] – which represents a rate of growth slightly *less* than the growth of Civil Service white-collar manpower as a whole. But these figures do not tell the whole story. There are another 500 or so qualified accountants in the Civil Service, but they do not belong to the Accountancy Group. The biggest single group are Tax Inspectors, with their own Inland Revenue career structure. On the other hand, within the Accountancy Group, the number engaged on policy-oriented work is small; half the group work in the Ministry of Defence on non-competitive Government contracts. So although comparison of crude numbers can be misleading, the picture that Fulton described – and condemned – remains broadly true.

This point emerged with stark clarity when Sharp appeared before the English Committee. The subject of 'internal audit' was raised. This is a modern and sophisticated system, used by every major business in the western world, to monitor management decisions and control systems. It is a task that requires qualified accountants. When the Conservative MP Nicholas Ridley raised the subject, this exchange followed:

> *Sharp:* 'There are in fact very few accountants at present employed on internal audit in the Civil Service. The Ministry of Defence has the bulk of those who are so employed . . . The actual forms of internal audit in the Civil Service vary. Some are more developed than others, but there is a general move at the moment towards an improvement in this direction. I believe that more accountants in this field could be of great benefit in the development of modern internal audit with a modern approach.'
> *Ridley:* 'Are you saying that, apart from the Ministry of Defence, internal audit has not hitherto been done by auditors?'
> *Sharp:* 'Yes, I am saying that.'
> *Ridley:* 'Is that not rather extraordinary?'
> *Sharp:* 'Extraordinary it may be, but it is a fact.'
> *Ridley:* 'Surely the internal audit as you describe it, not just checking that the figures are right, but as a tool of management, is one of the most important things in terms of control in the Civil

Service that there could be?'
Sharp: 'Yes, very much so . . . I should like to see many more accountants in internal audit.'[26]

(Sharp conducted a survey soon after his appointment and found that 1700 civil servants were engaged in internal audit, but only thirty of these were qualified accountants.)

That exchange took place in December 1976. On 1 January, 1977 there were 384 accountants in the Government Accountancy Service.[27] Two years later, far from there being the 'many more' that Sharp told the English Committee he wanted, there were actually twenty fewer.

It would be unfair to blame Sharp for this state of affairs. Within the limits of Whitehall discretion, he makes no secret of his wish to reform the role of accountants within the Civil Service along the lines that Fulton and Melville-Burney recommended. Indeed, when talking to outsiders, he is one of the very few Permanent Secretaries who does not instinctively defend the status quo – not least, perhaps, because he is one of the very few Permanent Secretaries who has been in the Civil Service for less than twenty years. He does, however, have an uphill struggle. The first problem is that the Civil Service does not pay nearly enough to attract good accountants. For young accountants – in their late twenties, say – the rates of pay seem comparable; but those who stay in the Civil Service can expect their pay to rise only gradually, while in the private sector the pay of good accountants tends to rise rapidly in their thirties and then level off. For good experienced accountants the figures are way out of line. Sir Douglas Allen, then Head of the Civil Service, made the point forcibly to the English Committee when he described the difficulties of filling the post Kenneth Sharp now holds:

We tried to recruit at Deputy Secretary level and found that we could not get them . . . The fact is that some time back when the highest rate of pay in the Service, at Permanent Secretary level, was around £17,000 I was told when I went and discussed our accountant recruiting problems with the profession that the average member who was going into partnership was expecting to receive at least £23,000 and they would not be interested in the possibility of coming into a Service where the highest rate of pay was £17,000.[28]

There is also a more fundamental issue that takes us back to Fulton's central thesis that the Civil Service needs to be more professional. Policy divisions are run by administrators, and administrators traditionally see accountants like other specialists – as people to turn to when an 'accountancy problem' turns up. Coming from the private sector, where accountants and managers are jumbled together as decision-makers, Sharp found the Civil Service mentality archaic. He wants to integrate accountants into policy divisions, but there is a long way to go. Soon after his appointment he went to talk individually to the Permanent Secretaries who run each Government department. One department, he found, had no qualified accountants at all: the Permanent Secretary, it seems, did not see where one could be fitted in. Sharp persuaded the Permanent Secretary to start appointing some – four in the first instance, with more to come later.

So there is progress, but the pace is arthritic. It is not that anyone actively wants internal audit to be incompetent, or policy-making to be ill-informed, but that the traditions and organization of the Civil Service, and not a few careers, weigh heavily on the side of leaving things as they are. For the consequence of giving accountants an active policy-making role would challenge the very principle that policy-makers should rise above specialist interests and therefore not be beholden to any specialism themselves. If it is accountants today, who will it be tomorrow? Scientists, civil engineers, doctors, architects?

So far Sharp's main success has been in raising the number of senior accountants (at the grade of Assistant Director – equivalent to Senior Principal – or above) from twenty-five in 1968 to forty in 1977.[29] This modest gain seems to be about the only thing that the Government can point to when its record is criticized.

The Government's preferred response, however, is to say as little as possible. The English Committee's report underlined Fulton's diagnosis on the lack of accountants, and criticized the lack of progress since then.[30] When the Government subsequently issued a White Paper in answer to the English Committee, it simply ignored the point; another victory for the generalist administrators.

Fulton regarded its proposal to set up a Civil Service College as so important that it persuaded the Government to accept this recommendation on the day of publication. The College was formally opened two years later. Though the building stands its main purpose has been lost.

As conceived by Fulton the College had three main objectives. First it was to provide relevant post-entry training for those graduates who were recruited to be economic and financial administrators and for those who were to be social administrators; this would then equip the new breed of non-generalist administrators with a thorough knowledge of the subject matter in their respective fields. Secondly, it would provide courses for specialists (e.g. scientists, engineers, architects, etc.) who needed training in administration and management to make them more like their French counterparts. Thirdly, the College was to have two important research functions:

> It will be uniquely placed to conduct research into problems of administration and those of machinery of government. In addition, however, we hope the Planning Units in departments . . . will commission the College to undertake specific research into problems of present or future policy on which they need assistance. Publication and open discussion are important to research; the College should encourage this to the greatest possible extent . . . This combination of major teaching and research functions will enable the College to fill a role that we believe is greatly needed. It should become a focus for discussion of many of the most important problems of the Civil Service as a whole – discussion in which we hope that many outside the Service will share.

So the College was to be an internal spur to better government.

In fact the College has never worked as Fulton intended. Since proposals about administrative specialization were rejected, that put paid to the first of Fulton's objectives. Since the proposals for an open structure from the top to the bottom of the Service have also fallen by the wayside, any courses for specialists in administration and management lost much of their point. But in its failure to become a major research establishment the performance of the College has been most dismal – especially in the light of what Harold Wilson promised after Fulton's report was published.

In November 1968, when the Commons debated the Fulton report, Sir Edward Boyle, a member of the Fulton Committee and then a Conservative MP, specifically asked Harold Wilson, the Prime Minister: 'whether the Government have formed any view on the recommendation in paragraph 102 that the college should also have research functions and conduct research into the problems of administering the machinery of government?' Wilson replied: 'The answer to that question is, very clearly, yes. . . . It is intended that it shall be a major centre of research for major studies, but particularly for the functions and needs of the Civil Service itself. We thought that was one of the very useful recommendations and we support it.'[31]

The man placed in charge of this 'major centre of research' was Eugene Grebenik. On paper Grebenik had the kind of qualities Fulton admired: as a demographic statistician, he had acquired experience in government and the academic world, and in the variety of Government inquiries and advisory bodies that live in between. Grebenik's initial hopes, and his subsequent disillusion, can be clearly traced through the college's annual reports. In his first report, for 1970-71, Grebenik wrote:

> If the college is to attract academic staff of a calibre comparable to those teaching in the university, it is essential that they should be given the facilities for research and publication which are necessary for personal advancement. In the second place, it is generally accepted in institutions of higher education that teaching without research tends to become routinized and dull. . . . Research is essential for the maintenance of the College's standards and morale.[32]

To demonstrate his intentions, Grebenik proposed five ambitious studies: the setting up of passenger transport authorities – their administrative and managerial problems; regional administration by Government departments; comparative administration ('It might consist of a long case study of a major project in Anglo-French co-operation, such as the Channel Tunnel or Concorde'); the management of science and technology in government; the anatomy and physiology of a government department.[33]

A year later Grebenik was more cautious:

> Like Janus we must look in two opposite directions at the same time. Our activities will be under constant scrutiny – and rightly so – by the clients whom we serve, the Civil Service. But we also have to earn the respect of . . . the academic community. . . . The recruitment situation for teaching staff . . . continues to give us some cause for concern. . . . The selection and initiation of research studies moved somewhat slowly during the year because of the need both to recruit the necessary staff and to discuss with the policy divisions of the Civil Service Department and with other departments the projects which had been suggested by Directors of Studies.[34]

Of the five research projects outlined the year before, two had been dropped (on passenger transport authorities, and on science and technology), and only one was in progress (on regional administration).[35]

Then, in 1973:

> At the end of its third year the college may claim to have survived the perils of infancy. But it still faces the problems of growth and expansion, and it would be wrong to suggest that there is entire unanimity about its ultimate size or shape, or about the precise role that it should play in the Service.[36]

There was no mention of research into comparative administration or the anatomy and physiology of a government department. Only regional administration survived.

Relations between Grebenik and the rest of the Civil Service Department (of which the college was, and is, formally part) grew steadily more icy. In 1973 the CSD asked Ralph Heaton, a retired Deputy Secretary, and Sir Leslie Williams, the recently-retired Secretary-General of the staff side of the National Whitley Council, to mount a fresh inquiry into Civil Service training. Their report, in 1974, found that the College was suffering from the diversity of its objectives: 'It is as though the same institution were expected to combine the roles of All Souls and an adult education centre, with some elements of technical education and teacher training thrown in for good measure.'[37]

On the College's research programme, the report said:

> Considered as a whole, the College has not won the complete confidence of the Civil Service. Its research effort has been slight. . . . It has not hitherto been the forum to which one would instinctively turn either for the discussion of important Civil Service problems, or for the promotion of greater understanding between the Civil Service and the outside world.[38]

In 1975 Grebenik responded with his own counter-charges:

> We have not always obtained as much assistance from departments as we would have liked. . . . Research is an academic activity which is unlikely to flourish under conditions where the academic staff have to spend the greater part of their time in repetitive teaching at a non-academic level.[39]

And in 1976:

> I must confess to a feeling of disappointment with the attitudes that I discern in some quarters of the Civil Service, even among those responsible for training, towards scholarship and research. . . . Such attitudes can only have discouraging effects on the morale of academic teachers working in the College. . . .
>
> I now regard it as a matter for regret that the pressure to expand training facilities in 1970 diverted our energies from giving greater attention to more fundamental problems of College objectives. Unless the role that the College is expected to play in the life of the Civil Service is properly defined, the task of its Principal will continue to be one of difficulty and frustration, and the results of his labour unlikely to please anyone.[40]

By now Grebenik was in such open combat with his CSD colleagues that a parting of the ways was inevitable. In 1976 Grebenik retired early. He was succeeded by his deputy, Mrs Barbara Sloman; and to confirm finally that the College was no longer even expected to fulfil Wilson's and Fulton's ambitions, the post of Principal of the College was downgraded from Deputy Secretary to Under Secretary.

One of the curiosities of Grebenik's controversial tenure is that much of the debate was carried on in public. Normally disputes within departments are regarded as private affairs; one of the things that irked more than one senior CSD man was the way Grebenik would use his – published – annual reports to criticize those around him. But even then, Grebenik never spelt out the depth of his disagreements, with Sir William Armstrong in particular.

From the beginning, in fact, Armstrong disagreed with Grebenik about the real purpose of the College. Grebenik (like Fulton) wanted research in depth; Armstrong preferred training in breadth: 'A week at Sunningdale could be the crown of a messenger's career,' Armstrong once wrote in an internal minute. (Sunningdale, in Berkshire, is the College's residential centre.) Grebenik wanted to attract good academics with high salaries and security of tenure; Armstrong overruled him and enforced a three- to five-year contract system, which has never ceased to cause problems. 'The contract system *is* a bit of a stinker,' says one senior College official who is by no means an uncritical admirer of Grebenik.

Finally Grebenik wanted to adopt Fulton's proposal of a College run by an independent governing body 'consisting not only of civil servants but also of men and women drawn from a wide range of interests outside the Service.' Armstrong downgraded this idea to an 'Advisory Council', which meets once a year and has little say in the direction of the College. Armstrong argued that as the College came off the CSD vote, he should call the piper's tune. So when Grebenik failed to secure the co-operation of Government departments for his research projects, all he could do was complain to his impotent Advisory Council.

Since the departure of Grebenik and his attempts to implement Fulton's ambitious plans, the College has settled into a quieter, less controversial phase. It runs 500 courses a year, with an average length of two weeks, covering 9000 students – a thousand of them from outside the Civil Service. It has recorded its successes: a high pass rate, for example, in students it has entered for the British Computer Society examinations. Although it still has problems – nobody thinks the system for training Administration Trainees is yet quite as it should be – there is general consent that the College does a useful job.

It does not, however, do the job Fulton wanted. It is not independent; it is not a major centre of research; it provides no critical spur to better government. Wilson announced one thing to the Commons; Armstrong wanted something different. And as with unified grading, Armstrong won.

Many of the 'lost reforms' we have already considered were at least partly, and usually indirectly, designed to make the Service more efficient. We can see that objective in the proposals for a Civil Service Department for Administrative specialization, for Planning Units, for more late entry, for the abolition of classes, for the Civil Service College, for adding the dimensions of management and administration to the skills of specialists. As these reforms were gradually lost or weakened, so was the cause of greater efficiency.

But Fulton also had a battery of proposals designed for a direct and frontal assault. The most important of these was the creation of a Management Service Unit in each major department which would have the constant job of promoting departmental efficiency. Also in the cause of efficiency Departments were to be divided into 'Accountable Units' so that costs of particular operations could be measured against output. Again, in the cause of efficiency parallel and joint hierarchies were to be abolished.

Not much has happened as far as the last two of these proposals are concerned. And though each major department now has a Management Service Unit, the cause of efficiency does not appear to have been greatly improved. Certainly this was the message which came from exchanges in the English Committee when it started by considering the O and M (Organization and Methods) work of Management Services Units against what Fulton had actually proposed.

Fulton had acknowledged that the Civil Service 'has played a major part in the development of organization and methods (O and M) in this country'. But the report went on to say that 'the work of departmental O and M divisions in promoting efficiency is at present often inadequate.'[41] One reason Fulton gave was the separation of O and M staff from another batch of civil servants concerned with efficiency – staff inspectors. Fulton said:

> The separation of staff inspection (assessing the numbers of staff required for the efficient performance of a given amount of work) and O and M (analysing the tasks and the methods by which they are performed as well as the organization required for the purpose) divides what should be a unified operation.

Fulton recommended that: 'The function of O and M and staff inspection should be combined in the same unit, which would mount operations of varying scale and depth according to the problem.'[42]

This has not been done. The CSD checklist, however, sidesteps the issue. First, in summarizing the Fulton recommendation, the CSD subtly redefines it: 'O and M and staff inspection should be combined *at the operational level*' (emphasis added). The CSD goes on to suggest that in practice that is almost what now happens: 'There is close co-operation between staff inspection and O and M staff.[43]

If the intention was to pull the wool over the English Committee's eyes, it was never likely to succeed. For one of the Labour MPs on the Committee was John Garrett, who had been a management consultant working for the Fulton Committee. When Sir Douglas Allen, as Head of the Civil Service, and John Moore, a CSD Deputy Secretary, gave evidence to the English Committee, Garrett asked them why the reform had not been implemented. Allen said: 'In the discussion which took place in the two or three years after the Fulton Committee reported . . . the Service felt that it was best to leave things as they were as regards the management of these two operations.'[44] Moore added: 'We are building up a general regime under which the CSD will be able to monitor the Service as a whole.[45] What is especially unusual about Allen's response is that it lacked any pretence about who had decided what. Fulton said the Service was doing things wrongly, but 'the Service felt that it was best to leave things as they were'. So Fulton was defied.

The importance of this defiance goes beyond the specific reform, which might appear somewhat arcane to anyone not passionately interested in management techniques. It was part of an attempt by Fulton to bring order to the chaos of Civil Service efficiency checks. And, as the English Committee discovered, the resistance to reform meant that a fair degree of chaos remained. One vivid example concerned the Inland Revenue, whose efficiency had been examined by a management review jointly conducted by the CSD and the Inland Revenue. Who is responsible, the Committee wondered, for ensuring that our taxes are collected efficiently? First, Nicholas Ridley put the point to the CSD's Richard Wilding:

> *Ridley:* 'Do you have figures showing what it costs to collect each tax which the Revenue collects now, five years ago or ten years ago, what it costs to collect similar taxes in other countries and other comparable data about output?'
> *Wilding:* 'I think that this is mainly a question which should be directed to the Inland Revenue.'
> *Ridley:* 'With respect, it is not. It is a question of management. I am asking you, who purport to have done an assignment in the Inland Revenue, whether you believe that our taxes are collected cheaply or expensively. . . . Do you know that?'
> *Wilding:* 'Not in that case.'
> *Ridley:* 'Then who is to do it?'
> *Wilding:* 'I think it is a matter for the Inland Revenue and for the Treasury.'[46]

A few days later the chairman (equivalent to Permanent Secretary) of the Inland Revenue, Sir Norman Price, came to give evidence. Michael English pursued the point with him:

> *English:* 'It is said (in the Layfield report on taxation) that if every mortgagee in the country paid his mortgage repayments net of interest relief and the appropriate amount was given as a grant to the Building Societies . . . your organization could save 4,500 staff at a cost of £18m. Presumably Layfield got this statistic from you?'
> *Price:* 'Indeed, yes.'
> *English:* 'When did anybody first think of this? Presumably there are 4,500 people working in the Department who . . . could have been saved in terms of public expenditure?'
> *Price:* 'Yes, but if I may say so, with respect, that is not our business.'[47]

Price argued that savings on that scale involved policy decisions, and policy was the responsibility of Parliament. Which is, of course, true – but it is not the whole truth. Many instances of inefficiency can, it is true, be traced back to political decisions. Yet those decisions are themselves based on advice – from civil servants. So a rigorous management review ought to show up two sorts of efficiency savings: those that do not involve policy decisions (say, the reorganization of a Department's regional and local structure), and those that do (altering the tax system, or the method of paying social security benefits, for example). The English Committee therefore wanted to see the papers submitted to the Inland Revenue management review teams. Price told the Committee: 'We have nothing to hide; we have no objection at all.'[48] A year later, the English Committee reported: 'We did not, however, receive them and must assume from this reluctance to produce such papers that they would not be likely to alter our view that current management reviews, substantially by Departments of themselves, are weak instruments.'[49]

The English Committee called for a tougher system of centrally-organized efficiency checks on departmental work, under the control of the Treasury. ('The CSD obviously lacks the Treasury's "clout".')[50] More specifically, the Committee repeated Fulton's recommendation for the combining of O and M and staff inspection. The subsequent Government White Paper sidestepped both points. On transferring powers from the CSD to the Treasury, it said this was 'a matter for the Prime Minister. . . . He has not yet reached any view on this particular recommendation.'[51] On O and M and staff inspection the White Paper demonstrated that *chutzpah* is alive and well and living in Whitehall: it repeated the CSD checklist trick of misquoting the proposal, and then saying something like it was being done. According to the White Paper, 'it is important, *as the Committee implies*' that the two groups 'should work in very close co-operation . . . whether in joint *or separate* assignments. Current organization *normally* reflects this principle'[52] (emphasis added). Well it would, wouldn't it?

The issues discussed above touch on only a few of Fulton's 158 recommendations: many others, it must be emphasized, have been carried out. The pattern that emerges is that the old Administrative Class largely chose for itself which recommendations to carry out and which to ignore. Those reforms at the heart of Fulton to make the Civil Service more professional and accountable were either ditched or fudged, even though Fulton ostensibly had government support. The specific consequences for the relations between civil servants and ministers are discussed further in Chapter 9.

That any institution under attack and threatened with reform should resist change is scarcely surprising. In retrospect, that the Civil Service should succeed so completely in its resistance was even predictable. For after the initial policy decisions to implement Fulton, politicians and other outsiders were largely excluded from the process of change. The Civil Service handled it itself. If anyone felt a conflict of interest, he concealed it with ease.

Indeed, the strength of the Civil Service to resist unwanted change was – and is – greater still. It is a sacred rule that ministers carry responsibility for their departments. Now, the ministers responsible for Civil Service reform have been the Prime Minister (one of whose titles is 'Minister for the Civil Service') and the Lord Privy Seal (until 1979 responsible for the day-to-day running of the Civil Service; the Conservative Government transferred this responsibility to the Lord President). If civil servants have failed to carry out reform, it is not they but their political masters who must take the public blame. Which means that ministers are locked into a relationship that forces them to defend their officials.

It is arguable that ministers of both Labour and Conservative governments have – precisely because of their political responsibility – failed to pay sufficient attention themselves to the progress of Civil Service reform. But even a keenly reformist Lord Privy Seal who tried to push reform through would still face acute problems. All the advice and information reaching him, on a host of detailed issues, would come from civil servants themselves. If necessary they could spend man-years putting together facts and arguments that he would often have only hours to consider. And anyway, if the civil servants hold out long enough, there is always the likelihood that in a year or two there will be a ministerial reshuffle and a more pliable ('realistic' is the word civil servants would use) man placed in charge.

Indeed, in one highly relevant case it took just seven months. When Labour came to power in March 1974, Robert Sheldon was made Minister of State at the Civil Service Department. John Garrett, a newly elected Labour MP, became his Parliamentary Private Secretary. It could have been a powerful double-act – the ex-member of the Fulton Committee working with one of the committee's management consultants to reactivate reform. While Labour was in a minority in the Commons, Sheldon and Garrett could do little more than wait and hope for a new Parliament with a working majority, to give them the time and backing to bring about change. But after the October 1974 election Sheldon was moved to the Treasury, and Garrett also departed from the CSD. The impetus to shake up Whitehall was lost.

But then there is little political capital to be made out of reforming Whitehall. It is not a subject that wins elections, or in the past has greatly excited MPs. The English Committee itself observed:

> It is 104 years since a Select Committee of the House of Commons enquired into the Civil Service as a whole, and we recommend that in future the various aspects of the Civil Service should be regularly reviewed by appropriate committee of the House.[53]

Actually, the Committee was wrong; it doubtless gave some pleasure to the CSD officials who drafted the Government's White Paper in response to say: 'The enquiry . . . was the first review of the Civil Service by a Select Committee of the House of Commons since 1942.'[54] Even so, an inquiry every three-and-a-half decades scarcely suggests the watchfulness of a hawk.

PART TWO
THE ROUTE TO THE TOP

6

RECRUITING AN ÉLITE

ONE OF THE MAIN ATTRACTIONS of working for the Civil Service is job security. Once they let you in, you have to do something spectacularly improper to get kicked out. In 1978 out of 567,000 non-industrial civil servants, just 55 were sacked for disciplinary reasons; 57 were retired early 'on grounds of inefficiency or limited efficiency'; 123 were retired early 'on grounds of redundancy'.[1] In practice, a modest dose of common sense and propriety allows you to stay a civil servant until you retire. In the middle and senior administration grades many do just that. 82 per cent of Permanent Secretaries have been in the Civil Service for 25 years or more; so have 79 per cent of Deputy Secretaries, 62 per cent of Under Secretaries and 70 per cent of Senior Executive Officers.[2]

This makes the recruitment of recent school and university leavers – the great majority of administrative civil servant recruits are under 25 – more than usually important. In private industry middle managers and senior executives can be tempted away from rival companies, and frequently are, as the appointments pages of the quality newspapers constantly prove. The Civil Service, on the other hand, seldom looks outside its own ranks to fill any job paying more than £5,000 a year. Recruiting civil servants means picking as many potential high flyers as possible – and at the same time as few potential albatrosses. It is a task carried out by the Civil Service Commission – with scrupulous honesty, but questionable efficiency.

The Commission (CSC) was originally created in 1855 to combat the corruption and incompetence of Britain's ruling élite. A generation of argument had crystallized by the 1840s into a strangely familiar political debate – how to curb the worrying trend of rising government spending. A House of Commons Select Committee on Miscellaneous Expenditure questioned Charles Trevelyan, the independently-minded Assistant Secretary at the Treasury, about government waste. Trevelyan replied that much government work was indeed superfluous; a number of offices were 'completely effete as practical offices for the transaction of business, and exist merely for the preservation of antiquated forms'. Between the late 1840s and early 1850s Trevelyan, together with Sir Stafford Northcote, William Gladstone's Secretary at the Board of Trade, investigated ten government departments. Then, in 1854, they published their conclusions in 'The Organization of the Permanent Civil Service'.

The Northcote-Trevelyan report caused a sensation by its outspoken language. Nowhere was it more pointed than in its description of the people that the Civil Service recruited:

> Admission into the Civil Service is indeed eagerly sought after, but it is for the unambitious, and the indolent or incapable, that it is chiefly desired. Those whose abilities do not warrant an expectation that they will succeed in the open professions, where they must encounter the competition of their contemporaries, and those whom indolence of temperament, or physical infirmities unfit for active exertions, are placed in the Civil Service, where they may obtain an honourable livelihood with little labour, and with no risk. . . . The character of the young men admitted to the public service depends chiefly upon the discretion with which the heads of departments, and others who are entrusted with the distribution of patronage, exercise that privilege.[3]

The report proposed that this system should be scrapped:

> The general principle, then, which we advocate, is that the public service should be carried on by admission into its lower ranks of a carefully selected body of young men who should be employed from the first upon work suited to their capacities and their education. . . The first step towards carrying this principle into effect should be the establishment of a proper system of examination before appointment. . . We recommend that a central Board should be constituted for conducting the examination of all

candidates for the public service whom it may be thought right to subject to a test. . . No other means can be devised of avoiding the evils of patronage.[4]

The massed ranks of the establishment were appalled. Queen Victoria feared that examinations would open up high office to 'low people without breeding or feelings of gentlemen'. H. U. Addington, a former Under-Secretary of State for the Foreign Department, equated privilege with freedom (an equation that continues to stalk British political debate 125 years later): 'Jobbing is a part, though an ugly part, of the price which a free people must pay for their constitutional liberty.'[5]

The reformers, however, received a well-timed if unpleasant boost in October 1854. The British Army fighting in the Crimea was displaying the same qualities of patronage and incompetence that Northcote and Trevelyan had pointed to in the Civil Service; one consequence that month was the Charge of the Light Brigade. Four months later, in the scandal that ensued, Lord Aberdeen's Government fell; and the incoming Palmerston administration, though by no means radical by inclination, felt that expediency demanded action on both Army and Civil Service reform. In May 1855 the Civil Service Commission was born.

The Commission's methods of working have, naturally, changed greatly since 1855 – but its governing principle has not: the Civil Service Commissioners alone are ultimately responsible for the appointment of all permanent civil servants, and the Commissioners are not answerable to ministers or anyone else for their decisions. The Order in Council that enshrines this principle is updated from time to time, but its essentials remain the same. In the words of the 1969 Order,

> The qualifications of all persons proposed for permanent appointment shall, before they are appointed, be approved by the Commissioners, whose decision shall be final, and no person shall be so appointed until a certificate of his qualification has been issued by the Commissioners.

Those words lie at the heart of the Civil Service's freedom from personal or political patronage.

From time to time that freedom is tested, and the boundaries of CSC responsibility are subtly redrawn. How permanent, for example, must a 'permanent appointment' be to require CSC approval? Until 1978 the rule was five years – so ministers could give shorter assignments to political nominees without subjecting them to the CSC recruitment process. By the spring of 1978, however, this rule was beginning to trouble James Callaghan's Labour Government. On coming to office in March 1974 a number of Labour ministers had appointed special political advisers. All were committed Labour supporters, and many had worked for the shadow cabinet when Labour was in opposition. They came to work in ministers' private offices, and in the policy unit at 10 Downing Street for the Prime Minister. Their status was that of temporary civil servant, which meant they were governed by the five-year rule.

In March 1979 the five years would be up. Callaghan realized that the advisers would then need to be replaced – or fight for their jobs in open competition for a 'certificate of qualification' from the CSC. Callaghan instructed the head of the Civil Service, Sir Ian Bancroft, to devise a scheme to allow the advisers to stay on as long as Labour remained in office. With some deft legal footwork Bancroft, and the Commissioners, avoided either a bruising confrontation with the Prime Minister or an abject surrender of their independence. Charles Morris, Minister of State in the Civil Service Department, announced their verdict in a written reply in the House of Commons on 1 August, 1978. The Commissioners' legal advisers had considered what the courts might make of the term, 'permanent appointment'. They concluded that:

the natural meaning of a 'permanent appointment' is one which may continue until the individual appointed reaches pensionable age, and that an appointment which is intended to end at a point of time well short of the completion of a career would not be readily understood to be permanent.

Such finesse! You do not *change* the rules: that would cause all sorts of problems. Instead you *discover they are different* from what you thought: So special advisers could stay on more than five years, while the CSC's independence remained formally intact.

The CSC's independence, as a principle, has survived all the criticisms that the Civil Service is not sufficiently under ministerial control. Indeed, in 1977 when the House of Commons Expenditure Committee produced its own critical report on the Civil Service it argued that in one sense it was not independent-minded enough:

> There may be something wrong with the constitution of the Commission. All its four members are civil servants in the Civil Service Department of Deputy or Under Secretary rank, three of whom have been civil servants all their working lives. We consider that this may make the Commission rather inbred and therefore suggest keeping its existing full-time civil servant membership but adding to them part-time outside Commissioners, so that these outsiders form a majority of the new Commission.[6]

The Government met the Expenditure Committee half way, and agreed to appoint two part-time outsiders to the Commission. In October 1978 the first of these appointments was announced – Miss Patricia Downs, the director of personnel at Woolworths.

The idea of outside commissioners was opposed by Dr Fergus Allen, the First Commissioner. Allen is the Expenditure Committee's odd-man-out: he has *not* been a civil servant all his working life. He began his working life as a civil engineer, and joined the Civil Service as a scientific officer in 1952 at the age of 31. He presents himself as living proof that the critics are wrong when they say only Oxbridge classicists get the top Civil Service jobs. (Allen took his degree at Trinity College, Dublin.) Allen's defence of the CSC is essentially that it has all the experience and professionalism it needs. It is the private sector that has learned from the Civil Service, and there is no need to reverse that process now.

The operation that Allen oversees is indeed considerable. Even though Civil Service manning levels have been reduced since 1975, the turnover of staff still requires the CSC to find more than 50,000 recruits a year, excluding the blue-collar industrial workers employed in the service. To keep this task manageable, and the size of the CSC itself within bounds, the CSC only processes a minority of applications itself. Most recruitment work – finding 40,000 or so new clerical officers and assistants, typists, and local officers – is subcontracted to individual ministries and done locally. The CSC's role is to set the ground rules and monitor the results.

Clerical Assistants comprise the largest number of new recruits – almost 26,000 in 1978 out of 62,700 non-industrial Civil Service recruits.[7] Most are under 20 when they join, and almost three-quarters are women. They need two O-levels, including English language. This is how the CSC describes the job in one of its recruitment leaflets for school leavers:

> The Clerical Assistant is on the first rung of the administrative staff ladder. The duties typically involve keeping records, sorting and filing papers, and some simple figure work – perhaps using a calculator. There may be some straight-forward letter-writing, and time spent dealing with inquiries from the public. The job is very much like that of a junior clerk in a large business firm.[8]

A further 10,000 people, two-thirds of them women, are recruited as Clerical Officers, or to equivalent grades. These are the front-line infantry in dealing with the public. They are the people at the counter in Social Security Offices; they answer many of the letters and telephone calls to do with, say, driving licences and tax returns. They need five O-levels, including English language. Like Clerical Assistants, Clerical Officers have traditionally been school-leavers, but in recent years an increasing proportion have joined the Civil Service later: in 1978, 39 per cent of male recruits and 43 per cent of female recruits were in their twenties.[9] An increasing minority are even graduates, reflecting something of a chasm between the widespread opportunities for entering higher education and the scarcity of challenging jobs afterwards. In particular the CSC finds that the job of Clerical Officer appeals to a number of married graduate women: it offers the chance of a job near home, and more interesting work than that available to most secretaries.

Examinations have only recently started to intrude into the

world of Clerical Assistant and Officer selection. They are principally for people without the necessary GCE qualifications, and test whether the applicant is adequately numerate and literate. One of the exercises, on comprehension, requires ten questions to be answered in ten minutes:

> Each question consists of a pair of sentences. *One* of the sentences does not read sensibly because two of its words have been interchanged. You have to find these two words and put a tick through each, making sure the ticks go clearly through the words you intend to mark. (There is no need to make any mark on the sentence that is correct.)
> Example:
> Our station leaves the train in 5 minutes.
> The weather next day was no better.[10]

The first round of Clerical Officer tests, from which that sample was taken, was found by the CSC to be not wholly satisfactory, and future tests are likely to be rather different.

The CSC is directly concerned with the recruitment of up to 12,000 civil servants a year by open competition; it also sets 'limited competitions' which allow 4-5,000 civil servants a year to achieve promotion faster than they would by the normal route within their own department. The cutback in Civil Service manning levels has been harshest in its impact on open competition places, which allow outsiders to try for Executive Officer and more senior jobs in the administrative grades, and their equivalents in the more specialized grades. When vacancies arise, they tend to be filled more slowly than before, and then to be filled with promoted rather than newly recruited staff. Between 1974 and 1978 the number of civil servants recruited by open competition fell from 12,000 a year to 5,500, reducing candidates' chances of success from one in six to one in fourteen[11]. The CSC's open competitions normally provide more jobs for new graduates than any other single employer, so the cutback had a significant national impact on graduate employment prospects.

About half the civil servants recruited centrally are Executive Officers. According to the CSD,

There are four main types of work that Executive Officers do. They may be in charge of a section of Clerical Officers and Clerical Assistants in – say – a Department of Health and Social Security Office. Here it is the Executive Officer's responsibility to see that the clerical staff are manning the counters, and working properly. The clerical staff will be trained to deal with routine matters, but anything out of the ordinary will be referred to the Executive Officer. A second area of work is acting as an assistant to a senior civil servant – arranging meetings, collecting and collating information, and generally taking charge of the spade-work that is involved in any policy matter. Thirdly, Executive Officers are the people who will go, on their own initiative, outside the office to take the department's work to the public. They may visit a factory to discuss a VAT return, or call on an old person to explain about supplementary benefits. Finally about a third of Executive Officers undergo special training and take up more specialized work, often with their own job titles. The Inland Revenue has a large staff working on the assessment of taxes and on their collection. District Auditors in the Department of the Environment keep a check on local authority expenditure, and the Department of Trade has executive staff who investigate companies in compulsory liquidation or bankruptcy . . .[12]

Until 1948 the recruitment of Executive Officers was almost wholly confined to grammar-school leavers. The upper age limit was 19. The method of choice was examination only, and places were fiercely contested. In the 1930s success guaranteed a secure place in the middle class at a time when jobs were scarce and university places were far fewer than today. After the Second World War the school-leavers' examination was replaced by an interview and graduates were also allowed to compete. Today the age limit is 28, but even that will soon be scrapped. In November 1977 a 37-year-old woman complained to an industrial tribunal that she had suffered discrimination; although the age limit applied to both sexes, she argued that in practice this put women at a disadvantage, because in their twenties many women were busy looking after young children. The tribunal upheld the woman's case, and ordered the Civil Service Department to sort out a different, non-discriminatory recruitment system by 1980.[13]

In 1976, when the cutback in recruitment started to bite, written examinations were reintroduced to select candidates for interview. The Executive Officer Qualifying test (EOQT) is specifically intended as a valve, to be opened more widely or closed more tightly according to the numbers of EO recruits that the Civil Service requires. A candidate could 'pass' the EOQT one year, while a better candidate might 'fail' the following year if the need for recruits suddenly falls. That is precisely what happened in 1977. Unknown to candidates, the CSC simply raised the pass mark. In a letter to the chairmen of EO interviewing boards, the CSC explained its decision: 'Because the number of applications is again likely to be very high while available posts will be much fewer than last year, the qualifying standard has been raised in the EOQT and no candidate with a pass mark of less than 108 will be invited for interview.'[14]

The EOQT consists of three papers. The first is similar to a standard intelligence test. For example: Which one of the following words would look the same if the two middle letters were turned from top to bottom? KILT, AXIS, DROP, FACT, SHUN. (Answer, AXIS.)[15] The second paper tests numeracy. Originally it was entitled 'Graphs and Tables'; but this was felt not to convey the spirit of practical Civil Service office work, so in 1977 it was renamed 'Enquiries from Management'.

The third paper is called an Executive Problems Test. The CSC describes it as consisting 'of a number of problems of the kind that can arise in administration'. In fact it is a souped-up intelligence test. For example:

> You are a school secretary making arrangements for the annual outing. The children have been given details of five possible outings, called A, B, C, D and E, and have been asked to place them in their order of preference. When the orders of preference were scrutinized it was found that they could be arranged in seven groups. The table shows the order of preference of each of the seven groups of children. It will not be possible to arrange five different outings; but it will be possible to arrange two, and the headmaster has told you to choose the two which will permit every child to have either his first or his second choice. In order to do this, which two will you choose?

Table of preferences

Group of children	Outings in order of preference
1	B A C E D
2	E D B C A
3	A B E C D
4	C B A E D
5	D E C A B
6	A B D C E
7	A D B E C (Answer: B and D)[16]

Those candidates who show themselves capable of turning letters on their head and organizing school outings then go before one of the twelve interviewing boards that sit in different parts of Britain. Each interview lasts about thirty minutes.

There is nothing remotely casual about Civil Service interviews. The CSC goes to considerable lengths to make sure the interview boards operate to a uniform standard. In 1977 the CSC issued its interviewing panel members with a 31-page guide, 'An introduction to Selection Interviewing'. Although the guide could be applied to any large organization looking for staff, it gives an illuminating insight into the methods of Civil Service recruitment boards. It says that interviewing boards should have three or five members. A board of two is too small: the two will either agree, with the risk of reinforcing each other's prejudices, or they may be so unlike that 'there is the possibility of deadlock or of uneasy compromise'. More than five makes the board unwieldy; and 'having an odd number of people on the Board avoids a cleavage of opinion into two equal groups.' Hence, three or five are the favoured numbers: 'generally speaking, three is the ideal number. . . . A board of three contains some variety without being unduly formidable.'[17] (In Executive Officer interviews the three normally consist of a retired civil servant as chairman, together with two representatives of Government departments.)

Interviewers are advised to 'be friendly but purposeful. . ... The first essential is to get the candidate talking freely. One can start with simple questions which are easy for him to answer, and progress to more searching questions which require time for reflection.'[18] One important rule is to avoid leading questions: 'A certain candidate had failed his A levels the first time he took them and said "I did not work too hard that year". Instead of asking "Why?" the interviewer said "You had other interests?" and smiled knowingly. The candidate just said "Yes".'[19] Open-ended questions are preferred: 'The most inefficient way to conduct an interview is to ask a series of questions and on each occasion to obtain a plain Yes or No.'[20]

The guide then gives a cautionary example of how brief replies to persistent open-ended questioning revealed the true attitude of a candidate from Edinburgh for a post in the National Gallery:

'You have a good Fine Arts degree from Edinburgh and an M Phil. from Sussex; which branch of the Arts interests you most?'
'Painting.'
'Any particular period?'
'Renaissance and nineteenth and twentieth century.'
'What interested you particularly in the Royal Scottish Academy Exhibition this year?'
'I didn't see it. I only get an hour for lunch.'
'But it is open until 9pm.'
'My evenings are fully occupied.'
'What is the attraction to you of working for the National Gallery?'
'I hate the commercialism of dealers' galleries and the atmosphere would be so different.'
'Do you know the collection in the National Gallery?'
'Oh, very well.'
'Fine. Do you have a favourite school?'
'French nineteenth century.'
'How would you like to see this school strengthened in the Gallery?'
A blank look and an inadequate reply.[21]

Each board member has a form which he starts to fill in while the interview is in progress. In Executive Officer interviews a five-point scale is used to assess each of seven qualities: appearance and bearing; clarity of expression; speed on the uptake; reasoning powers; independence of mind; initiative; range and depth of interests. After each half-hour interview the board compares notes, finally distilling its impressions into a single mark, on a one (excellent) to nine (very poor) scale, and the chairman adds some comments on the form which then goes to the CSC's headquarters in Basingstoke. This is one chairman's report on a woman who scored five, and just passed.

> Miss C has the force of personality which comes to a woman who has worked in a man's world (in charge of a petrol station) and she has the self-confidence and the ready tongue of those who have had to live by it. She is devious rather than subtle but she would get results and would not lack courage. She has her share of general intelligence but for a time does not seem to have put it to best use. She would be acceptable to Employment Services Agency as an employment adviser.[22]

The normal pass mark is six, but in Basingstoke the CSC raises or lowers the pass mark to obtain the right number of successful candidates for the jobs available. Candidates are not told their board mark; they are simply told whether they have been recommended for appointment or not.

There can be no doubt that the CSC goes to great lengths to operate a system that is fair, in the sense that a candidate's chances do not vary much with the vagaries of board membership. This concern for uniformity is clearly proper, and it is a reasonable – if somewhat crude – measure of the CSC's success that it is seldom criticized for lack of uniformity. To say the system is as uniform as it can be is, however, by no means the same thing as saying it is unbiased: merely that if there are biases, they operate in a standard way.

Selection bias is an emotive topic, and also a difficult one. The existence of bias can be suggested, but not proved, by statistical tests. Figures supplied to the House of Commons Expenditure Committee in 1977 showed that candidates with first-class degrees had no better chance of succeeding in the Executive Officer Competition than did candidates with third-class degrees.[23] But does this mean that the qualifying tests for interviewing boards are inefficient at spotting bright candidates – or that they are properly looking for different qualities from those tested in university examinations? In the words of one Civil Service Commissioner, who had no doubt that the system worked well, 'EO boards may well reject candidates with firsts because they are wet.'[24] But that does not fully answer the problem. Statistics here are about the aggregates of individual performances: *in aggregate,* there is no reason to expect first-class graduates to be 'wetter' than third-class graduates – while there is some reason to expect them to be cleverer and have greater application to cerebral work.

There is another piece of suggestive evidence of bias. It concerns race, and the EO qualifying test. The Civil Service Department has a policy of non-discrimination; but doubts have been expressed as to how completely this policy is implemented on the ground. To gather data the Civil Service Department commissioned the Tavistock Institute of Human Relations to do a survey; its results, published in 1978, suggest that non-white candidates have a harder time at each stage of the selection process than white candidates. One of the more striking tables shows *that in 1976, non-white candidates who failed the EOQT were more likely to have degrees than white candidates who passed.* Only 20 per cent of non-white graduates passed the EOQT, compared with 80 per cent of white graduates.[25] The Tavistock survey contains a number of studies; in any one of them the small sample sizes might explain the statistical biases. But repeatedly, in different parts of the Civil Service and at different levels, Tavistock found that successful non-white candidates generally needed to be more highly qualified than successful white candidates.

Tavistock is careful to avoid jumping to conclusions, usually suggesting that further monitoring is needed. On the EOQT, Tavistock says:

> It would be difficult to discriminate unfairly and deliberately against coloured candidates in a highly organized competition such as the one in question. The data available does however lead us to recommend most strongly that a special monitoring study should be made of the role of the qualifying test in this competition, both for sifting and interview, and of the performances in it of white and coloured candidates of varying origin and background.[26]

In other words, there is a suspicion of a bias that is inherent in the EOQT, but the discrimination is not deliberate.

The significance of such a bias, in this, and in other Civil Service selection processes, is partly about race: governments that pass laws about racial equality have a self-evident duty to apply fully the spirit and letter of those laws within their own fiefdom. The significance of the bias is also partly about the nature of the Civil Service Commission: the CSC has constructed an impressive superstructure to ensure a uniform selection system – but if the foundations are faulty, the superstructure must be approached with extreme caution.

But there is a more fundamental point. The most likely kind of bias is, in the broadest sense, a social/cultural one: each generation of civil servants favours people like themselves. If this is the case, then the defects in the selection system go to the heart of the problem identified by Fulton, of a Civil Service that has insulated itself from many of the pressures and requirements of a modern industrial power, and instinctively seeks to preserve its own out-dated image of itself.

That hypothesis needs testing, and there can be no better place to look than the entrance gate to the citadel of the Service: the competition to become administration trainees (ATs). This is the test that most people who want the senior policy-advice jobs in Whitehall must first pass. The numbers involved are small: 100 to 200 new ATs a year are recruited, compared with the total Civil Service recruitment of more than 50,000. But from the pool of ATs are drawn the people who both influence ministers and control the Civil Service itself. They join together, progress together, and wield influence together. In 1946 three young men met for the first time when they competed together to become Assistant Principals (the predecessors of Administration Trainees). They were Robert Cox, Douglas Wass and Ian Bancroft. Today Sir Robert Cox runs the government's Property Services Agency (which is responsible for all Government buildings, from Post Offices and Army barracks to 10 Downing Street and the Whitehall ministries); Sir Douglas Wass runs the Treasury; and Sir Ian Bancroft is head of the Home Civil Service. As Bancroft describes it, their lives and careers have crossed and recrossed like those of the characters in 'A Dance To The Music Of Time' by Anthony Powell – one of Bancroft's favourite authors.

Some people escape early and achieve eminence in other fields. Edward Heath left the Civil Service after a year to pursue a political career. Mike Brearley, the England cricket captain, achieved one of the highest marks in the 1964 entrance competition, but never took up his place. But in general, those who pass the competition join the Civil Service; and those who join stay. So the way the Civil Service picks men and women in their early twenties is of no little importance for the future of Britain's government. If the system does not radically change, the new ATs of the late 1970s will be the Permanent Secretaries of the year 2010.

Fulton found that the damaging concept of the generalist administrator was reflected in the entry competition, which was biased towards candidates who had been to public school, then Oxford or Cambridge, and had studied classics or ancient history. On the face of it, new recruits were very much sought in the mould of their elders. But this did not happen in isolation. In 1946 the Civil Service sought the help of an eminent psychologist – a specialist, therefore, and not a generalist – to identify and spell out the qualities to be desired in new administrators. His advice was followed, and most of today's most senior civil servants are people who thirty years ago were deemed to possess the qualities he listed. What nobody realized at the time was that the psychologist was an academic con-man, Sir Cyril Burt, whose influential eugenic theories about inherited, class-related, mental abilities, were derived from fraudulent 'studies' and faked 'results': many of his published figures were simply made up.

Burt's faked figures lent great support to the ideology of the 'all-rounder' élite. A paper from Burt was incorporated into the Spens Report in 1938, which led to the creation of the 11-plus exam. In the following passage it takes little effort to change 'child' to 'civil servant', and 'childhood' and 'classroom' to 'Civil Service' to obtain the general principles by which the pre-Fulton Civil Service operated:

Intellectual development during childhood appears to progress as if it were governed by a single central factor usually known as 'general intelligence', which may be broadly described as innate all-round intellectual ability. It appears to enter into everything which the child attempts to think, or say, or do, and seems on the whole to be the most important factor in determining his work in the classroom.[27]

Burt's work and theories are now discredited, but echoes of them can still be found in the Civil Service. His specification for administrative recruits has been revised; yet the very first requirement is still for 'a good all-round intellect'. That is not in itself, of course, a heinous quality either to possess or to seek: the point is, who defines it and how. What Burt did was to underpin the Civil Service's own instincts with spurious theoretical foundations. Fulton wanted to tilt the bias away from the old 'generalist' élite. The committee proposed 'preference for relevance', so that candidates with degrees in subjects like engineering, economics and the social sciences should have a better chance of becoming administrators and policy-makers;[28] more generally Fulton said: 'There should be an inquiry into the methods of selection to consider ways of making the process of selection more objective in character . . .'[29]

The Government quickly rejected 'preference for relevance', but did set up an inquiry into the selection process. It was chaired by Jack Davies, then assistant to the Governor of the Bank of England, and twenty-five years previously the chief psychologist in the War Office's directorate for personnel selection. (That was the time when the War Office was pioneering the selection techniques – for choosing army officers – that the Civil Service subsequently adopted.)

The conclusions of the Davies Committee contained none of Fulton's reforming zeal:

Method II [the system devised with Burt's help that by the 1960s had largely transplanted 'Method I' – written examination – as the selection system for choosing administrators] is a selection system to which the Public Service can point with pride . . . We think that the make-up of the entry . . . reflects the character of the field of candidates who chose to compete rather than the choice made by the selectors from within that field. We found no evidence of bias in Method II itself, either in the procedures or on the part of the assessors . . . With certain modifications we have endorsed the

Method II procedure as a suitable means of selecting potential Administrative Class civil servants.[30]

The reformers' reaction was sharp. According to Lord Balogh,

> How could an employee of The Old Lady, sitting in the innermost nook of the old boy network, impartially adjudicate whether an interview (with the old boy network) would or would not yield the happiest of results? By condemning it, he would condemn himself.[31]

Reviewing the Davies report for the English Committee eight years later, Lord Crowther-Hunt attacked the conclusion that no biases existed rather more clinically:

> This really was a white-washing conclusion which in fact ran counter to the Davies Committee's own statistics. For example, the Davies Report showed that in 1968 Oxford and Cambridge provided only 35 per cent of the candidates for Method II – but they provided 59 per cent of the successes. More important, the Davies Report showed that while the majority of those applying to get into the Administrative Class came from LEA Schools (56 per cent in 1968) the LEA Schools provided only a minority of the *successful* candidates (37 per cent). Conversely – while the public and other fee-paying schools provided 44 per cent of the candidates, their candidates formed 63 per cent of the successes.
>
> In other words – the successful candidates were very far from being an accurate reflection of the different proportion of candidates – in spite of the Davies Committee's contrary conclusion.[32]

In 1977, when MPs on the English Committee examining the Civil Service met to prepare their final report, the committee divided between the critics and the agnostics. The critics – most Labour MPs on the committee – said in their minority report:

> We recognize 'a bias of the Civil Service recruiting in its own image', a bias of the Civil Service paying too much attention to certain literary skills; a bias of the Civil Service in favour of the rounded individual of the sort created by the atmosphere of Oxford and Cambridge; and a bias of class, caste and cast of mind.[33]

The majority report conceded that the statistics showed biases; but:

The pro-Oxford and Cambridge bias may be expected if the Civil Service Commission 'is seeking to recruit the most able' graduates. Whether the pro-independent school bias is due to the same cause is more doubtful; one cannot be certain from the statistics. The pro-arts bias may result from fewer of the ablest scientists applying but again one cannot be certain of this.[34]

The most recent year for which figures are available in detail is 1978. They help isolate at which, if any, of four points in the selection process bias might occur:

1) Bias in the self-selection of candidates – in other words, are good classicists more attracted than good economists to the Civil Service?

2) Bias in the written qualifying test that all candidates take.

3) Bias in 'Cizbee' – the Civil Service Selection Board that invites promising candidates to London and subjects them to an ingenious cocktail of tests, exercises and interviews.

4) The Final Selection Board, a formal interview that reviews the mark awarded by Cizbee and finally decides who is acceptable as future administrators (or as diplomats or tax inspectors, where the procedure is almost identical).

During 1978 more than 3,000 candidates took the qualifying test; 2,500 were external candidates; another 600 were internal – principally Executive Officers hoping to speed up their career progress.[35] (These figures include all candidates who entered administrative trainee as one of their choices. It therefore includes some people whose first preference was the Diplomatic Service or the Inland Revenue; but it excludes those whose sole ambition in entering the competition was to become, say, a tax inspector.)

The qualifying test consists of a series of written papers. Typically a candidate must: reduce an article of 1,500 words to a summary of 300 to 350; give advice on an imaginary government problem (like – should a seaside town in peril from subsidence caused by disused mineshafts be evacuated?); analyse some tables of social statistics; and answer tests on verbal intelligence, comprehension and 'data sufficiency'.

These are the figures for external candidates passing the qualifying test in 1978:[36]

Type of School	Number who sat qualifying test	Number who passed test	Percentage who passed
Private/Direct Grant	838	310	37
Maintained	1,616	400	25
University			
Oxbridge	612	305	50
Non-Oxbridge	1,909	418	22
Degree subject			
Arts	1,221	403	33
Science & technology	313	92	29
Social Sciences	926	216	33

The most marked statistical bias appears to be towards Oxbridge candidates. But the CSC:

> has little doubt that this familiar pattern arises largely if not entirely because the overall calibre of candidates from Oxford and Cambridge who apply for Civil Service administration is higher than that of the generality of applicants from other universities . . . Oxford and Cambridge still attract more than their share of the most able school-leavers as measured by A-level grades.[37]

Equally, the apparent dominance of arts graduates among applicants is explained by the CSC in terms of the mix of candidates:

> It is a fair assumption that the best social scientists and scientists will seek careers in their specialisms, whereas Civil Service administration is high on the list of career choices for many of the most able graduates in non-vocational arts and humanities courses.[38]

The interesting point about this comment is that in order to demonstrate the qualifying test's objectivity, the CSC upholds the principle of future mandarins being drawn in large measure from the ranks of 'non-vocational arts and humanities' students – a group that closely approximates to the generalists condemned by Fulton.

The one statistical bias that the CSC cannot offer a ready explanation for is that which seems to benefit pupils from private schools: 'There can be no question of subjective bias,' the CSC says, 'since the marking is done anonymously.'[39] The problem for the CSC here is that either conclusion would be embarrassing: if the bias flows from the nature of the qualifying test, then the figures would suggest a clear class bias and lend support to the Labour MPs' criticism of the Civil Service 'recruiting in its own image'. But if the bias is not in the tests but in the self-selection of candidates, then the Civil Service is failing to broaden the social base of its administrators by attracting enough of the brightest ex-pupils from state schools to apply. Indeed, the fact that the public schools educate less than one in fifteen children but provide four out of ten applicants to the administrative Civil Service, suggests such a trend.

It may well be true that the candidates who pass the qualifying tests are, broadly, the most capable people who take it: in which case, the CSC has a large problem in making a career in the administrative grades attractive to a wider cross-section of Britain's graduates. To some measure the selection biases are bound to reflect class bias in the educational system itself; but the CSC's Dr Fergus Allen maintains it has no business interfering with these:

> Our function is to fill permanent pensionable posts in the Civil Service by open competition and on merit. It is not to indulge in our own theories about how the educational system should be changed, if at all. We have to accept the output of the educational system as it is.[40]

Yet that is precisely what the Civil Service has not done. The 'output of the educational system' has changed markedly during the last thirty years: the great majority of graduates are now non-Oxbridge, non-public school, and non-arts and humanities. If the results of the administrative qualifying test are taken as an objective reflection of the calibre of the candidates; and if it is thought important that the Civil Service should attract a cross-section of Britain's brightest graduates – then, quite simply, the Civil Service is attracting the wrong candidates.

According to one Oxbridge careers adviser, the image of the Civil Service as an employer of ex-public school Oxbridge arts graduates is still potent:

> One of the attractions is not the work as such, but the fact that
> people are conscious that they want stimulating colleagues: it's the
> environment, rather than the job. The Civil Service is one of the
> few employers who look kindly on post-graduate students in
> mediaeval history.
> I get some chemists who come and see me who don't know what
> they want to do. I would ask first, 'Do you want to use your
> chemistry?' I would also ask whether someone specifically wanted
> to work in the public or private sector. The scientists who apply to
> become civil servants tend to be ones who are not sure what they
> want to do, except that they don't want to use their discipline;
> often they are people who have been active in student societies and
> have an interest in public affairs. Sometimes they want to leave
> their subject because they are weak in it.[41]

Once the qualifying test has sifted the candidates, however, the
initial biases ought to disappear. More than half the candidates
have already been eliminated, and these are likely to include the
failed chemists and incompetent redbrick students – the victims
of over-optimism, as well as of any selection bias. From now on
the survivors should be on an equal footing.

They are not. Following a recommendation by the Commons
Expenditure Committee to give fuller information, the Civil
Service Commission reported the following pattern for 1978 for
the second, and most exhaustive (not to say most exhausting),
stage of the selection process – the Civil Service Selection Board
(CSSB, or Cizbee as it is always called):[42]

Type of School	Number who attended CSSB	Number who passed CSSB	Percentage who passed CSSB
Private/Direct Grant	253	146	58
Maintained	316	143	45
University			
Oxbridge	243	153	63
Non-Oxbridge	335	140	42
Degree subject			
Arts	328	164	50
Science & technology	74	37	50
Social Sciences	168	86	51

Two points stand out from these figures. First, your chances of passing Cizbee do not seem to be affected by your degree subject, once you get through the qualifying test. But second, a clear bias still remained in favour of Oxbridge and public school candidates – *even though a disproportionate number of them had already survived the first hurdle.* The significance of this is that the class bias in degree subject is relatively small; while the class bias in school and university attendance is relatively large. In other words, the Cizbee system appears not to mind what you have studied, but it does favour a privileged background.

Cizbee's staff are highly sensitive to such charges. They have evolved what they believe to be one of the most thorough, rigorous and fair systems of selection in the world – one that teases out the hidden qualities of nervous candidates, and tests the real merits of the smooth-talking customers. The care Cizbee takes flows directly from the cardinal, century-old principle that the Civil Service selection process should be objective and fair. What has gone wrong?

Until 1949 Cizbee operated from a secluded country house at Stoke D'Abernon in Surrey. Candidates lived with their examiners for two days, and many felt that their table manners counted as much as their intellect. Today Cizbee is housed in modern functional offices in Northumberland Avenue; the rooms where Britain's future mandarins are assessed are furnished with plain, standard-issue tables and chairs, and little else.

As the surroundings have become plainer, the tests have become more sophisticated. According to one survivor of the system, 'When I did the tests in 1966 there was hardly a figure in sight. When I went back as a part-time board member in 1970 the influence of Fulton was already in evidence. The appreciation included cash flow figures – already discounted to net present values, mind you . . .'[43]

To gain an insight into the way Cizbee works today, I* was allowed to follow the fortunes of a group of candidates through their two-day ordeal. The principal condition was that none of

*PK

the candidates or their assessors should be identified. In the account that follows, therefore, some licence has been taken with the characters, though each event and quotation closely follows the notes I made at the time. (The one exception to anonymity is Clarence Tuck, the director of Cizbee, whose identity can anyway be discovered from *Who's Who* and the *Civil Service Yearbook*.)

At nine o'clock on the first morning twenty-one candidates gather in a room on the sixth floor of Standard House. They sit at small sloping school desks as Clarence Tuck tells them what they have let themselves in for. Tuck says they will be split into groups of five or six. Each group will be assessed by a panel of three: a chairman, who is usually a retired Permanent Secretary; a psychologist; and an observer, who is a youngish civil servant who passed Cizbee a few years ago. Although candidates will be assessed in groups, they will be marked against an independent standard, not against each other. Successful candidates will hear the following week; they will then go to a short formal interview, with the Final Selection Board (FSB). Almost 80 per cent of candidates who reach the FSB are then offered jobs as Administration Trainees (or equivalent posts in the Inland Revenue or the Diplomatic Service, who also recruit their future élites through Cizbee).

Tuck cannot resist a jibe at private companies who recruit graduates: 'We do not give you lunch. The public purse, I'm afraid, doesn't run to the hospitality you might have received from some of our competitors.' Tuck and the assessors then leave the room, while candidates are given a form to complete. For candidates who have not done their homework it is the first inkling that some of the selection techniques will be unfamiliar in the extreme. They are asked to describe themselves – twice: once through the eyes of a friend, then through the eyes of a critic. They must also write down three or four subjects they would like to discuss with their assessors. These must be set down as a point of view, like a debating society motion, with the candidate saying whether he is for or against.

Meanwhile the assessors meet to discuss the background of each of their five candidates, and draw up a preliminary list of points to watch for:

(Chairman) 'This chap has a model school and college record. Have you ever seen a better candidate on paper?'

(Psychologist) 'There is some suggestion of verbal weakness. We may have to look at potential rather than performance. But I agree, he does look good.'

(Chairman) 'We had a chap last year who scored 377 in his QT and we marked him F. He had a first-class mind and talked like a well-oiled machine, but when it came to the point of decision he couldn't make up his mind. No good for us.' (377 in the qualifying test is exceptionally high: the pass mark varies at around 280. At Cizbee, F is a bad failure.)

When the candidates' forms arrive, with their self-assessments and points for discussion, the assessors look for more clues.

(Psychologist) 'X has put "oppose" against each of his statements, like "Capital punishment is sometimes justified – oppose". Does this mean he is pessimistic in his outlook?'

After an hour the five candidates file into the assessors' room. Three are internal candidates: they already have jobs at Executive Officer or equivalent level, and want to speed up their promotion prospects. The other two are external candidates. After ten minutes of mingling over coffee and biscuits – Cizbee timekeeping is strict, despite the attempts at informality – the five are invited to sit in a semi-circle facing the assessors. The observer then speaks: 'This first exercise is a group discussion. I want you to discuss with each other the subjects I give you. From time to time I will change the topic. There will be no chairman. This is the first topic: Is British society decadent?'

For fifteen seconds nobody speaks. The candidates glance nervously at each other, and even more nervously at the assessors. Eventually one of them says: 'Yes, Britain used to be a vibrant industrial society. Now there is a sense of decay.'

The other candidates agree, though somewhat uncertainly – except for one who argues: 'Britain is more moral that it used to be – in Charles I's day, for example. We are more open, and that means there is less hypocrisy.'

During the next half hour another three topics are covered:

the political activities of civil servants, the use of North Sea oil revenues, and the desirability of foreign tourists. After the candidates have left the assessors mull over what they have said. One candidate seemed eager to defend the status quo: why? Another said very little: is he nervous, or out of his depth? Of the candidate who broke the fifteen-second silence, the psychologist says: 'I was grateful to him for breaking the longest silence I can remember. But was this, I wonder, because he was nervous. Sometimes it's the nervous man who can stand the silence least – he can't hold himself in.'

Up to this point the candidates are not, in theory, being 'marked': the assessors are simply sizing them up, trying to work out what weak points and strong points to look for in each. Does one of them have a rigorous mind? Does another have enough penetration? One 'is not as narrow as we thought'.

By the end of the first morning the candidates and assessors are settling into a rhythm – the day alternates between candidates working on their own, and working together. When they are away on their own doing written exercises, the assessors read what they have done previously and discuss the group. It is á process of continuous assessment, not just in the sense that candidates are marked as they go along, but in the sense that the final judgment on each one is formed by gradually refining and revising early impressions. This is one of the reasons why the eventual mark decided on for each candidate is a letter rather than a number: there used to be numbers, but this gave the misleading impression that the performance in different exercises was added up. In fact the whole process is both more flexible and more subjective than that.

To help in their task, each assessor has a thick loose-leaf book, 'Notes for Assessors', always called the 'bible'. The bible lists the qualities the assessors should look for:

A good all-round intellect. The candidate need not be of the highest academic level, but he must be capable of putting his intellectual ability to good practical use. Penetration and judgment are of the highest importance . . . He must be able to express himself clearly on paper and in an orderly manner. In an increasing number of jobs numeracy will be almost as important. . . . He must be able to work with and handle other people, and to make ready and easy contact, at different levels both inside and outside the Service . . . His attitude, as developed, must be one of tolerance and humanity, i.e. he must have, or develop, a feeling of how his administrative decisions could affect 'ordinary people' . . . He will need drive and determination . . . the emotional ability to work under stress.

As we have seen, this list of qualities is adapted from the ideas of Sir Cyril Burt; and the flavour of an élite injected with *Boy's Own Paper* attitudes still survives: penetration, judgment, ready and easy contact, drive and determination, emotional stability. Above all, there is that give-away phrase about 'his' decisions (not ministers'?) affecting 'ordinary people' – by implication a separate breed of countrymen for whom he must 'develop' a feeling.

Judgment, determination, and so on are not, even so, qualities that even the most fervent egalitarian would despise. But how do you measure them – and who does the measuring? Cizbee's answer is that good assessors know how, and Cizbee knows how to pick good assessors. Yet even if that is so, the qualities listed in the bible are as significant for their omissions as their inclusions. The ex-assessor quoted earlier says: 'Words like "committed", "inquiring", "concerned", and "original", do not [go down well with the Board]. With the undergraduates and just graduated candidates I often had the feeling that what we were really looking for was the prematurely mature.'[44]

While the assessors discuss the group discussion and begin to compare each candidate with the qualities demanded by the bible, the candidates themselves are served the red meat of Cizbee. They are given a fictitious file on a government 'problem'. The file contains notional minutes of meetings, letters between ministers and civil servants, ministerial statements, press cuttings and so on. The problem has three possible solutions. In two-and-a-quarter hours each candidate must read and digest the file, then write a note on each of the three options; finally he must choose one option as the best, stating his reasons. There is no 'right' answer: the appreciation is marked according to the accuracy and completeness of the analysis, and the marshalling of the arguments leading to the final choice. This particular exercise is the 'written appreciation', but the make-believe problem it sets up forms the basis of much of the rest of Cizbee.

The 1978 exercise looked ahead to 1985. Commercial quantities of natural gas (the file says) have been found in the Celtic channel, and a decision has been made to refine it for export in liquefied form. The problem is where to site a terminal to process and liquefy the gas. The cheapest place is 'Morton'; but this is near a holiday camp and a national park. The second cheapest is 'Wellingport', a town across the channel: the terminal would create much needed employment, but the site would be next to a council estate and there is a small danger of an explosion. The most expensive solution would be to construct an offshore terminal; but there are technical uncertainties and it would take longest to come on stream.

The exercise is a parody of the administrative Civil Service at work; like all parodies it is constructed round an exaggerated truth: ministerial advice on complex subjects often is tendered in a hurry by people with no special knowledge, and for whom the principal objective is to write a clear brief rather than provide the right answer. Because the 'written appreciation' is, in the most serious sense, a game, however, nobody questions the rules. No candidate responds by saying: 'I cannot possibly give you an answer in this time and on this information; it is wrong to formulate advice in this way. There is much more I would want to find out first, and these are the questions I would want answered. . . .' Such a candidate might well end up providing ministers with better advice, but only by breaking the rules of the game. He would not make an acceptable civil servant.

Sometimes the parodies contain deliberate in-jokes. Shortly after the Fulton report was published, a Cizbee exercise centred on a large provincial town: 'The regional offices of several Government Departments are here in the glassy skyscraper of Fulton House, known locally as The Kremlin.' The significance of such remarks, and of even more private in-jokes, generally eludes the candidates.

The first afternoon comprises a mixture of individual interviews, the marking of the written appreciation, and a new exercise based on the gas terminal problem. At some stage during Cizbee each candidate spends forty minutes alone with each assessor. The psychologist probes each candidate's personal background and forms a judgment on his maturity and emotional stability. The chairman and the observer conduct more general interviews, in which they explore one or two of the subjects that the candidates wrote at the start of the day they would like to talk about. On this, as on every detail of Cizbee, the bible gives advice: 'Candidates should leave the interview feeling reasonably happy, and for a poor candidate it is advisable to keep some subject up one's sleeve for the end of the interview on which it is known that the candidate will feel at home.'

It does not always work. At the end of one difficult interview the assessor asks about the cinema, one of the candidate's stated interests.

'You like the cinema, then?'

'I love it. I sit in front of a screen and watch anything. I go a lot.'

'What did you see last?'

'Oh, er, I can't remember. It was a little time ago. But I'm going to see *Star Wars* tonight.'

Between interviews the assessors mark the written appreciations. Most candidates choose the offshore site, but their papers are marked according to the range of factors they have included, and the way they construct their conclusions. One candidate pleases and surprises the assessors by mentioning a fresh problem nobody had thought of before – and solving it. Suppose there was bad weather, and ships could not dock at the offshore terminal to take the liquefied gas away: storage problems might quickly mount up. The candidate thought the excess gas might be flared off, if production could not be slowed down. He is awarded six on a one (bad) to seven (excellent) scale; very few candidates ever get seven.

The second written exercise is the diplomatic letter. The scene has moved on a few years, and the terminal has been built. Gas is being sold to a country called Omdala, which is run by a dictator. ('The President of Omdala is frequently criticized in the liberal press for his autocratic and, some would say, repressive rule but has proved a valuable ally of the West and of Britain in particular.' The language bears an uncanny resemblance to that used by Dr David Owen as Foreign Secretary to defend the Shah of Iran.) The President's wife faces a demonstration when she attends the terminal's opening ceremony; among the demonstrators are radical students from Omdala. Three students are subsequently fined £20 for a breach of the peace, but Omdala's angry President is not satisfied. He sends a sharp cable to the British Prime Minister demanding the students' imprisonment. Candidates then receive their instructions:

'You are an official of the Department of Foreign Affairs instructed to draft a reply for the PM, who has commented, "We cannot afford to lose these contracts".'

The bible's guidance on the perfect answer gives a modest but intriguing glimpse of Britain's diplomatic table manners:

> Candidates can and must give an apology but they cannot give the assurance requested. They should explain that the three demonstrators who committed an offence have been punished (and might add that £20 is a significant part of an undergraduate's income) . . . Candidates should neither deprecate the fact that demonstrators are allowed such latitude in this country nor contrast the position with that which prevails in Omdala.
>
> Clearly, candidates should express in simple and sincere terms the Prime Minister's regret at the distress experienced by the President's wife. They might go on to suggest a suitable conciliatory gesture but must be careful not to overdo this: there must be no question of 'buying' contracts in this way. A visit to the gas terminal by the President's son and some of his school friends might be an appropriate gesture.
>
> Finally, candidates should refer to the mutual benefit which Britain and Omdala would derive from the contracts and express the hope that this will not be jeopardized by a distressing and atypical occurrence.

It is scarcely surprising that few candidates do well on this test: indeed it is questionable whether a young graduate who *did* do well would make an attractive public servant in later years.

The required cynical balancing act, devoid of moral content, may be necessary in the Prime Minister's private office, but seems positively undesirable in twenty-one-year-olds. In the event, all the candidates are marked down, either because they let their democratic principles show through, or because they take such care to obliterate those principles that they veer to the opposite extreme. For example: '. . . Justice has been visited, and without delay, on three of the ill-mannered louts whom we managed to apprehend. You would not be alone, your Excellency, in regretting that the laws of my country do not permit much severer penalties . . .'

At the end of the first day the assessors swap views. In most cases it is already clear what kind of mark each candidate will get. One candidate with an impeccable school and university career, about to take a science degree, is doing well. The observer-assessor says he holds his ground well, and is exceptionally well-informed. The chairman is agreeably surprised: 'That's unusual for a scientist.'

At the other end of the scale, the psychologist reports on one of his interviews with another candidate:

> I have difficulty expressing myself with moderation. He's as daft as anyone can be without actually being insane. He said he didn't like the appreciation test because he doesn't like writing – he didn't seem to realize that this was a large part of a civil servant's work. He's a completely self-absorbed and self-indulgent character making no attempt to impress or even give a coherent answer. I can't see him making anywhere near the grade. It's months since I've come across such a gormless candidate.

The second morning starts with the 'committee exercise'. Once more the subject is the gas terminal. The candidates take it in turn to chair a fifteen-minute meeting with the other four. Before the session starts each candidate has thirty minutes to read a 300-word outline of the specific problem the committee must resolve under his chairmanship. As each 'meeting' starts, the other four candidates have just two minutes to read the same brief. The idea is to force the leading role on the chairman, while seeing how quickly the other candidates can grasp the intricacies of the problem. As with the written appreciation the day before, nobody says it is a daft way to reach a decision; but like the day before, the parody of official committee work contains a depressing proportion of Civil Service reality.

The exercise produces one big surprise. A candidate who had impressed none of the assessors the day before turns out to have a remarkable knack at handling a committee. With skill and confidence he chaired a discussion on the problems of housing short-term construction workers on building a terminal. A short while later, as an ordinary committee member, he took over a floundering discussion about how to handle an embarrassing discovery of archeological remains uncovered while preparing the terminal's foundations. He demonstrates impressive technique – calm, coherent, and persuasive without being overbearing. The other candidates broadly reinforce the impression the assessors have already formed.

The rest of the day is spent completing the round of individual interviews, and doing intelligence and general knowledge tests. There is one additional exercise – 'the buddy ratings'. Each candidate is asked to rate the other four: who would make the best two civil servants, and who would make the best two holiday companions? This test originated in America, and is designed to give some idea of how people are likely to get on with others of their age and experience. Few assessors seem to take much notice of it, though it can help an intelligent candidate who is thought unpleasant by the assessors, but liked by his fellow candidates. According to the psychologist-assessor, 'Girls normally score well as holiday companions, because all the men think it's our way of finding out if they are homosexuals.'

At the end of the second day the assessors gather in all the evidence and have a general discussion about the candidates. But they leave their full discussion until the next morning, after the candidates have gone. By then the assessors will each have worked out their marks for each candidate.

The marking system is a thing of wonder. The first stage is to mark each candidate out of seven for each exercise. The four main marks are for the gas terminal problems: written appreciation, letter drafting, committee chairman and committee member. There is then a battery of subsidiary marks for the intelligence tests, summed up as a 'verbal test index' and a 'non-verbal test index'. These marks accumulate during the two days of exercises and tests.

The second stage takes place on the third morning. Each candidate is judged on eleven personal qualities: penetration, fertility of ideas, judgment, written expression, oral expression, personal contacts, influence, drive, determination, emotional stability, and maturity. These marks, also on a one to seven scale, have an oddly ill-defined relationship with the exercise marks that have been so laboriously compiled. Indeed, assessors are specifically instructed on the marking sheet: '*All* the available evidence is taken into account, and not merely performance at CSSB.'

The third stage, again only loosely linked to the stage before, is to award each candidate an overall mark. The test is whether he stands a good chance of reaching Principal level, with some hope of taking the short cut through the 'HEO(A)' grade (a special designation for Higher Executive Officers earmarked for rapid promotion). The scale is:

A: 'Has the potential to merit promotion to HEO(A), to become Principal two or three years later, and thereafter to reach Assistant Secretary.'
   A1: 'Outstanding.'
   A2: 'Above average.'
   A3: 'Acceptable.'
B: 'Acceptable – but at this stage uncertain whether likely to merit promotion to HEO(A) or not.'
C: 'Acceptable: will probably not merit promotion to HEO(A) but should reach at least Principal.'
D: 'Near miss.'
E: 'Below acceptable level.'
F: 'Well below acceptable level.'
G: 'Not in the running.'

Some effort is made to reach unanimous verdict on each candidate, and it is rare for discussion not to yield a consensus. Every candidate awarded D or above is invited to the Final Selection Board, but many assessors are reluctant to give Ds. One candidate who hovers between D and E finally receives an

E after the chairman says: 'From my FSB experience I'm in principle against Ds unless we are really unsure. We should make this one E.'

Candidates who survive Cizbee and are invited to the FSB (two out of the five in this case) have passed the worst. The board lasts thirty-five minutes, during which the candidate faces a Civil Service Commissioner, two other senior civil servants, an academic and an industrial manager or trade union official. In the words of one commissioner, 'The philosophy of the Final Selection Board is not to examine the candidate but to review the Cizbee report with the aid of the candidate.'[45]

FSB interviews have a set routine. The commissioner first questions the candidate for ten minutes or so, then one of the outsiders has his turn, and finally one of the two civil servants. The other outsider and civil servant observe and take notes.

Stories abound of the quaintness of the FSB. George Cunningham, a former civil servant who subsequently became a Labour MP, described his own experiences in the third person in the *New Statesman*:

> The candidate sat nervously before his examiners at the end of the horseshoe table in the old Burlington House, anxious lest in this his final interview he should prove unfitted after all for service in the higher reaches of Whitehall. 'Tell me,' said the chairman, 'how much economics do you know?' 'Well,' said the candidate, 'I find bits of the *Economist* difficult each week.' The examiners laughed. 'So do we,' they said. 'You say that you have heard Indian students claim that the British partitioned India to further our own interests. What did you reply?' – 'I said I didn't believe it.' 'A learned professor has said: 'The irrational is not always the unreasonable.' What do you think he meant?' Since the professor had been the candidate's own tutor, he was able to satisfy the board on that.[46]

In practice Cunningham's answers probably mattered little. The FSB confirms 80 per cent of the marks awarded by Cizbee, and most of the 20 per cent they change are inconsequential: an A2 to an A3, or a B to a C. Candidates who are invited to the FSB and then told they have failed have usually been marked Ds by Cizbee in the first place.

The FSB's verdict is the end of the process. The commissioner distils the reports from the qualifying test and Cizbee and sets our future mandarins on their course. An A1 grade is seldom awarded – more than a year might elapse without one – but this is what one commissioner recorded about one of the most highly regarded A2s of recent years:

> . . . He is certainly among the cleverest two or three young people I have seen in my eight years in the Commission. . . . At FSB our only (slight) difficulty was in explaining to ourselves why we – and CSSB – withheld the A1 accolade. If he has any shortcomings it is on the human side. Austere is the adjective that springs to mind, with the tiniest flavour of a prig. . . . He has had a protected life so far and his base of experience is very narrow. This may account for the streak of naivete to which the CSSB team refers.
>
> I hope that he will join the Service for, as well as being highly qualified, he is full of surprises. For example, once his exams are over he hopes to devote time to writing humorous pieces, having been encouraged by successes in the *Punch* caption competitions. Not much sign of coldness of temperament here.

The complexity of the recruitment process for Administration Trainees is defended by the need to find the very best people, and to be seen to do so objectively. There is a sense in which the Civil Service succeeds admirably: from its premise (the need for all-round intellect and the other 'generalist' qualities) it proceeds rigorously towards its conclusion. Indeed, if anything the system is over-engineered, in the sense that Cizbee could probably be shortened by at least half, without any perceptible change in the mix of successful candidates. Anyone who observes the process cannot fail to be impressed by the care and compassion of the assessors.

So why do the statistics repeatedly show such biases towards public school and Oxbridge-educated candidates? The most obvious explanation is that the flexible marking system leads to subjective assessments: however unwittingly, most assessors are likely to look for the qualities they think they have (or should have) in themselves. And since most assessors are themselves past products of similar recruitment exercises, it would scarcely be surprising if they seek to recruit in their own image. To do otherwise would be to confess that the Civil

Service might have been wrong to choose people like themselves in the past.

But that is precisely the central point that Fulton made: the Civil Service is dominated by the philosophy of the generalist. It proposed 'preference for relevance' in recruitment: this was rejected by the government. It proposed a unified class structure to break the monopoly of the generalists on policy work: this was stifled by Armstrong's rearguard action. And it proposed a fresh look at the recruitment system to find out where it had gone wrong.

Looking at the selection process for Administration Trainees ten years later, the overwhelming impression is that Fulton has been thwarted here too. There have been changes: more of the exercises involve numbers; some of the latest psychological tests are employed. But the outcome is little different. In the mid-1970s, of external AT candidates who finally passed the Final Selection Board, more than half came from public schools, almost two-thirds came from Oxbridge, and most were arts graduates. In all probability that will closely resemble the mix of Permanent Secretaries in thirty years' time.

The biases remain, and so do their long-term consequences. Tinkering with Cizbec, however, would change little. Cizbee is a carefully designed vehicle, well-tuned and expertly driven. Its problem is that it is taking the wrong passengers in the wrong direction.

HOW TO BECOME
A MANDARIN

THERE IS NOTHING CASUAL about the way Britain finds its Permanent Secretaries. The process is nowhere written down as a set of rules, and there is no job specification; but a hidden hand guided by custom and practice leads the Civil Service's high-flyers from their twenties towards the top of the profession with uncannily uniform results.

Almost all today's Permanent Secretaries are aged between 53 and 59. Almost all became Assistant Principals (then the first step on the mandarin ladder) in the late 1940s. Half of them had been to Oxford, and most of the rest to Cambridge. LSE graduates mounted a brief challenge to the Oxbridge duopoly in the early 1970s, but the retirement of Sir Douglas Allen as Head of the Civil Service in December 1977, followed by the departure of Sir Claus Moser from the head of the Government Statistical Service a few months later, depleted their ranks. A new Permanent Secretary is typically a 53-year-old Oxbridge graduate with almost thirty years' experience in the Civil Service; and for once the word 'typically' does not embrace a fictitious identikit man drawn from unreal averages: there are very few Permanent Secretaries who do not closely resemble that picture.

Stage One: Administration Trainee
Despite Fulton, the prospects for today's Administration Trainees (ATs) are not vastly different from those of the Assistant Principals of thirty years ago. Some obvious changes have been made in the management of new graduate recruits –

but ironically it is this aspect of the mandarin career path that has recently come in for the most severe criticism. Before Fulton, Assistant Principals were a select breed: around one hundred a year were chosen, and the act of choosing them almost guaranteed their place among the administrative élite. As Assistant Principals they received training in small groups at the Civil Service's Centre for Administrative Studies.

Today, Cizbee is asked to spot not just potential high-flyers but a wider group of people who might eventually make the grade even though they are not obviously top-rank entrants. The idea is to delay the final choice of high-flyer until more people have had a chance to prove themselves; and at the same time to seek out more internal candidates among Executive Officers for fast-streaming.

The opportunities for Executive Officers are, not surprisingly, pushed with great vigour by the Society of Civil and Public Servants, the trade union for the executive grades. Without passing Cizbee to become ATs, their members have little chance of rapid promotion up the ladder. The standard career progression for a successful EO who does *not* take the AT path is: Higher Executive Officer (HEO) after eight years; Senior Executive Officer (SEO) eight years later; Principal six years later; Senior Principal six years later; Assistant Secretary four years later: total thirty-two years. The standard promotion rate for successful ATs, however, is: AT to Higher Executive Officer (A), two and a half years; HEO(A) to Principal two and a half years; Principal to Assistant Secretary seven years: total, twelve years.[1] A successful AT can hope to be an Assistant Secretary – one of the 1700 most senior administrative civil servants in Britain – by his late thirties, working in Whitehall and helping to shape Government policy. An optimistic EO not embarking on this route might hope to become an Assistant Secretary – in his fifties; but the most likely terminus for his career will be as a Senior Executive Officer or Principal, managing a local office and applying rules and policies he has had no part in forming.

This is not to say that local office manager is other than a respectable career grade to reach. It is that the Civil Service itself still applies the mentality of the pre-Fulton class structures to what should be, and theoretically is, a unified 'Administration Group'. Before Fulton, the Executive Class had grades like Chief Executive Officer, Senior Chief Executive Officer, and Principal Executive Officer. Only the names have changed: while an EO can now hope through normal promotion to become a Principal, it is nothing like the same job done by a young high-flyer in Whitehall – it is merely Chief Executive Officer under another name.

A decade after Fulton two worlds remain within the Administration Group: the world of policy-makers, whose promotion is rapid, and who work mainly in London; and the world of the clerical and executive staffs, where promotion is usually slow, and whose managerial work is scattered round Britain.

Despite – or even because of – this rigidity in career structures, it would seem that the opportunity to navigate Cizbee and become an AT would be welcome to many EOs. When the AT scheme was launched in 1971, the CSD hoped that between one-third and one-half of all ATs (who would total 250-300 a year, almost three times the old AP intake) would be recruited from the ranks of the EOs. That proportion has never been reached. Instead it has wavered between one in five and one in nine – chiefly because the number of in-service applicants has been lower than expected. In a note to the English Committee in 1975, the CSD could only guess at the reasons why, out of 21,000 EO's in their twenties, fewer than 600 a year applied:

> The reasons why the number of in-service appointments as AT has been lower than anticipated are not known with certainty, but internal applicants (who must either be Honours graduates or have two years' service) are of course already settled in jobs and homes and there has, in recent years, been an increased reluctance on the part of younger staff (and staff in general) to move to London where virtually all AT posts are to be found. A number of departments have mentioned this reluctance as a factor which has discouraged many good EOs from applying for the scheme.[2]

One other reason suggested by the CSD has the smell of Catch 22. A good EO with the confidence to apply to be an AT is also likely to gain promotion anyway to HEO. In the long run, of course, the AT route opens up some exciting possibilities; but in the short run it means no more money (except for a London allowance), besides the upheaval of a move to the capital. Whereas staying put and becoming an HEO locally means more money and no upheaval. For young EOs who have recently embarked on a mortgage and a family, a decision against taking the AT route is by no means irrational.

There are other criticisms of the way the AT system has worked out. It is disliked not only by anti-élitists like the Society of Civil and Public Servants, which feels it is still stacked too heavily in favour of newly-graduated high-flyers; it is also disliked by a number of senior civil servants who think the system is not élitist enough. According to one Assistant Secretary:

> One of the changes for the worse has been the replacement of the Centre for Administrative Studies by the Civil Service College. The CAS people were shit hot. It was a centre of excellence. I was taught economics there by people like Roger Opie, Maurice Peston and Nicky Kaldor. I once asked Peston why he gave courses there – everyone knew the pay was lousy. 'Because you're the brightest students I have,' he said. If you had 30 APs on a course, you had 30 top-flight people. Today, if you have 30 people on an AT course, there are only 10 top-flight people. If you try and get really top people to come and teach at the college regularly, they will laugh in your face.[3]

The English Committee, finding few people willing to defend the AT system in public, concluded by recommending its abolition. They gave this alternative recipe for graduate recruits:

> After short Departmental induction courses (as at present) they should be placed in and tried out in jobs which, if they prove able, can be of steadily increasing responsibility. . . . They should compete on even terms with others in the service, graduates and non-graduates, for entry to a course designed to train those who will reach the highest management levels of the service.[4]

In effect, English wanted the choice of the real élite to wait until civil servants had already become Assistant Secretaries. The Government did not respond immediately because a committee of civil servants, under John Moore of the CSD, had already started to reassess the whole AT scheme.

When it reported in December 1978, the Moore committee agreed that 'many of the criticisms of the AT scheme do have some validity'. Notably:

> There is in-Service talent which is not being drawn into the AT scheme and, because of this, is not being adequately developed. We agree and believe that the scheme has not attracted all potential in-Service candidates, particularly those who work outside London. We also accept that the scheme may to some extent have hindered the development of talent within the EO grade. This is because it has absorbed the resources and some of the better development posts, without attracting as many serving civil servants as had been expected.[5]

Moore still felt, however, that the élite should be selected young.

The essence of the Moore proposals is to separate the recruitment of ambitious graduates from the encouragement and selection of good Executive Officers. For graduates Moore proposes something akin to a return to the old AP system: the selection of a smaller number of graduates of higher average calibre than are now recruited. These would then undergo a two-year probation 'involving a series of testing postings in a representative range of a department's work'. Those who succeed would then be marked down as fast-streamers; those who fail 'would be required to leave the Service or would be regraded to EO.'[6]

A more radical change is proposed for the in-Service candidates that the present AT system fails to attract. At present passing Cizbee provides no certainty of promotion or more money. To remove the disincentive, Moore wants bright Executive Officers selected for an Executive Officer Development Scheme, which would give EOs the opportunity to demonstrate their skills without the upheaval of the AT scheme. After two or three years' successful service within the scheme, EOs would *then* go through Cizbee – with success automatically bringing promotion and conferring fast-stream status.

Until the AT system is changed, and possibly even then, the present techniques of turning out generalists to run Whitehall will continue. In a CSD booklet, *Careers in Administration,* the point comes across with force and even pride. The booklet gives brief first-hand accounts of civil servants at different steps up the mandarin ladder. This is part of the account of the Administration Trainee sent to the Welsh office:

> Two years ago, I left university with a doctorate in history and a vague notion of wanting to serve the community. The marketing side of industry interested me first, but after a closer look I decided it was not for me. The Civil Service attracted me since it seemed more concerned with broad social and economic issues. . . .
>
> I had . . . said at the interview that I was hopeless at figures, so I was rather surprised when my first job had to do with housing statistics! This proved a very interesting nine months. . . . From there, I joined a team concerned with planning for the development of the Celtic Sea. Most of my time was spent in helping to prepare briefs on this and other subjects related to the Welsh economy.[7]

ATs have two spells at the Civil Service College, an undistinguished modern building behind Victoria Station. It has the feel not of a place of learning, but of anonymous Government offices – which it once was, when it housed the Crown Agents. ATs receive their college training in groups of around forty, in ten-week courses at the end of their first and second years. The courses are wide rather than deep; the first course provides lectures and exercises on: the political parties; the relations between civil servants and ministers; the structure of Whitehall; statistics (for two weeks); economics (for four weeks); the legal system; devolution; and the Common Market. The second course is more concerned with the machinery of Government, and the management of staff and finances within departments.

One of the curiosities of the College's AT course is that none of the ATs are assessed on their performance, so their individual departments, who must determine the speed and direction of their career progression, receive no direct reports on whether a trainee has learned a lot or wasted his time. The college courses are, in fact, the only times when a civil servant knows he is not being assessed; throughout the rest of his career anything he does may be noticed and counted towards the annual staff report filled in by his superior. The decision not to send college reports to departments was taken in 1972 (the CAS did send reports, and so did the College in the early days of the AT scheme), and is evidently approved of by even the more studious trainees. According to one, 'I don't want to feel I'm being tested yet again – certainly not by some of the tutors we have here.'[8]

For equal and opposite reasons, some tutors would like reporting back to be resumed. It would restore some of the morale and authority which they feel the turbulent early years of the College have undermined. One of them says, 'Some trainees let things go to their heads when they realize they have ten weeks of not being assessed when they come here. It would be much better if they were assessed. A course director can size people up after ten weeks at least as well as an AT's line manager with less day-to-day contact over a year.'[9]

With or without the discipline of reporting back, any ambitious trainee would be prudent to give the courses close attention. For in their emphasis on 'practical' tuition and exercises (compared with the 'theoretical' courses of the CAS), they supply a number of the tricks of the trade that are worth learning young. For example, the picture of relations between ministers and civil servants contains refreshingly few illusions or constitutional myths, not least because of the mildly irreverent humour with which Gerry Bradshaw, the AT course director, leads the exercises.

A typical day starts with Bradshaw asking ATs to draft a briefing paper for a minister. Briefing papers are the arteries through which a fair proportion of the Civil Service influence flows. Bradshaw reads out a minute sent out by James Callaghan when he was Prime Minister: 'The papers addressed to me are too long. We can't afford inflation in words and papers any more than in currency.' (The ATs groan in unison at the parallel.) Bradshaw then draws the blunt conclusion:

'If you are going to be short, it means choice. Ministers prefer clear advice. If you are firm, you won't often get the response from ministers that you are trespassing on their power.

Secretaries of State are very busy: paper is always flying across their desk. The great trick is persuasiveness. You mustn't appear to annoy anyone. You must allow the minister to believe he's thinking for himself – so employ a tone of reasonableness to make the minister think, "Yes, this is right".'

Bradshaw does not in any way suggest that his prescription is aimed at chipping away at ministerial power – merely that efficient government requires a clear understanding of the true relationship between ministers and officials. His introduction sets the tone for the rest of the exercise, which is to demonstrate the techniques of clarity and brevity. He then distributes some copies of a (real) Overseas Development Ministry paper on Common Market aid policy – the sort of thing a civil servant may have to digest at short notice for his minister – and asks the ATs to read it.

After about two minutes Bradshaw picks on a random AT and asks what the paper is about. The AT says he has not finished reading it. A second AT thinks the key paragraph is paragraph nine, but he can't find any conclusions. A third says the exercise is unfair: it is a technical paper, but anyone initiated in the subject would know what it was about; it was wrong to inflict it as an example of incomprehensible officialese on an audience with no background in the subject. He is deflated by another AT who says he had actually been at the Overseas Development Ministry at the relevant time, and the paper was the sort of thing that might well have crossed his desk; but he couldn't understand it either. Bradshaw agrees. (He is an ex-ODM man himself.) It is essential to write papers, even on complex subjects, that non-experts can understand. 'Often you have to write briefs on something you know nothing about – and you are lost if all you have to go on is something you cannot understand.'

The ATs then do a practice exercise: to prepare a brief for a Secretary of State who has to meet the deputy Prime Minister of Pelagria ('an imaginary country bordering the Mediterranean Sea') at short notice. It is a tricky problem about Pelagria's fear that Britain will curb imports of Pelagrian footwear – something that is under discussion by a Cabinet Committee, but is not yet Government policy. One enterprising AT recommends in his brief: 'Try to steer him off footwear and into his visits to other EEC capitals.' Bradshaw's response: 'Very good, but it's worrying to see such cynicism in one so young.'

The ideology of the generalist strikes young civil servants from a number of directions. As ATs they are unlikely to spend more than a year in any division of their department. The Civil Service College courses are designed to give all ATs the same smattering of knowledge across a broad area of Government activity – and things like the drafting exercise stress the need to master papers and write ministerial briefs on, in Bradshaw's words, 'something you know nothing about'.

Occasionally, ATs get a glimpse of a different world, showing that other ways of working are possible. When their work puts them in contact with other governments, especially the French government, it can come as something of a shock. One AT, sent for no particular reason that he could fathom to the Department of Industry, found himself dealing with French officials over Concorde:

> All the French I dealt with had pilot's licences, and were highly technologically trained. I don't think anyone on our side had ever been a pilot; they seemed mostly to have backgrounds in things like history and English, like me. At most meetings the UK delegations tended to be bigger than the French ones – to be honest, our side were usually better prepared in terms of political tactics. But looking back over the history of Concorde, we do seem to have made more of a mess of it than the French, don't we?[10]

Stage Two: Higher Executive Officer (A)
ATs who are deemed likely to make the highest grades of the Civil Service soon have any lingering specialist impulses washed away. After two years the best ATs are 'fast-streamed' and are promoted to Higher Executive Officer (A). With this grade comes the opportunity to serve as private secretary to a Permanent Secretary or junior minister – and the chance to watch the heart of the government machine at work. (Cabinet ministers have Principals as private secretaries.) ATs who have not achieved HEO(A) status after four years becoming 'main-streamed': they become ordinary HEOs, without the fast-

stream 'A' suffix. After Cizbee and the AT selection process this is the most crucial point in the career of would-be mandarins: at about the age of twenty-six they are divided into fast-moving goats and plodding sheep.

The CSD's booklet *Careers in Administration* gives this account by an HEO(A):

> On becoming a Higher Executive Officer (A), I was given my most interesting job so far – private secretary to a junior minister. This has often meant long hours of basic administrative work, but it has been fascinating – drafting speeches, seeing the House of Commons in action, knowing about current affairs before they hit the headlines, finding out from the top how a government department operates. Moreover, in my eighteen months in this job, I've visited Rome, The Hague, Dublin, Copenhagen, and – most memorable of all – spent ten days working and travelling in the United States.[11]

There are 350 HEO(A)s. They have the same pay, and notional status, as 22,000 other HEOs – people who have been promoted up the longer and slower executive ladder, or who have been mainstreamed after their times as ATs. These HEOs typically have junior managerial duties: for example, overseeing the work of six Executive Officers and a dozen Clerical Officers in a Social Security office – checking work, having the knottier problems referred up to them, and so on.

The difference between an HEO(A) and other HEOs is not simply – or even mainly – the difference between glamour and routine: it represents the decisive division within the Administration Group between the policy-making élite and the policy-implementing mass. Before Fulton the division into two classes was explicit; in the unified Administration Group, however, the division is no less real. Although the choice of the élite is made in two stages, with the selection of ATs and then of HEO(A)s succeeding the one-off selection of Assistant Principals, the result is much the same. In their middle or late twenties a small group of people – around ninety a year – is picked to acquire a unique expertise that no other civil servants can hope to match. As HEO(A)s or as Principals, most will spend some time observing Whitehall from the vantage point of a private office, and discover how Britain is really governed.

A cabinet minister's private office consists typically of nine people: two private secretaries, three clerks, two typists, a messenger and a photocopier. The private offices of Permanent Secretaries and junior ministers are smaller; those of some very senior ministers, like the Chancellor of the Exchequer, are larger, and the principal private secretary has the rank of Assistant Secretary. The two most important pieces of furniture in a private office are the door and the telephone. Together they comprise the drawbridge linking the minister to the outside world, and it is one of a private secretary's most important functions to raise them and lower them with skill.

Elaborate etiquette governs the manipulation of the drawbridge. In the Treasury, for example, when Denis Healey, as Chancellor, wanted to speak to Sir Douglas Wass, the Permanent Secretary, Healey would get one of his own private secretaries to contact Wass's. It is not the done thing for the two men to dial each other direct. Whenever Wass called to see Healey, he would enter Healey's private office and ask whether the Chancellor was free. The Private Secretary would know, but rather than just say 'Yes', he would go into Healey's office and say the Permanent Secretary would like a word. For Joel Barnett, however – Healey's ministerial number two, and a member of the Labour cabinet in his own right – the procedure was subtly different. If the Private Secretary said Healey was free, Barnett would walk straight in.

Every minister has a direct telephone line for personal and party calls – 'it was used most of the day during the 1976 leadership contest', says the private secretary of one of the contenders for the Labour leadership. All other calls are routed via the private office. Incoming calls flash up on a concentrator; the direct line to 10 Downing Street is marked, and when that line flashes it takes precedence over all other calls. Every call processed through the private office is listened to, and a note of each conversation is made.

Equally, a private secretary goes everywhere with his minister, and after each engagement writes up a note of what the minister said and was told. The main exceptions to this rule are – as with telephone conversations – when the minister is on personal or party calls, though it is also an accepted convention that a minister can slip his private secretary's leash when he wants to have an off-the-record lunch with a friendly journalist. (Telephone calls between ministers and journalists form a grey area. In their offices, ministers are supposed to talk to the press only when the private office is listening, although it would be something of an overstatement to say this always happens. Even so, some ministers will only talk freely to journalist friends when they are away from their ministry building.)

There is a simple, and arguably overpowering, reason for private secretaries keeping such close tabs on their ministers. Ministers lead very busy lives; when they are told things of importance they need a reliable note to refer to later; when they say things to outsiders they equally need a reliable contemporaneous note if there is any subsequent dispute over what happened. Precisely such a dispute occurred in 1978 when Mr 'Tiny' Rowland, chief executive of the company Lonrho Ltd, accused the then Foreign Secretary, David Owen, of breaking his word over an agreement Rowland said the two men had reached concerning Lonrho and Rhodesian sanctions-busting. As Rowland had nobody with him at the relevant meeting, it was not just Rowland's word against Owen's, but Rowland's against Owen's *and his private secretary's* – a point Owen lost no time in making when the row became public.[12]

But ministers of both parties occasionally feel oppressed by the system. The problem is most acute when they want to talk privately to ministerial or departmental colleagues about sensitive government decisions. Under the rules of the game, unless these involve specifically personal or party issues, they must talk in the presence of their private secretary. This, they sometimes fear, is like having an enemy spy at your shoulder: word will get back immediately to precisely the people you do not want to tell. Moreover, when this happens, the Civil Service has a built-in advantage, for everything ministers do or say is likely to be recounted to the relevant civil servants – while there is no mechanism for the indiscreet discussions of civil servants being reported to ministers. The information transfer tends to be one-way, with private secretaries acting as the valve.

Private secretaries agree this happens, but are apt to defend the practice. For one thing, they all know each other. Some have trained as ATs together; all of them have regular contact, fixing up meetings between ministers and sorting out the consequences. Throughout their careers they are likely to bump into each other in various capacities, whereas any given minister may soon be out of sight – a victim of old age, electoral defeat, or Prime Ministerial disapproval. It is therefore not surprising that each generation of Whitehall high-flyers develops its own tribal village loyalties, with its network of smoke signals and drumbeats, where information spreads rapidly. To a minister finding his tactics upset, this network can appear subversive. To the Civil Service it is an example of an efficient government machine, lubricated by the easy flow of internal information.

It is not easy to be a good private secretary. Sir Ian Bancroft has recommended 'an ability in any period when you are in a private office to read papers upside down'.[13] The hours are long and the work is exhausting. There are also two different masters to serve – the minister, and the hierarchy of officials within the department. The two masters may have a different idea of what 'good' in this context means, especially when the minister is at odds with his department over a policy decision. While the minister is the private secretary's formal day-to-day master, career prospects depend on the judgment of officials and not ministers. The path is difficult to tread, as one private secretary explained:

> A good private secretary sometimes has to anger the Permanent Secretary. If necessary he must stop a submission and say 'This paper is badly constructed – the minister won't accept it like this'. I've done it myself, though only when I have known more about the particular subject than the Permanent Secretary. I wouldn't care to do it too often.[14]

A private secretary can find himself caught between his minister and the Permanent Secretary in other ways. When the Conservatives came to power in 1970 and Peter Walker became Minister for Housing and Local Government, he called in all his junior ministers on the first morning for a talk. The requests, naturally, went out through the private office. Walker recalls:

To my surprise, when we met, one of the private secretaries came in. 'What are you doing here?' I asked. 'I've come to take the minutes,' he replied. I asked him to leave. Later that day my Permanent Secretary, Sir Matthew Stevenson, came in to see me. Steve, a wonderful man, said in his broad Scottish accent, 'You're making a great mistake. People will think you have a lack of confidence in your officials'. I told him it meant nothing of the sort. I just wanted to have a political and strategic talk with my ministers. Sometimes we might want to talk about civil servants. Often they would be party matters. It would be quite wrong for officials to attend. If any decisions were reached concerning the department I would naturally tell my private office.[15]

It is, however, extremely rare for a minister to establish his authority and overturn tradition in that way.

Much depends on the personal relations between the private secretary and the minister. One of Denis Healey's former private secretaries – Healey has been one of the more popular ministers to work for in recent years – gave this account:

Denis is the last Renaissance man. He has a sharp brain – the intellectual equal of anyone in the Treasury from Douglas Wass down or up, depending on how you judge Douglas Wass. He was always kind to young officials – in the private office we quickly learned to call him Denis – but he could be impatient with older officials he regarded as his intellectual inferiors.

He draws and paints a lot. When he is in a meeting and he is bored, he will draw caricatures of his colleagues. I've seen some of them, they are very good. He is also musical. I used to get opera stars ringing up the private office inviting him to opening nights and saying they wouldn't sing unless he was there. And he chatted – all the time. He came into our office to tell funny stories. Sometimes if he had some tedious person in to see him he would follow them out posing as a hunchback and pulling funny faces. Once I went to a television studio with him when he was recording an interview. He went up to the girl at reception and said, 'Mike Yarwood's the name'. The girl fell about.[16]

At a more functional level, trust is needed because any minister needs a private secretary to filter the torrent of paperwork that passes through:

Denis saw only ten per cent of what came in. The other ninety per cent consisted of information, or advice that could be channelled to junior ministers, or things that were so straightforward that we could respond on his behalf. When we did send a paper into Denis we seldom did it cold. We would add a covering note summarizing the points, listing the decisions that had to be taken, and defining the options. Usually we would make suggestions as to the course of action to follow.

In Healey's case, the response was often strong, but imprecise:

> He would put an exclamation mark, or a cross, or 'Bollocks' in the margin, and we had to distil his comments into memos that said, 'The Chancellor has some doubts about your proposal'.[17]

With a strong but sympathetic minister like Healey, work in the Private Office is usually stimulating, even if it takes some tact to remain on good terms with the rest of the department; although, in Healey's case he was popular with most senior officials because when it came to battles in Cabinet, Healey usually won. Officials like ministers who can do that. (In the Chancellor's office, the principal private secretary is at Assistant Secretary level, so a greater than usual amount of Whitehall expertise resides in his private office.) But when a minister – like Tony Benn – finds himself in frequent conflict within his department and also with his Cabinet colleagues, the life of a private secretary can be more difficult. During one of the rounds of public expenditure cuts, a spending programme that Benn was anyway not keen on was canvassed as a potential victim. A Deputy Secretary who regularly sided with the industry lobby in question submitted a paper saying the proposed cut would be disastrous. One of Benn's private secretaries passed the paper on, but added his own comment saying that the advice could be countered – and suggesting how.

Benn scribbled his decision, which accorded with the advice of his private secretary, on the same piece of paper. This was then photocopied and circulated to the Permanent Secretary and Deputy Secretaries. The Deputy Secretary who had written the original paper was furious, and complained to the private secretary for undermining departmental advice. The young, and fearful, private secretary replied: 'Tell me honestly, when you did your spell in private office, didn't you sometimes give different advice from the rest of the department?' 'Of course I did,' replied the Deputy Secretary, with commendable candour. 'But I never put it in writing.' It would have been a daft thing to do with any minister, but especially with a controversial one like Benn.

It would be wrong to suggest that private secretaries *wield* power – even in the example above involving Tony Benn, the private secretary was simply working on what he believed Benn's views to be. What they do is *observe* power being wielded, both through the formal channels of Cabinets, committees, and exchange of memos, and through more informal processes, where officials swap ideas and information, and where temporary alliances are forged to fight particular battles. By gaining this experience so young (most private secretaries are in their late twenties or early thirties), private secretaries acquire the knowledge that nobody else can hope to get until much later in life – inside knowledge of the way decisions are taken and policies made.

Stage Three: Principal

The level of Principal provides, perhaps, the greatest contrast between the ex-members of the old Executive Class and the administrative élite. An 'executive' Principal is typically in his late forties or fifties, running (say) a fair-sized Social Security office and in charge of a staff of 150. An 'administrative' Principal is usually about thirty, with a minimal staff, working at a Department's headquarters on a range of policy-related problems. This is how one Principal describes her job in *Careers in Administration*:

> Most civil servants emphasize the variety of the work, and certainly for me this is one of the great attractions. Maybe I am particularly aware of this diversity, working in the Home Office – which has been described as the rag-bag of government departments. I've been involved with immigration, Northern Ireland affairs, and the police. In my present job I am concerned with letters received from Members of Parliament. A ministerial decision can give rise to a great deal of correspondence; on for instance, a television programme or newspaper article, which can draw people's attention to a problem, and start a campaign to get things changed. I'm likely to be busy with whatever topics in the Home Office are attracting public attention.[18]

As a Principal the high-flying civil servant makes the gradual transition from learning the ropes to helping to run the machine. If he has not been a private secretary as an HEO(A), it is likely that he will spend part of his time as one now. Also at Principal or Assistant Secretary level another opportunity to master the private workings of Whitehall may arise – a secondment to one of the 'central departments': the Treasury, the Cabinet Office or the Civil Service Department. The CSD's responsibility is primarily the internal operation of government departments – staffing levels, codes of behaviour, manpower planning and so on. The Treasury and Cabinet Office, on the other hand, are involved with almost every major policy decision that any department takes. Where a private office gives a young civil servant a chance to examine the 'vertical' line of decision-taking – how particular policies are developed within ministries and then percolate up to the cabinet – a secondment to the Treasury or Cabinet Office opens up the 'horizontal' line of decision-taking: the debates at senior civil servant and ministerial level between departments over political and economic priorities, and the trade-offs that take place between them.

The level of Principal is the highest at which an administrator is largely protected from personal responsibility for judgments on policy advice. He usually works within a framework laid down at AS and more senior levels. For an enterprising and intelligent Principal it can be a trying time, as Peter Jay found before becoming an economic journalist and, subsequently, British Ambassador to Washington. In the mid-1960s Jay was one of the Treasury's young high-flyers; but he resigned at the time the Fulton Committee was sitting, and in evidence to the Committee he indicated some of the frustrations of being a Principal:

> A Principal in the Treasury may be responsible as such for naval equipment or health or home information or balance of payments statistics or national savings. Only incidentally and intermittently will he be responsible for working out new budgeting techniques, for analysing the costs and benefits of a selected chunk of defence strategy, for formulating a new policy for regulating expenditure on drugs or for designing a new approach to personal savings. . . .

People leave because they are frustrated; they are frustrated because they cannot identify with their work; they cannot identify with their work because they cannot build up expertise on a problem and see it through to a successful conclusion; and they cannot do this because individuals are too rigidly allocated to 'seats' which deal from one viewpoint with a continuous stream of different problems in a given subject area.[19]

Unlike Jay, most Principals do not leave the Civil Service; so it is reasonable to suppose that most do not share his frustrations quite so acutely. Indeed, as Fulton's Management Consultancy Group observed, Principals doing policy work have jobs that range from 'rather poor content, given the intellectual calibre of the generality of this grade',[20] to jobs that require considerable skill and judgment. A few senior civil servants, later in their careers, look back with nostalgia to their days as Principal, when they grappled with the fine details of policy questions and briefly became the department's 'expert' on a particular topic. A Principal who has a good relationship with his Assistant Secretary (or who simply has a bone idle Assistant Secretary) can feel that he is making policy – albeit in a narrow area – more directly than at any other stage in his career.

Such people, however, are in a minority. Either Principals dart from topic to topic (like the CSD's own *Careers in Administration* example, 'busy with whatever topics in the Home Office are attracting public attention'), or find that their opportunity for fresh, critical analysis is cramped by prevailing orthodoxies. According to one recently-promoted Principal who is mildly critical of the system, but not frustrated enough to leave:

The normal process seems to be for all initiative to be drummed out of Principals. They are not given real responsibility, and their work gets overlaid by the judgments and prejudices of more senior people. By the time Principals are promoted to Assistant Secretary, they are conformist in their attitudes.[21]

Put another way, Assistant Secretaries tend to be chosen from those Principals who demonstrate not only certain skills that make them worthy of promotion, but a degree of reliability (or conformity, depending on your point of view) that is thought necessary in a senior administrator. Work in a private office and in the Treasury or Cabinet Office does not only tell the rising civil servant much about the system: it also helps him to become part of its smooth operation – 'a bit too smooth', Rab Butler, one of the most experienced post-war Conservative ministers, once observed: 'it needs *rubbing up* a bit.'

Some idea of the value of private office and Treasury or Cabinet Office experience can be gained from an analysis of civil servants who joined as Assistant Principals in the late 1940s. This analysis shows that by 1971 fifty-seven per cent had reached at least the level of Under Secretary. But of those who had served in a senior minister's private office, and/or had experience of the Treasury or Cabinet Office, almost eighty per cent had reached this level.[22] Some care is needed in interpreting this figure, for there is a chicken-and-egg problem. Do civil servants succeed because they gain this experience – or do they get the experience because they are high-flyers who have been spotted young? There is no statistically watertight answer, but the most likely explanation of the figures is that both are true: high-flyers are spotted young, and given the experience – which then tends to reinforce their position as future candidates for the highest posts.

Either way, the special grooming that takes place at these early stages in a future mandarin's career is reserved for administrators. Specialists have narrower, more conventional career structures within their specialism. They move less frequently between departments, fewer have experience of the Treasury or the Cabinet Office, and hardly any work in private offices. The normal explanation is that specialists need to concentrate their efforts in the areas for which they are qualified: they would be wasting their expertise making notes in a private office of a minister's telephone calls, or drafting the minutes of cabinet committee meetings.

It is an appealing argument: harness the boffins to what they are good at, and let the administrators do the tedious work of keeping the bureaucracy going. The consequence, however, is that specialists are denied access to much of the experience that is needed in senior policy-makers: knowledge of how Whitehall itself gets things done. As a result the post-Fulton reform of the open structure, which nominally removes all barriers between administrators and specialists at Under Secretary level and above, has changed next to nothing, as we have seen. This fact is not merely conceded, but stoutly defended by some people in the CSD who oversee the Civil Service's career systems. One of them explains it this way:

> There is a consensus of opinion that if someone is going to move across he mustn't leave it to the last minute. X, for example (the head of a well-known Ministry of Defence establishment), is an excellent man, but he could never make a Permanent Secretary. He's never answered a PQ (Parliamentary Question from an MP); he's never had to sit at a minister's elbow scribbling notes during some difficult negotiation. This is the sort of thing that administrators spend thirty years doing. People who try to catch on late don't have much of a chance. It's the same in politics: outsiders who become ministers, like Frank Cousins and John Davies*, don't usually do very well. It's not that they don't have talent, but that they don't have the right experience.[23]

One of the interesting phrases used there is 'move across'. What the Civil Service does allow is specialists to seek to become administrators. In practice, however, this rarely happens. If someone is experienced in his specialism, and wants to move across to an administrative post where he can exert more influence on policy, there are two reasons why he is likely to be disappointed. The first is that he lacks the kind of 'political' experience gained by administrators; the second is that if he were to move across, about the only thing he can be certain of is that he will *not* have anything to do with his own special expertise. Like all administrators he will need the ability to handle subjects of which he has no prior knowledge, and the kind of posts he will be given in his first few years after becoming an administrator will reflect this. An economist who specializes in the economics of the labour market, for example, might transfer to become Principal in the Administration

---

*Frank Cousins, a former leader of the Transport Workers' Union, was briefly Minister of Technology in the 1964 Labour Government; John Davies, a former director of Shell and of the Confederation of British Industry, served in the 1970 Conservative cabinet.

Group. If he does, he could find himself working on anything from nuclear fuel reprocessing to homosexual law reform. It is certain he will not be allowed within a mile of policies to help cure unemployment. If he is a good economist, the prospect of moving across may well nòt appeal to him; and if he is a poor economist looking for a more promising career, the prospect is unlikely to appeal to the Civil Service Department. Ergo, few specialists become administrators – or mandarins.

Stage Four: Assistant Secretary
After Principal the next step for a budding mandarin is Assistant Secretary. There is an intermediate rank of Senior Principal, but this is almost wholly reserved for executive rather than policy posts. In *Careers in Administration,* this is how one Assistant Secretary describes his progress:

> I joined the then Board of Trade in 1958 as an Assistant Principal. . . . In my early years, I was involved with such varied matters as productivity, weights and measures, and the engineering industries. After being promoted to Principal, my work covered trade with Africa. . . . Then, as a complete contrast, I was put in charge of the Queen's Award to Industry. Ten years after joining, I was seconded to the newly-formed Civil Service Department. This period covered a change of government, and was a particularly fascinating time.
> I was later promoted to Assistant Secretary, and headed a division concerned with the pay of all public employees except non-industrial civil servants – from foresters to judges. Pay was high policy in those days. . . . On one memorable occasion I was the (innocent) excuse for a walk-out by civilian workers in an army establishment. . . .
> After spells in the Treasury and then Department of Trade and Industry, I now deal with certain financial aspects of coal supply in the new Department of Energy. I am particularly involved with issues arising out of membership of the European Economic Community. . . . I am now thirty-nine, and I suppose some people might describe me as a dyed-in-the-wool civil servant. My career has been eventful, and I have had jobs in five different departments, while remaining essentially a trade and industry man.[24]

There are two main clues in that account to suggest a mandarin in the making. The first is his age: at thirty-nine, he has evidently been an Assistant Secretary some years. Thirty-five is the critical age for promotion to Assistant Secretary. Promotions above that age are decided within individual departments. But any department wanting to promote a Principal to Assistant Secretary below thirty-five must have the permission of the Civil Service Department. An Under Secretary in the CSD reads the latest two or three annual reports on the candidate. According to one who has done this job, 'What I look for is someone with sufficient experience in a variety of jobs, so he has been tested in a variety of skills; I look for "flyer quality" – someone who can be expected to reach Deputy Secretary level; and I want to make sure he is the best man for the job.'[25] Up to a dozen civil servants a year become Assistant Secretaries who have not yet turned thirty-five. Not all of them will become Deputy Secretaries or Permanent Secretaries: nor is a failure to be promoted so young an inevitable sign of a career petering out. But the select group who have passed through this CSD sieve are getting their names on the right files for the future experience that will help them on their way.

The second clue about our high-flying Assistant Secretary concerns that experience. He speaks of his 'spell in the Treasury'. High flyers are normally lent to the Treasury at either Principal or Assistant Secretary level. One senior Treasury man familiar with the process describes it as follows: 'One of the important ideas is cross-fertilization: people get to know each other. When they go back to their departments they know who we are, and how the public expenditure system ticks.'[26] It sounds very civilized. In many ways it is. At the same time it is an integral part of the way Whitehall establishes its own village community. As in a village, people get to know one another well, and over the years they develop shared assumptions of what is right and what is wrong, what is acceptable behaviour and what is not. As in a village, they often have fierce rows, but (almost) always they contain these within their community. Like proud villagers they distrust outsiders.

Secondments to the Cabinet Office – the secretariat for Cabinet and Cabinet Committee meetings – serve a similar purpose: they help make the machine work smoothly, by the technique of initiating a select few into the intimate mysteries of cabinet government. Or, to give the different slant of one Cabinet Office insider:

> We need to have constant contact with departments; we are the custodians of a lot of departmental information. They must know we respect their confidences – not only on formal papers, but when they tell us they are thinking of doing this or that. They are likely to feel happier if one of their own men is working with us.[27]

One of the odd things about the construction of this private community is that a number of senior civil servants seem genuinely baffled by public ignorance of the way government works. They acknowledge that the system encourages the creation of an informal village community, but they deny that it is inbred, or that its activities are inaccessible to outsiders. Lord Armstrong, when he was head of the Civil Service, was just one such person. Since becoming chairman of the Midland Bank he has changed his view markedly:

> Since I have left Government service, I have felt quite frequently to be in some terrible fog. It's quite extraordinary how while I was inside I felt we were straining every nerve to explain ourselves, and that on the whole we were managing it. Any reasonable person who paid attention to what we said would have understood what we were about. But it looks very different from outside.[28]

One of the curiosities of the Civil Service is that its efficient operation depends, in different ways, both on extreme informality and on rigid rules. A new Assistant Secretary has the opportunity to acquire some of the keys to the inner sanctums of government authority. He also acquires a Wilton carpet; an office 200 to 250 square feet in size (50 square feet bigger than the office of a Principal, who is not automatically entitled to a carpet); an oak or teak desk; an oak or teak committee table six foot by three foot; an oak or teak side table three foot by two foot; a swivel desk chair, a black-coated aluminium wastepaper bin, a hanging mirror with a plywood back, and a regulation range of storage units and book cases. His right to a pair of curtains must wait until he is an Under Secretary; when he becomes a Deputy Secretary he gains the right to an office suite *in walnut* (not to mention an office 400 to 450 square feet in size). Civil Service rules do not define the power of a civil servant, but they do define the size of his desk.[29]

Settled in his swivel chair a new Assistant Secretary joins the 2,000 or so people who really count in Whitehall: those with direct responsibility for mastering, and advising on, specific policy issues. The grander, strategic decisions are handled by Under and Deputy Secretaries; but for practical purposes many government decisions depend crucially on the work done and conclusions reached by Assistant Secretaries. Here, for example, is a selection of some of the Home Office divisions, each one headed by an Assistant Secretary:

> *C.1 Division:* Policy on the sentencing powers of the courts and the treatment of offenders; on criminological research and statistics; and on the Criminal Injuries Compensation scheme. The Advisory Council on the Penal System.
> *F.2 Division:* Police powers and procedures; discipline and complaints against the police.
> *F.4 Division:* Public order; subversive activities; terrorism; arming the police; security of explosives.
> *T.2 Division:* BBC and IBA finance and sponsorship functions. Wired services (including broadcast relay services) and their licensing. Broadcast receiving (television) licence matters in liaison with the Post Office. Co-ordination of decisions on the future of broadcasting.
> *I.1 Division:* Legislation against racial and sex discrimination; liaison with Commission for Racial Equality and Equal Opportunities Commission. Local race relations issues.
> *B.2 Division:* Immigration rules; patriality and exemption from control; appeal system; control of immigration of United Kingdom passport holders, and of citizens of Pakistan.[30]

In normal times – that is, other than when there is some major public row over immigration or police powers, say – the Assistant Secretary is the senior official directly concerned with constructing policy advice. A capable Assistant Secretary working to a sympathetic Under Secretary will find that his briefs for ministers, draft answers to Parliamentary Questions, and draft replies to MPs, are scarcely changed.

There is an inherent tension in all good senior civil servants that starts to appear at Assistant Secretary level. On the one hand he is expected to master his subject; on the other hand he is expected to be sufficiently detached emotionally from the content of his work to be able to reverse a previous policy at a moment's notice. An Assistant Secretary in the Department of the Environment said:

> People do get committed to specific policies. My former colleagues on local land planning devised a system of control which only made sense if there were unitary local government. They were devoted to it. Then Peter Walker decided to have a two-tier system, with each tier having some planning responsibility. Their work went to waste. So they went out and got very drunk. I'd have thought the worse for them if they hadn't.
>
> The next day they came in and knuckled down to their new job. Administrators are better at this than professionals. A road engineer will always believe in building roads, so he's not much use if your policy is to encourage railways.[31]

A different perspective on the same problem was given by one of the most successful post-war civil servants – in career terms – who was destined for the rare honour of promotion to Permanent Secretary in his forties, but resigned to go into industry: 'One senior civil servant told me when I was an Assistant Secretary of someone on my staff, "He gets emotionally involved". It was a criticism. The trouble is, you need some commitment to have the motivation to do a job well. You can't just say, "Oh well, that failed, let's move on to the next subject".'[32]

About the worst thing that can happen to an ambitious Assistant Secretary, short of being caught accepting bribes, is to 'go native' – to stay in the same division so long that he is thought to be irredeemably lost to a particular specialism. The corollary – that highly regarded Assistant Secretaries switch responsibilities every two or three years – was, as we have seen, severely criticized by the Management Consultancy Group reporting to the Fulton Committee in 1967.

Little has changed since then. Some Assistant Secretaries stay in one place long enough to command the detail of their subject, and even to become committed to the success of what they are working on. But the perceived dangers of excessive commitment, of 'going native' and losing all detachment, are minimized by 'giving chaps wider experience' – that is, moving them around.

In some ways an Assistant Secretary is a minister's most useful shield against attack. Precisely because the greatest body of detailed policy knowledge resides at Assistant Secretary level, much of the work in fending off MPs is done here. It is, supremely, the kind of work that stresses the need to avoid mistakes, rather than the impulse to suggest bold initiatives. A junior civil servant who gives a wrong answer to a member of the public is unlikely to cause a major upset: a minister's signature over an Assistant Secretary's error can cause acute embarrassment. So ministers rely on Assistant Secretaries to check the information – and to get it right. These political realities have clear lessons for the public, as one Assistant Secretary in the Department of the Environment explained: 'If you want to write to a minister, get your MP to do it for you. The answer will be drafted by a Principal and carefully checked by an Assistant Secretary. If you write direct as a member of the public it will be answered by an Executive Officer, and you will get a much less satisfactory reply.'[33]

The emphasis, however, is on not giving MPs false information, rather than offering extra correct information. The art of handling Parliamentary Questions (especially written ones, where factual details are sought) illustrates this. The difficulties for MPs are considerable. If the question is too broad, it can be fobbed off to avoid revealing information the Government wishes to remain confidential. For example:

> *Mr Rooker* asked the Secretary of State for Transport if he will publish the background papers which he has received from oil companies on the subject of lead additives.
> *Mr Horam:* [a junior transport minister]: I am not sure what papers the hon. member has in mind, but if he will write and tell me more specifically what he is seeking, I will look into the matter.[34]

That question and answer between a back-bench Labour MP and a Labour minister formed part of a protracted attempt to extract information about lead additives. It was a 'fishing' question: Jeff Rooker did not know what, if anything, the oil companies had told the Department of Transport on the subject. In order to have asked the question effectively, Rooker would have had to know part of the answer already – say, that a particular company had done a study on the impact of additives on air pollution and had submitted its findings to the Government. But because he did not know, he could not ask a precise question; and because he could not ask a precise question, he was not given a helpful answer. The reasonable tone of the reply ('if he will write and tell me more specifically what he is seeking . . .') concealed a confidence that only the Department could furnish the basic knowledge on which such a letter could be based. In reality, Rooker (with some other MPs) had to pursue the issue by asking various detailed questions, briefed by outside experts. At the other extreme, some questions are deemed too specific:

> *Mr Morgan* asked the Secretary of State for the Environment what percentage of appeals by ratepayers in England to local valuation courts for reductions of their rating assessments, during the years 1975, 1976 and 1977, respectively, were successful.
> *Mr Guy Barnett* [a junior Environment minister]: This information is not available.[35]

In between come a host of questions where answers are available. The central point is that the MP is often seen as an actual or potential adversary, to be helped as *little* as possible – whereas departmental ministers need to be buttressed with as *much* help as possible. One seasoned Assistant Secretary with experience of handling questions to the Chancellor of the Exchequer explained:

> There is no comparison. With a minister you give a full and quick answer to what he wants. With an MP, you often know what point he is trying to make, but you answer no more than the precise question he has asked. If he has not asked the right question, that's his problem. Often the answers to PQs are deliberately misleading.[36]

The word 'misleading' needs qualification. Apart from some accepted special cases – like denials of impending devaluation – Assistant Secretaries go to considerable lengths not to prepare actually untrue answers: not least because there is the self-evident risk of being caught out. It is more that the art of answering awkward questions (as any journalist or press officer also knows) is to try and steer the questioner away from his chosen course and down some more harmless path. It is in this sense that some MPs complain of being misled: the information they are given is true, but not what they wanted.

The adversary relationship between the executive and MPs over Parliamentary Questions is heightened by the bizarre ritual of oral answers every afternoon from Monday to Thursday. The questions here, as a rule, are deliberately vague. What MPs then do is to use follow-up questions (of which the minister has no warning) to dent the carefully-prepared surface of smooth government administration. Equally, each time it is a minister's turn to face oral questions his officials – and in particular the relevant Assistant Secretaries – try to prepare for as many contingencies as possible by guessing what supplementary questions will follow, and briefing the minister accordingly. It is a tense time, because ministers hate looking foolish in Parliament – and the uncertainties of question time provide ample opportunities for foolish answers. One Assistant Secretary who had just come from a 45-minute bull-session with ministers in the Department of the Environment said: 'The place goes crazy on days like this. They don't know what to expect, they are very uptight. They start getting bogged down in detail, suddenly asking irrelevant questions about some £1½ million programme when they have a budget of £2½ billion. They're mad.'[37]

A typical example of the way a simple oral question (of which ministers have warning) conceals the 'real' question is:

Mr Nelson asked the Secretary of State for Industry, when he intends next to meet the chairman of the Confederation of British Industry.

There was evidently a simple answer, which Eric Varley, the then Industry Secretary in the 1974-9 Labour Government duly gave: 'I meet the president and other leaders of the CBI at regular meetings of the NEDC.'

But, of course, that was not the real issue. What was the Conservative MP Anthony Nelson really after? Varley's officials would have spent some hours preparing notes for alternative follow-up questions. They could cover almost any aspect of Government industrial policy. When Varley sat down, having given his trivial answer to the trivial question, Nelson said:

> At his next meeting with the CBI, will the Secretary of State discuss the important recommendations of the Corfield report to the NEDC on improving industrial design? What is the right hon. Gentleman's response to suggestions that State financial assistance might be partly replaced by assistance directed towards improving industrial design in the country?

Varley's brief (or his memory) was equal to the occasion:

> The Corfield report was discussed at the last meeting of the NEDC and was very well received. Industrial design and product development are important features of our approach and I hope that we can carry them further within the NEDC. I have no hesitation in saying that if public funds are required we shall take sufficient powers to obtain them.[38]

The point about this exchange, and many similar ones, is how little emerged. Parliamentary questions are governed by a framework that prevents the efficient dissemination of information and encourages an adversary relationship even on an issue such as industrial design, where neither ideological pride nor government secrets are at stake.

Yet from the viewpoint of almost all parliamentarians, question time in the Commons is central to the principle of parliamentary government. According to Sir Harold Wilson: 'It has been said that Harold Macmillan, a highly successful performer at question time, used to be physically sick, or very near to it, before questions on Tuesday and Thursdays. In my address to the British Academy I said that, if Britain ever had a Prime Minister who did not fear questions, our parliamentary system would be in danger.'[39] The role of the Prime Minister in parliamentary questions is different from departmental ministers: he must be willing to speak twice a week on almost any subject; while departmental ministers have less frequent ordeals more or less confined to their specific responsibilities. That does not, however, alter the underlying belief of some parliamentarians (for example, Michael Foot) that the unpredictability of question time provides an important check on the power of ministers and the Civil Service.

Certainly without some formal procedure such as question time the opportunities for challenging the executive would diminish. But that should not obscure the fact that one of the main impacts of parliamentary questions, as they are presently organized, is to force ministers and civil servants to close ranks. It is usually more important to say nothing that is provably false than to say something that is revealingly true.

Handling MPs' questions is a special example of a more general phenomenon observed by Sir Derek Rayner, a joint managing director of Marks and Spencer who was seconded in the early 1970s to the Ministry of Defence to advise on procurement policy. Rayner told the English Committee:

> Whereas in business one is judged by overall success, in my experience the civil servant tends to be judged by failure. This inevitably conditions his approach to his work in dealing with the elimination of unnecessary paper work, and in eliminating excessive monitoring, and leads to the creation of an unnecessary number of large committees, all of which leads to delays in decision-taking and the blurring of responsibility.[40]

Principals and Assistant Secretaries drafting answers to MPs are classically in the business of failure-avoidance.

Stage Five: Open Structure

By the time a civil servant is ripe to join the highest ranks of the Service – Under Secretary, Deputy Secretary and Permanent Secretary – he needs to have acquired various qualities. According to Sir Ian Bancroft, to reach the top you need '75 per cent will-power and 25 per cent intellect'[41]. He admitted to the English Committee that in the Civil Service, unlike industry, 'It has been the case until the fairly recent past, as I am sure all of you recognize, that the way to the top has so often been via a series of what one might call, in short-hand, policy-mongering jobs, without much experience of managing and organizing work and people.'[42]

Even if – as Sir Ian then hinted – the Civil Service plans to give high-flyers more managerial jobs as part of their career structure, this does not alter the essential characteristics that the Civil Service, as currently constructed, requires in its senior policy advisers: an intimate knowledge of the government machine, and an ability to react to the day-to-day needs of ministers. These remain the preserve of the traditional general administrator, with his experience of private office work, the Treasury or Cabinet Office, preparing policy briefs and drafting answers to letters and questions from MPs.

As we have already seen, one modest genuflection to Fulton's proposals for a unified class structure was the creation of an 'open structure' covering the three top grades in the Civil Service. In principle, any civil servant, whatever his background, once he reaches Assistant Secretary or the equivalent specialist level, can be promoted to any of the jobs in the open structure. In fact, as the evidence of the Institution of Professional Civil Servants to the English Committee showed, very little has changed: about sixty per cent of open structure posts are essentially policy administrative posts, and are filled by generalist administrators; the other forty per cent are essentially specialist posts, filled by people with specialist backgrounds.[43] To have a good chance of reaching Permanent Secretary, promotion to Under Secretary needs to come by the early forties. Compared with an Assistant Secretary, according to one high flyer, 'The Under Secretary has a more supervisory role, like a company director. He is there to pour oil on troubled waters when there's a row.'[44] The Under Secretary takes the detailed policy work of subordinates and either rubber-stamps it, if it is routine, or argues it through with other officials in the department, or other departments (above all the Treasury), if it is not routine. More than the Assistant Secretary, the Under Secretary inhabits a world of official committees and hurriedly called meetings with ministers.

When cabinet ministers and ex-ministers speak of their relationships with civil servants they normally mean Under Secretaries and above; apart from their private secretaries, they seldom have routine contact with more junior officials. So although much (indeed, all) detailed policy work on a specific issue may be done by an Assistant Secretary with a couple of

Principals, it will be the Under Secretary or Deputy Secretary who discusses the matter most frequently with the relevant minister. (Indeed, it is one of the complaints of ministers – of both parties – that they have difficulty in discovering what is going on in the policy engine-rooms of their own departments, where Assistant Secretaries and Principals may be engaged in a discussion of wider and fuller options than percolate up to ministers.)

Precisely because of the etiquette of communication, the subtleties of responsibilities and relationships between Assistant Secretaries and Under Secretaries become important. When Thomas Bingham QC conducted an inquiry into the breaking of oil sanctions against Rhodesia, the actions of two Assistant Secretaries in the Ministry of Power were described in some detail. The two officials – Barry Powell and Alan Gregory – handled detailed discussions with BP and Shell in 1968 over a 'swap' arrangement with the French oil company Total: a cosmetic device that allowed the two oil giants to keep their share of the southern African oil market while ensuring that no specifically *British* oil reached Rhodesia.

But were Powell and Gregory solely responsible for executing a policy that ten years later, with the publication of the Bingham report, rebounded so devastatingly on the probity of British government? Jeremy Bray, who had been a junior minister at the Ministry of Power from April 1966 to January 1967 – the early months of sanctions-busting – mounted a remarkable attack on Powell's and Gregory's Under Secretary when the Bingham report was debated in November 1978:

> On an issue of such sensitivity, Assistant Secretaries do not act alone or without the knowledge and support of their seniors, and subject to their guidance. The Under Secretary of the petroleum division was Mr Angus Beckett, whose name appears less frequently in the Bingham report. Mr Beckett had been in and out of oil matters in Government since the 1940s. He had a knowledge of the jargon, gossip and personalities of the oil industry unequalled in Whitehall. He was largely responsible for the first four rounds of North Sea oil and gas licensing, and had been publicly quoted by Sir Laurence Helsby as an example of how versatile and expert an administrative civil servant could be.
> In fact, I found that whenever I pressed Mr Beckett on any

business, financial or economic question, he quickly took refuge in generalities. His view was that whatever was good for the oil companies was good for Britain. He passed on to Ministers the views of the oil companies regarding their own supra-national status and the folly of any Government intervention, adding pepper and salt of his own. He was so obviously in the pocket of the oil companies that I do not think they had any great respect for him. Certainly when he retired and sought the reward that, alas, seems now to be the expectation of many civil servants who have had responsibilities for industry, he did not get a job in any of the oil majors but obtained one with William Press, the North Sea oil contractors. . . .

In my experience, Mr Beckett deliberately blocked information going to ministers. We were a small Department with only two Ministers, Richard Marsh and myself. As well as some specific responsibilities, Dick Marsh gave me free reign in the Department. When I asked for some information on refinery capacity and throughputs, the petroleum division was unable to supply it. I asked the statistics division and it produced some data. When Mr Beckett found out, he blocked any further such information coming to me, not only from his own division, but from the statistics division.[45]

Bray's experience may have been unusual; stating it publicly certainly was. But the central idea of the pivotal role (for good or bad) of the Under Secretary is widely acknowledged. Discussing his knowledge of his staff, the Permanent Secretary of one of the larger departments says: 'I now know people down to Under Secretary level. In my first year it was a struggle to get to know all the Under Secretaries. Within the department this is the critical level for decisions. He is the key man; he should be able to see the problem in the round, yet know enough about the small print to dip into it'.[46]

As a broad guide, where Assistant Secretaries handle the details of specific issues, Under Secretaries supervise wide areas of policy. In the Department of Trade, for example, one Under Secretary oversees government policy on insurance; four Assistant Secretaries each then control some aspect of it; another Under Secretary heads the Civil Aviation Policy Division, with five Assistant Secretaries; the Under Secretary who heads the Shipping Policy Division has three Assistant Secretaries.

Deputy Secretaries – the rank just below Permanent Secretary

– tend to become more involved in department-wide issues. Their numbers (about 150, compared with more than 500 Under Secretaries) are too small to allow any of them to have too narrow or detailed a responsibility; furthermore, it is a common practice for departments to have weekly internal 'cabinet' meetings of Permanent and Deputy Secretaries. In the Treasury this is formalized into a Policy Co-ordinating Committee, which meets every Tuesday morning (more often in a crisis) at 9.30 in the office of Sir Douglas Wass, the Permanent Secretary. There is an agenda, and minutes are produced. The PCC has a designated secretary – the Under Secretary in charge of policy co-ordination. Other departments have less formal cabinets. At the Department of Health and Social Security, for example, Sir Patrick Nairne instituted informal Monday meetings at noon: there is no agenda, and no minute-taking. The purpose is to have a free-ranging discussion of mainly tactical issues – are things under control?, are there any immediate problems?, should we respond to this or that newspaper article? (In most departments the chief press officer also takes part in departmental cabinet meetings.)

Whether a cabinet minister's knowledge of his officials, in terms of day-to-day contact, extends down to Deputy or Under Secretary, or even Assistant Secretary, level, depends greatly on the character of the minister and the nature of the department. Ministers in small departments with an appetite for detail may even get to know some Assistant Secretaries well – especially if the Deputy Secretary concerned is tolerant about being by-passed, or lazy, or both. Otherwise, Under and Assistant Secretaries exist on the fringes of ministers' (especially senior ministers') lives – on tap when a specific problem becomes politically sensitive, but otherwise invisible.

One Permanent Secretary described why a number of cabinet ministers do not generally look further than Deputy Secretary for advice:

> Some ministers more than others don't like large meetings. A psychologist once said that the best place for decisions was in the intimacy of the boudoir. Many people don't like large meetings with people they don't know. Winston Churchill hated them. If you worked with Winston it was a great day when, maybe after

two years, you realized that he had grasped your name. You knew then he might listen to you. Mr Callaghan's a bit like that. He prefers small meetings with people he knows.[47]

It is an understandable view. The policy work of 2,000 Assistant Secretaries and above are channelled through to 100 ministers. It is inevitable that even hard-working ministers can only see a small fraction of the policy work that is done for them. Information, analysis, and policy options must be carefully selected in order to provide ministers with manageable briefs on which to pass judgment. That process of selection is done – and self-evidently must be done – by civil servants. At the same time the *method* of selection and presentation can make a decisive difference to the view any minister then takes. The control over this process gives senior civil servants considerable power. The issue is not whether this power exists, but how it is wielded – and by whom. A diligent Deputy Secretary working to an enthusiastic minister can open up the choices available on any given subject; a less flexible Deputy Secretary working to a more idle minister is likely to limit the choices *and to receive the gratitude of the minister for having done so.*

The style of the minister matters greatly; and a change of minister can transform the working lives of senior civil servants. When Barbara Castle was Minister of Transport, from 1965 until 1968, she sought out different views and encouraged officials down to Assistant Secretary level to debate with each other in her presence. (Castle is probably more responsible than anyone outside the Treasury for bringing economists into policy-making. One of her reasons for expanding the role of economists in each department she went to was to have an alternative conduit for policy advice, so that Deputy Secretaries could not wield a monopoly over the information and advice reaching her.) In 1968 Castle was succeeded by Richard Marsh. Marsh preferred clear advice, with the arguments thrashed out by his officials beforehand. The life of Deputy and Under Secretaries became easier, if less stimulating.

The reverse happened when Peter Walker succeeded John

Davies as the Conservative Secretary for Trade and Industry in 1972: Davies liked clear advice, while Walker would often seek to open a debate up. (This did not produce unanimously appreciated results: Walker received much of the blame for mishandling Britain's energy policy in the autumn of 1973, when the price of oil quadrupled and the miners threatened to strike, and Edward Heath effectively demoted Walker by removing all energy responsibilities from him in January 1974.)

If senior civil servants must adapt to the different *administrative* styles of the ministers, they must also learn to live with different *political* styles. When Anthony Crosland was Secretary of State for the Environment, from 1974 to 1976, he embarked on an ambitious housing policy review. One of his aims was to tidy the rag-bag of subsidies, tax reliefs, controls and statutes to provide a proper balance between help for owner-occupiers and help for council tenants. As well as being a politically fraught subject, the intellectual problems surrounding the concept of even-handed treatment are immense. Crosland wanted to confront, and solve, the intellectual problems first, and then to construct his political solutions afterwards. Before the exercise was completed, however, Crosland moved to the Foreign Office, and Peter Shore took over at Environment. Shore had less patience with the details of the intellectual problem Crosland had set: he did, however, have as a clear political priority the need to help council tenants. Much of the work done by the Assistant and Under Secretaries under the Crosland regime was consigned to remote filing cabinets, and a completely different kind of policy review was prepared.

8

THE PERMANENT
SECRETARIES

TO PROGRESS WITHIN THE OPEN STRUCTURE – from
Under Secretary to Deputy Secretary, and finally to Permanent
Secretary – you must above all impress your fellow mandarins.
Ministers – the Prime Minister especially – have some power
over the most senior appointments, but their cards are carefully
marked for them by Whitehall. In the words of one insider:
'You must be clubbable. It's a team game. I worked for a while
with X. He's now a Deputy Secretary at Employment. Very
able, a first-class intellect, superb technique in preparing
advice: one of the brightest people in the Service. But he's a
loner, he gets up the nose of his colleagues, so he won't become
a Permanent Secretary'.[1] He was right. Not long after that
interview, X was moved sideways to run a Quango – one of the
fringe non-Civil Service organizations whose leadership is in
the gift of Whitehall.

The organization of careers within the open structure is one
of the main concerns of the head of the Civil Service. The first
occupant of that job when the CSD was created, Sir William
Armstrong, tried to devise a home-grown system for spotting
future Permanent Secretaries:

> I tried to look several years ahead. I did a great deal of it
> personally, starting in 1968. I built up a big chessboard, with
> departments listed along one side, using counters for people and
> moving them about to see what could happen. Today I suppose
> you would do it with a computer on a visual display terminal, but
> we didn't have that sort of thing in those days. I often used to
> spend most of Sunday at home playing with different possibilities.

I started looking at the Deputy Secretaries. But often the Deputy Secretaries were failed Permanent Secretaries, and not all that hot. So I had to look down to Under Secretary level. But there were some hundreds of them. I asked each Permanent Secretary to rank the Under Secretaries in his department – promotable immediately, promotable in time, not promotable. Then we interviewed all the Permanent Secretaries in turn. At first, some of them didn't quite catch the idea of the exercise. I would say, 'Look, you say all 30 of your Under Secretaries are promotable, you don't understand what we're looking for'. Things then settled down. We repeated the exercise annually.

I would then bring all this information to my chessboard, and move the counters around. First I would say, in a year's time these people will have retired, and there would be so many spaces to fill. Then I would look at the people, and move the counters in different ways to fill the spaces, until I had a number of pictures of what might happen one year ahead, two years ahead, and so on. In some cases, where a Permanent Secretary was 58 and might be replaced in two years by someone of 55, I would think seven years ahead to who might replace him.

I did a lot of this work myself. But I also had SASC – the Senior Appointments Selection Committee – which I chaired, with about six Permanent Secretaries and one or two specialists. Solly Zuckerman [Chief Scientific Adviser to the Government, now Lord Zuckerman] was on it for a while. I would bring these ideas to them. Normally we would have two meetings on each Permanent Secretary appointment – the first meeting with the retiring incumbent, who would tell us who he thought should get the job, and we would discuss it with him; the second SASC would be without him, when we would discuss it amongst ourselves. Sometimes our plans would be upset by a sudden death, like Andrew Cohen at Overseas Development.

I did not meet the Under Secretaries personally. But it is one of the advantages of moving people around departments that whenever SASC discussed an Under Secretary for possible promotion to Deputy Secretary, at least two people on the committee would know him. What I did was to have small lunches for newly promoted Deputy Secretaries. I would wait until there were about half a dozen of them, and we would go to a private room off the CSD canteen. It wasn't outstanding food, but it was a good place to meet them.[2]

The selection committee described by Armstrong, as it happens, provides a further example of a botched Fulton reform. Fulton wanted a small committee containing equal numbers of administrators and specialists, together with one or two outsiders, whose 'wide experience of business and other outside activities could in our view help to avoid an inbred and purely Civil Service attitude to these appointments.'[3] As with so many Fulton proposals the essential reforms were not carried out; administrators remained dominant, and outsiders were kept away. But the CSD's checklist for the English Committee gives the impression that the reform *was* implemented:

> In July 1968, with the Prime Minister's approval, a committee consisting of a number of senior officials, including senior professional civil servants, was set up to assist the official Head of the Home Civil Service in making his recommendations to the Prime Minister for the filling of Home Civil Service vacancies at Deputy Secretary level and above. The committee has met monthly since then.[4]

In 1974 Sir William departed, and so did his chessboard. Sir Douglas Allen, his successor, expanded the system, but removed much of the determinism. Each year he called for reports on all Under and Deputy Secretaries, together with those on all Principals and Assistant Secretaries regarded within their departments as high-flyers. Then two senior CSD people – Sir John Herbecq, the second Permanent Secretary, and John Moore, the Deputy Secretary in charge of the Personnel Management Group – would do their 'milk round'. They would visit each department and talk to the Permanent Secretaries about the people on their list.

Under this system (which has broadly survived under Allen's successor, Sir Ian Bancroft), when a vacancy arises for a post as Deputy Secretary in a department, that department puts forward one or two names, and the CSD produces a list of alternatives culled from the milk round. Both sets of names go to the committee of Permanent Secretaries, who decide in conjunction with the departmental Permanent Secretary (if he is not already a member). A consensus as to who is best then emerges; as used to be the case in the Cabinet, votes are unknown. The departmental Permanent Secretary then goes to his Secretary of State. The minister may choose another candidate, but given his limited knowledge of the field he seldom does. Finally, the head of the Civil Service sends a minute to the Prime Minister with his 'advice', arising out of this process.

Ministers have, in practice, greater control over the appointment of their Permanent Secretaries. The head of the Civil Service talks to the Secretary of State, and makes his suggestion. The minister can reject it, or argue against it: but his power is qualified by the involvement of the Prime Minister in the process. In the words of one ex-Permanent Secretary: 'If the minister wants to promote the office cat, the head of the Civil Service would go to the Prime Minister to sort it out.'[5]

Richard Crossman described the process of give-and-take when the then head of the Treasury, Sir Laurence Helsby (who then had some of the functions of the head of the Civil Service), visited Crossman in January 1965 to discuss the succession to Dame Evelyn Sharp:

> Punctually at ten thirty Sir Laurence Helsby arrived to have the expected conversation with me. When I looked at him I suddenly realized I had been at Oxford with him where we had both done Greats. He's a curious character, amiable and apparently pleasant, but with veiled eyes. He came straight to the point. He wanted to announce Sir Bruce Fraser as my next Permanent Secretary. . . . I said I was interested in Sir Philip Allen. He told me that Allen was more suitable for the Home Office and Bruce Fraser for my Department – though he didn't say the latter very convincingly. We sparred a good deal and I finally said I was prepared to give dinner to both men and then to give Helsby my opinion. He said I must appreciate that a Permanent Secretary would last longer than a minister and that therefore he was concerned to find one who not only got on with me but who was suitable for the Department. . . .[6]

In the event, the succession became something of a drawn-out battle: Crossman accepted Fraser – with strings attached – then changed his mind before Dame Evelyn left; eventually she was succeeded neither by Fraser nor Allen, but by Sir Matthew Stevenson.

On other occasions the smoothness of the process surprises even the participants. When Sir Philip Rogers retired as Permanent Secretary at the Department of Health and Social Security in 1975, the Department had no internal candidate whom Sir Douglas Allen thought adequate to take over. He spoke to the Prime Minister, Harold Wilson, and suggested Sir Patrick Nairne, the Second Permanent Secretary in the Cabinet Office. Most of Nairne's career had been spent in the Ministry of Defence, and Allen considered that his experience of a ministry with a large staff and many specialists would make him suitable for the DHSS. Wilson agreed, but warned Allen that the Secretary of State for Social Services, Barbara Castle, would never agree: as a left-winger she would distrust anyone so closely associated with the defence establishment. But Castle did agree, to Wilson's and Allen's surprise. It turned out that one of her Ministers of State, David Owen, had formed a high opinion of Nairne when Owen had been a junior minister at Defence. His recommendation helped to tilt the balance.

Two years later Barbara Castle spoke about Nairne on BBC radio. Her verdict, coming from one of the toughest and most demanding departmental ministers of the past two decades, is one any Permanent Secretary would treasure:

> Patrick Nairne . . . was a joy to me because I was embarked on the controversial policy of phasing private practice out of the National Health Service hospitals. I don't know what his personal views are – I would suspect that he would be instinctively against it if he'd been the minister. But the objective and efficient way in which he would sit down and say, 'right, now I can see this and it involves this and your strategy is that', helping in an objective working out of the strategy – you know, I don't know whether his training at the Ministry of Defence had something to do with this almost military obedience with which he served the policy of the minister. Now that is what you expect of your Permanent Secretary. You need to feel that in the end, when the chips are down, he was going to see the whole resources of the department were carrying out the minister's policy.[7]

Nairne, in Castle's view, provides an excellent example of a Permanent Secretary fulfilling his job description. This was most succinctly provided by Sir Douglas Allen in 1978 when he was Head of the Civil Service:

> He is responsible for the efficient organization of his Department, for instance its division into operational blocks of work, the allocation of sufficient staff (and no more) to different areas of work so that they can discharge their duties, and the co-ordination of the

work of those blocks. It is his duty as Accounting Officer to keep the Department's activities and expenditure within the bounds set by Parliament through its statutes and its vote procedure. He is responsible for the management of his Department's staff including their training and career development, and for the promotion policies of his Department, which usually follow lines agreed with the staff side. He has to ensure that his Department has satisfactory arrangements for safeguarding confidential information in its keeping, and for the preservation of its official records. On all this kind of work he is directly answerable to Parliament and though he cannot be questioned in the House as such he may be cross-examined by the appropriate Parliamentary Committees (normally either the Public Accounts Committee or a sub-committee of the Expenditure Committee). He will also be responsible for ensuring that the Minister is provided with the kind of service he wants from the Department; of which the elements most likely to be of interest to the Minister are the general organization of the Department, the disposition of senior officials and the arrangements for providing the Minister with his support services, including briefing him on both Departmental and general Government matters and handling his correspondence. The Permanent Secretary will also be the Minister's chief policy adviser but by no means the only one. . . . Official Heads of Departments also share in a collective responsibility for the Civil Service, especially since it is the individual Department which employs civil servants, not the Civil Service as such.[8]

That things do not always go smoothly is amply demonstrated by the Crossman Diaries. But a rare example of rows being disclosed by a civil servant came in November 1975 when Sir Antony Part, Permanent Secretary at the Department of Industry, was interviewed by Vincent Hanna on BBC television about his relationship with his former political master, Tony Benn:

Part: . . . 'Of course lots of his ideas are very radical, really turning the system upside down.'
Hanna: 'And did this offend, upset or worry you?'
Part: 'No, it didn't upset me as a technique at all. Some of the policies that he was suggesting were pretty radical but we slogged it out between us.'
Hanna: 'Now you say you slogged it out – what way did you slog it out with the minister, what's your style of slogging?'
Part: Well, first of all try and persuade him that he was wrong and if I thought I wasn't getting anywhere I'd try something a bit

harder and we'd really start hitting each other verbally across the table.'
Hanna: 'How hard did you hit him?'
Part: 'Oh, quite hard, quite hard and, you know, I would say "that's bloody nonsense" and he would say – "well that's the way I'm going to have it" and I said – "all right, you're the Secretary of State and if that's the way you want it, you have it that way".'[9]

Part, who was on the point of retirement, had little to lose by giving vent to his conflicts with Benn. Sir. Douglas Allen, however, could scarcely contain his anger. A few weeks later he sent all Permanent Secretaries a sharply worded letter headed 'Radio and TV interviews by officials – comments on individuals'. Allen warned that the danger

of commenting on any individuals with whom an official has come into contact in the course of his business, is particularly acute. But here guidance can be specific. No civil servant should make any comments whatever about the performance, working methods or personal characteristics of any Minister or ex-Minister, any MP, any member of a foreign government, or any other prominent public figure, with whom his work has brought him into contact, however innocuous comment may seem at the time. The risk that the comment may emerge out of context or in an edited or otherwise distorted form is too great to be run. It could do great harm to working relations. Moreover public comment on colleagues or on Ministers is quite out of keeping with the general spirit and behaviour of the Service.[10]

When Sir Ian Bancroft became head of the Civil Service in 1978 he confirmed Allen's view, and even went further. He advised Permanent Secretaries to keep all direct contact with the media – newspapers as well as radio and television – to a minimum. The episode illustrates two of the fundamental lessons for any aspiring mandarin. First, do not seek or expect public glory: your rewards, like your influence, depend on your anonymity. Second, heed that phrase of Sir Douglas Allen about 'the general spirit and behaviour of the Service': it embodies a long tradition that has survived wars, economic recessions, and the Fulton and English Committees; discover its secrets and the mysteries of government will be revealed unto you. In terms of protocol if not power, Britain's top civil servant is

Sir Ian Bancroft, the Head of the Home Civil Service. By some odd (and certainly genuine) accident, his office overlooking Horse Guards Parade sits symmetrically opposite the rooms at the back of 10 Downing Street where Britain's top politician works. Bancroft does not like being interviewed; nor does he like other Permanent Secretaries being interviewed. When the others want to speak on the record he likes to know: when he himself wants to speak on the record, he asks the Prime Minister. One of the lesser tasks that James Callaghan had in 1978 was to approve Bancroft's request to speak to me* about his background and his attitude to his job. It was the only time in 1978, his first year as Head of the Civil Service, that Bancroft talked publicly about himself.

For anyone ambitious for success as a civil servant, a synopsis of Bancroft's rise to the top provides as useful a guide as any:

> My father was a northern school teacher – he was the son of a Lancashire cotton spinner, and I don't mean mill owner. My mother had been a school teacher – she was the daughter of a North Wales miner, and I don't mean mine owner. So, you see, I don't come from a privileged background, but it does have the flavour of public service.

Following elementary school at Dalton-in-Furness, Bancroft won a Co-operative Wholesale Society Scholarship to a nearby grammar school. When the family moved to north Yorkshire, however, the scholarship could not be transferred; so Bancroft's father paid fees of five guineas a term to educate him at Sir William Turner's Grammar School in Coatham. In terms of 'public school bias', Bancroft is a marginal case. (The school recently went comprehensive.) He was the only boy of his year to go to Oxbridge.

From then on, however, Bancroft did all the right things. He studied English at Balliol College, Oxford. War service meant that he was in his mid-twenties when he started thinking about a career. With his 'flavour' of public service, and the tradition of Oxford arts graduates becoming successful civil servants, he filled in the forms for the Civil Service. 'I knew, truthfully, very little about the Civil Service. It was then somewhat mysterious,

*PK.

and I was partly curious. In the late 1940s there was a national mood – a post-war radical mood – that having won the bloody war, nothing was impossible. We had achieved what many had thought was impossible in winning the war after all.'

The Civil Service had ceased regular recruiting for the administrative class during the war. By the end of the war considerable catching up was needed; in addition, the expansion of peacetime government activity caused by the 1945-51 Labour Government created the need for even more administrative civil servants. In 1939 there had been 163,000 non-industrial civil servants; by 1949 the number had risen to 458,000. (In the 1950s, when the Conservatives dismantled many of the controls and tasks required by war and austerity, the figure never fell below 375,000, still more than double the pre-war level.)

Bancroft was one of the recruits in a massive three-year 'reconstruction' entry competition – a competition that produced most of today's Permanent Secretaries and Deputy Secretaries. That fact is not without significance, for it means that most of the top civil servants during the past few years were attracted to the Civil Service in circumstances very different from those today. One of the common themes that emerges from talking to a variety of them is an enthusiasm at that time for making Britain a better country – and a belief that the Civil Service was the place where the action would be. It amounted in some cases to a blind confidence in both the power and benevolence of Whitehall. One typical reminiscence of a 'reconstruction' entrant (not Bancroft):

At university I was a political animal with a small 'p'. In my final year I was trawling around, wondering what to do. I was interested in a career that would get me to the centre of things. It was soon after the war, a time of reconstruction; many of us were keen to get involved in it. Jobs in industry were not sold well. Instead of saying, 'Our company is growing; these are the kind of things you might be doing in ten or twenty years' time', they would say, 'This is how we make biscuits, or detergents, or whatever'. I was appalled at the thought of spending my life making biscuits. The Civil Service sold itself much better, with well-produced pamphlets describing the work of a Principal, and so on. My best friend said he was applying for the administrative class, and I decided to try as well.[11]

Bancroft's subsequent career gave him an unusually good opportunity to watch the frustrations that followed the post-war enthusiasms: he served in the Treasury as private secretary to a line of Chancellors – Rab Butler, Reginald Maudling and James Callaghan. According to Butler, Bancroft was 'the best private secretary I ever had. Absolutely charming, straightforward and efficient. The Treasury's hell, isn't it? He helped me all through that difficult time. And when I became Lord Privy Seal he offered to go with me. We had Winston's old rooms above the penguins. Not penguins – pelicans. I thoroughly enjoyed it.'[12] (These were in the same set of offices now occupied by Bancroft in his departmental role as Permanent Secretary of the Civil Service Department.)

After Butler, Bancroft returned to the Treasury where Maudling considered him 'an ideal private secretary. Hell of a nice chap; clear vision, great tact.' Callaghan also evidently found Bancroft agreeable at the Treasury, for a decade later it was Callaghan's decision as Prime Minister to make Bancroft Head of the Civil Service, preferring him to the two other discreet contenders, Sir Frank Cooper (Ministry of Defence) and Sir Patrick Nairne (Department of Health and Social Security).

Bancroft himself remains determinedly modest about his career progress:

> Like most people who joined the old administrative class my expectation – my 'career grade' – was Assistant Secretary, although I suppose I did hope to become an Under Secretary. It was when I became a Deputy Secretary in 1970 that I began to realise that I might become a Permanent Secretary. . . . Remember, I was an Assistant Secretary for nine years: there was nothing automatic about my rise. My philosophy is – never volunteer, never refuse. Things simply happened to me.[13]

Bancroft's career has certainly displayed the knack, or luck, of someone who has been in the right place at an awkward time, as when he helped Callaghan through his stormy period as Chancellor in the mid-1960s. Bancroft was in at the beginning of the Civil Service Department in 1968, when the Treasury's man-management work was hived off in obeisance to the Fulton report. As Deputy Secretary, Bancroft helped to set up one of the giant departments of the early 1970s, the Department of the Environment, where Bancroft ran the establishments division. Then, in 1973, he was brought back as Second Permanent Secretary to take charge of the the day-to-day work of the Civil Service Department: Sir William Armstrong had by then become almost wholly absorbed in the effort to make the Conservatives' income policy function.

In early 1974, with the incomes policy under siege from the miners, Armstrong suffered a nervous breakdown. Although the sudden disappearance of Britain's top civil servant from public life passed almost completely unreported, Bancroft won considerable respect within Whitehall, where it mattered, both for his personal help for Armstrong, and for briefly acting as uncrowned head of the Civil Service. Armstrong retired a few months after his breakdown. The events of early 1974 not only altered the face of British politics: they also changed life at the top of the Civil Service. One of the issues that the establishment of the CSD left unresolved was the relationship between the Permanent Secretary of the Treasury and the Head of the Civil Service. When the two posts were one, nobody had any doubt who the most important civil servant was. But with the splitting of the Treasury the matter became less clear-cut. Armstrong managed to gain the ascendancy largely by forming a very close relationship with Edward Heath. When Heath attempted to make a secret deal in July 1973 with the miners' leader, Joe Gormley, Armstrong was the only man at Heath's side in the garden of 10 Downing Street. When Heath gave a public press conference some months later to announce the next stage of his incomes policy, there again sat Armstrong, under the television lights, next to Heath.

Heath's defeat and Armstrong's breakdown undermined the power of the Head of the Civil Service. More generally, they finally destroyed the lingering post-war belief that Britain could be 'ruled' from Whitehall, in the sense that whatever policy decisions central government reached would be translated obediently into the desired actions with the desired consequences. Succeeding Armstrong, Sir Douglas Allen assumed a more modest policy role – parallel with the new modesty of Whitehall as the arbiter of the nation's fate.

Allen was never comfortable as head of the Civil Service. His forte was economic policy rather than man management. Before the incomes policy collapsed he had been tentatively approached about succeeding Armstrong, because Armstrong was already receiving tempting overtures from the Midland Bank to become the bank's chairman. Allen savoured the prospect of doing Armstrong's job – 'the Prime Minister's Permanent Secretary', as he would put it. But by the time the post was his, the job had changed its character. Where Armstrong was Heath's constant policy companion, Allen rarely visited 10 Downing Street at all: during almost two years when Harold Wilson was Prime Minister and Allen was head of the Civil Service, the two men had conversations of any substance only three or four times. Allen largely occupied himself with departmental CSD work: appointments within the open structure; preparing evidence for the English committee; morale and manpower problems within the Civil Service; handling the Civil Service unions. Allen's only major policy excursion was into the prickly thickets of open government (see chapter 11).

When Bancroft succeeded Allen at the beginning of 1978, he arrived without Allen's soon-to-be-dashed hopes. He never expected or wished to be the Prime Minister's Permanent Secretary. He defends his corner, nonetheless: 'It is a fallacy to think that concentrating on Civil Service issues means opting out of policy. Things like employment policy and union relations raise all sorts of policy issues.' Does that mean, then, that Bancroft is after all involved in the incomes policy debates in Whitehall – since he is the head of one of the largest employers in the country? 'No, it would be wrong to give the impression that I play a leading role.'[14]

Bancroft sees one of his main tasks as helping to restore both the internal morale and the external prestige of the Civil Service:

> The criticisms go deeper than merely complaints about civil servants. They are about the relationship of the Service with the community. The authority of large organizations generally has declined. Everything is subject to question and to debate. With the Civil Service it happens within departments, and between departments, as well as with the public.

The decline in authority and power of central and local government has been associated with greater intervention – though I would not like to say which is cause and which is effect. A wider debate is inevitable. It is not fruitful to stand in its way. There is a change in the way senior civil servants do their job; now they have to do a lot more explaining. They appear more often before Parliamentary select committees. There is an acknowledged effort by the legislature to get back more control over the executive. On the whole I think the process of questioning and debate is healthy. Decisions ought to be better and more acceptable, less of a mystery.[15]

There are a number of Permanent Secretaries who would say something like that in public, and give mouth to more pungent remarks in private. Bancroft is not like that. He is circumspect and mild in private too. The difficulty is often to distinguish understatement from blandness. During the October 1974 general election Denis Healey dropped a fearful clanger by claiming that inflation was running at only 8.4 per cent a year, when the true rate was well into double figures. One of Bancroft's close colleagues of the time recalls that Bancroft then made the most critical comment about a minister that the colleague could remember: 'The Chancellor was not at his best, was he?'

Such mildness of tongue – seldom with any hint of irony – gives Bancroft a formidable reputation as a committee chairman, especially of small meetings. When a few people sit round his table at the CSD to discuss (say) the use of computers, he is likely to interject at one point: 'I am a simple layman, I don't really know anything about this subject. There are three questions that occur to me, but *do* stop me if you think any of them are absurd . . .' The three questions will then go to the heart of the matter – and Bancroft is never 'stopped'.

Bancroft's problem is that, although he has considerable virtues in private, he is a public nonentity. He talks about the inevitability of wider debate, and of senior civil servants having 'to do a lot more explaining' – but he does not give a lead. To the critics Bancroft is a living example of many of their criticisms; he is an Oxbridge arts graduate who rose through the ranks of the Treasury and private offices, whose skills are those of the layman experienced in the intricacies of the government machine. He represents, to them, many of the weaknesses of the Service. According to some Permanent Secretaries, on the other hand, Bancroft represents many of the strengths of the Civil Service: the problem is, he does not represent them to the outside world.

Altogether there are almost fifty Permanent Secretaries. Half are heads of departments; the other half are mainly Second Permanent Secretaries in large or important departments (for example, the Treasury has three, Environment has two); a few, who were not always career civil servants, have special roles at Permanent Secretary level (e.g. Ombudsman, Director of Public Prosecutions, Chief Economic Adviser). Permanent Secretaries who are heads of departments seldom become involved in the details of policy-making. Their main roles are as 'chief executive' of the department, and as its ambassador. The 'chief executive' function includes being responsible for the *financial* (as opposed to policy) conduct of the department; when the Comptroller and Auditor General criticizes a department's acounts to the House of Commons Public Accounts Committee (PAC), it is the Permanent Secretary rather than the Secretary of State who is generally called to explain his department's actions.

The 'ambassador' function involves representing the departmental view. The concept of the departmental view is difficult to define, or to reconcile with any conventional constitutional theory. Broadly it consists of the ideas and assumptions that, independently of which party is in office, flow from the knowledge and experience that are generated by civil servants working together. However much civil servants as individuals move around, they add their increment of information to the pool of knowledge about motorway building, or kidney machines, or food subsidies. Such knowledge does not exist in a moral or political vacuum: and so, by an often complex chemistry, a department's knowledge translates into a departmental view. Some of the greatest conflicts between ministers and their Permanent Secretaries occur when the minister's intentions conflict with the departmental view – Richard Crossman with Dame Evelyn Sharp, for example, or Tony Benn with Sir Antony Part.

Together the Permanent Secretaries form a private and exclusive club. Every Wednesday morning, they meet for an hour informally under the chairmanship of the head of the Civil Service. On many other occasions groups of Permanent Secretaries meet together in official committees to prepare the ground for cabinet committees. (Permanent Secretaries live at the apex of a complicated structure of official committees that extend down to Assistant Secretary level. The difference is that the Permanent Secretaries all know each other, and many of them have been on first name terms for thirty years.)

Formally, however, Permanent Secretaries remain the servants of their ministers. There is one important exception to this formal rule. Before a budget speech, the Treasury consults with a number of Permanent Secretaries on a personal basis: each Permanent Secretary will be given an idea of the Treasury's thinking as it affects his own department, and invited to comment. The sacred, if unwritten, rule is that ministers are told nothing of these proceedings. The cabinet is told the budget details the evening before the speech to Parliament. Unlike their Permanent Secretaries, cabinet ministers play no part in the discussion of budget details beforehand (although broad strategy debates within the Cabinet have begun in recent years).

Less formally, Permanent Secretaries have considerable freedom to explore new ideas and policy options before ministers reach a decision. But there is a fine dividing line between the proper – indeed essential – Whitehall task of thinking ahead, and the more questionable work of preparing the ground so thoroughly that ministers are 'bounced' (as civil servants would put it) into accepting ready-made schemes that are then difficult to reject.

A remarkable example of one attempt to start a classic 'bouncing' operation is contained in a secret set of minutes of a meeting held on 30 May 1977, during the last Labour Government. Present were the Department of Industry's Permanent Secretary, Sir Peter Carey, with three of his most senior colleagues: the Managing Director of GEC, Sir Arnold Weinstock, with his deputy; the Chairman of Rolls Royce, Sir Kenneth Keith; and the Chairman and Deputy Chairman of the

National Enterprise Board, Lord Ryder and Leslie Murphy. Their meeting was to discuss a plan to transfer control of Rolls-Royce Ltd, most famous for making the RB 211 aero engine, from public ownership to GEC.

The minutes of this meeting are reproduced as Appendix Three. Because they were intended for strictly limited circulation, they could afford to be frank. And one issue on which the minutes are very clear was the need to keep the relevant industry ministers (Eric Varley and Gerald Kaufman) in the dark until the deal was well advanced. Towards the end of the meeting Carey proposed that the next step should be an agreed outline scheme of how the merger would operate:

> *Thereafter* it would be appropriate to broach the subject with ministers . . . Sir Arnold stressed the confidentiality of the proposition. He asked that no one else be consulted *at this stage.* [Emphasis added]

Eric Varley told me that he had sanctioned his officials to hold talks with companies like GEC to see if some kind of deal on *part* of Rolls-Royce's operation could be done. He added, emphatically, 'there was no question of Rolls-Royce leaving public ownership or control'. Yet the minutes record, 'Sir Arnold said that either he ran the new company or it would never be formed.' There is no suggestion in the minutes of Carey repeating Varley's instruction that this was out of the question: indeed, according to one participant at the meeting, the minutes actually understated Carey's enthusiasm for precisely the arrangement Weinstock wanted.

In the event the merger plan did not then get much further – but because Weinstock and Keith were unable to settle the details, not because they disagreed on the principle. Two years later Carey revived the idea when the Conservatives came to power; this time the enthusiasm of the new Industry Secretary, Sir Keith Joseph, was engaged from the beginning: the disposal of state-owned companies was now central to government policy, not anathema to it.

If Weinstock and Keith had agreed the details of a take-over in 1977, Varley might have vetoed it. The point, however, is that the pressures on him to agree would have been immense.

Department	Name	Year of birth	University	Private Office service?	Treasury service?	Cabinet Office service?
Head of Civil Service	Sir Ian Bancroft	1922	Oxford	Yes	Yes	No
Cabinet Office	Sir Robert Armstrong	1927	Oxford	Yes	Yes	Yes*
Treasury	Sir Douglas Wass	1923	Cambridge	Yes	Yes	No
Ag., Fish & Food	Sir Brian Hayes	1929	Cambridge	Yes	No	No
Customs & Excise	Sir Douglas Lovelock	1923	None	Yes	Yes	No
Defence	Sir Frank Cooper	1922	Oxford	Yes	No	No
Education	Sir James Hamilton	1923	Edinburgh	No	No	Yes
Employment	Sir Kenneth Barnes	1922	Oxford	No	No	Yes
Energy	Sir Jack Rampton	1920	Oxford	Yes	Yes	No
Environment	Sir John Garlick	1921	London	Yes	No	Yes
Exchequer & Audit	Sir Douglas Henley	1919	LSE	Yes	Yes	No
Foreign Office	Sir Michael Palliser	1922	Oxford	Yes	No	Yes*
Health & Social Security	Sir Patrick Nairne	1921	Oxford	Yes	No	Yes
Home Office	Sir Brian Cubbon	1928	Cambridge	Yes	No	Yes
Industry	Sir Peter Carey	1923	Oxford	Yes	No	Yes
Inland Revenue	Sir Lawrence Airey	1926	Cambridge	No	Yes	Yes
Lord Chancellor's Dept.	Sir Wilfred Bourne	1922	Oxford	No	No	No
Northern Ireland	Kenneth Stowe	1927	Oxford	Yes	No	Yes
Overseas Development	Sir Peter Preston	1922	None	No	No	No
Scottish Office	Sir William Fraser	1929	Glasgow	Yes	No	No
Trade	Sir Kenneth Clucas	1921	Cambridge	Yes	Yes	No
Transport	Sir Peter Baldwin	1922	Oxford	Yes	Yes	Yes
Welsh Office	Sir Hywel Evans	1920	Liverpool	Yes	No	No

*L. Prime Minister's Off

The very fact of keeping the full plan in its early stages secret from ministers would have changed the odds of affecting Government policy.

It is, of course,. perfectly possible to argue that this would have produced a better Government policy – rather in the fashion of senior officials who, in their more exasperated moments, think they could run the country better if there were no ministers at all. The issue is, who is to judge? At present Permanent Secretaries appear to do much of the judging for themselves – often away from close ministerial supervision, and hardly ever answerable directly to Parliament.

Who are they? The table opposite shows the Permanent Secretary heads of departments at the beginning of 1980.

These 23 Permanent Secretaries, taken together, neatly illustrate the patterns described in the last chapter. At the end of 1979 all were between 50 and 59 years old. This span of one decade contrasts with a span almost three times as great in the Conservative Cabinet that took power in May – from David Howell, aged 43, to Lord Hailsham, 71. Eleven of the Permanent Secretaries had been to Oxford, and five to Cambridge. Nineteen had experience of private office, and eighteen had experience of either the Treasury or the Cabinet or Prime Minister's Office. Civil servants who end up in the highest grades spend time in *either* the Treasury *or* the Cabinet Office – but seldom both. Of the twenty-three, only Sir Lawrence Airey, Sir Robert Armstrong and Sir Peter Baldwin served in both.

The evidence of Oxbridge, especially Oxford, bias over the years is confirmed by other studies. R. K. Kelsall found that in 1950, sixty-two out of ninety-six Permanent and Deputy Secretaries had been to Oxbridge, with Oxford outnumbering Cambridge by thirty-eight to twenty-four.[17] A more recent study by Peta Sherriff, published by the Civil Service Department, concluded: 'There is a significant difference between the two groups ['fast movers' and 'slow movers'] and a higher proportion of the fast movers have attended Oxford (but *not* Cambridge). . . . The only educational factor associated with career success is attendance at Oxford.'[18] (Peta Sherriff's emphasis: 'fast movers' were those who had reached or passed

Department	Principal and above			Dep. Sec. and above		
	Oxbridge grads.	Non-Oxbridge grads.	Oxbridge as % of all grads.	Oxbridge grads.	Non-Oxbridge grads.	Oxbridge as % of all grads.
Foreign & Commonwealth	630	170	79	42	7	86
Treasury	110	51	68	10	3	77
Cabinet Office	55	46	54	7	3	70
Education	42	50	46	6	2	75
Civil Service Department	70	89	44	3	2	60
Overseas Development	98	141	41	2	0	100
Energy	49	100	33	3	2	60
Environment/Transport	299	668	30	14	2	87
Home Office	97	230	30	5	2	71
Trade/Industry/Prices	293	897	25	16	3	84
Northern Ireland	20	66	23	1	1	50
Defence	349	1254	22	13	9	59
Employment	154	598	20	5	3	62
Health & Social Security	127	538	19	10	2	83
Agriculture	109	499	18	5	2	71
Wales	21	112	16	1	1	50
Scotland	48	375	11	3	5	37
TOTAL*	2582	6056	30	146	51	74

*Includes some small departments not itemised above – e.g. Privy Council office

the level of Under Secretary at the time of the study; 'slow movers' were those who had not.)

Sherriff's study concerned civil servants *after* they entered the Service: her figures should not, therefore, be confused with calculations of *recruitment* bias. In other words, if you go to Oxford, you appear to have an advantage both in competing for entry, and in climbing the career ladder; if you go to Cambridge, you are more likely than non-Oxbridge candidates to enter the Civil Service, but no more likely to do well subsequently.

Not all departments are, however, equal in their university biases. A series of written answers to questions from a Labour MP, Bob Mitchell, in July 1977 gave details of the number of Oxbridge and non-Oxbridge graduates in each department for two groups: first those at Principal level and above, and second those at Deputy or Permanent Secretary level. The answers (see table opposite) provide an intriguing ranking of departments by the origin of their graduates, with 'glamour' departments like the Foreign Office, the Treasury and the Cabinet Office still recording a majority of their Principal-level and above graduates as having had an Oxbridge education.[19]

One noticeable shift that has taken place in recent years concerns school education. In 1950 one-third of all Permanent Secretaries had been to a 'Clarendon' public school – Eton, Harrow, Winchester, Charterhouse, Rugby, St Paul's, Shrewsbury, Westminster or Merchant Taylors. (These were the old established public schools studied by the Clarendon Commission of 1861-64.) By 1970 the proportion was down to one in five.[20] It is now one in eight; and only two out of the twenty-three Permanent Secretaries who are heads of departments had 'Clarendon' educations – Sir Robert Armstrong and Sir Wilfred Bourne, who both went to Eton. The others mostly went to second-tier public schools, or to direct grant schools, with a minority going to state schools. Today's mandarins tend to come from families of great diligence and a little prosperity, rather than great prosperity and a little diligence.

Sir Ian Bancroft, as we have seen, exemplifies the rise of the middle-class mandarin. Even today his lifestyle reflects the fact. He lives in Wandsworth in a Victorian semi-detached house which he bought in 1955: 'some of the neighbours call it Putney'. And, as if to prove that democracy has finally penetrated the citadels of Whitehall, he drives a Mini.

Civil servants retire at sixty. Although this retirement age applies at most levels throughout the Service, it has a special importance for those who get to the top: their years operating the levers of Whitehall give them a kind of knowledge and experience that many private companies and other non-government organizations find useful, and retiring Permanent Secretaries (and those who resign early) are often still young and active enough to be of use for some years.

To the critics the message is clear. According to Brian Sedgemore, speaking in a Commons debate on the Civil Service in January 1979:

> I looked up all the civil servants that I could find at Permanent Secretary or equivalent level who had resigned or left the Civil Service in the period from 1974 to 1977. It was discovered that there were twenty-seven. One of them died. But what was instructive about the other twenty-six was that every one of them went into industry. Not one of them went into the trade union movement, charity, or back to the academic world. Some may have fallen through my net, but I believe that list to be reasonably comprehensive.
>
> If I am right, we first see that a job in industry is now part of the career structure of senior civil servants. That has to be viewed against a particular background. We have heard about quangos. About 10,000 jobs are associated with quangos. Theoretically, they are allocated by ministers, but one does not need to be very intelligent to know that most of those jobs must be in the patronage of Permanent Secretaries in government departments. They hand out 10,000 jobs, and senior industrialists are getting a fair slice of those part-time jobs. That is a fact.
>
> At the same time, Permanent Secretaries, on retirement, are going into industry. There is a suspicion, which, to be fair, needs further study, that there is a merry-go-round of jobs between industry, top civil servants and quangos . . . industry employs civil servants – despite its apparent dislike of them – because it believes that is the best way to sustain its values in government.[21]

Sedgemore's figures are wrong. According to the Civil Service Department thirty-two Permanent Secretaries left the Civil

Service between 1974 and 1977. One died; the other thirty-one retired or resigned. Of these thirty-one, twenty-three took up new posts. But these covered a variety of activities, by no means all of them in private industry or commerce, as the table shows:

Permanent Secretaries who left the Civil Service between 1974 and 1977 and took up new posts.[22]

Left in 1974	Final Department	Where they went
Lord Armstrong	Head of Civil Service	Midland Bank (chairman)
		Shell Transport & Trading
Sir Max Brown	Trade	Schroder International
		John Brown
		Ransome Hoffman Pollard
		Electrical Research Association
		Monopolies & Mergers Commission
Sir John Cuckney	Property Services	Port of London Authority
	Agency	Senior Crown Agent
		Abbey Capital Property Group
Sir James Dunnett	Defence	Imperial Group
Lord Rothschild	Central Policy Review Staff	Rothschild & Son
Left in 1975		
Sir James Jones	Environment	School of Advanced Urban Studies, Bristol Univ. (policy adviser)
Sir George Leitch	Defence (procurement)	Short Brothers & Harland (chairman)
Sir Philip Rogers	Health & Social Security	Outward Bound Trust (chairman)
Sir John Wilson	Defence (administration)	Crown Housing Assn (chairman)
Left in 1976		
Sir Denis Barnes	Manpower Services Commission	Manpower Society (president)
		Glynwed Ltd
		General Accident
Sir Richard King	Overseas Development	IMF/World Bank Development Cttee (Executive Secretary)
Sir Norman Price	Inland Revenue	European Court of Auditors
Sir Antony Part	Industry	Orion Insurance (chairman)
		Debenhams
		EMI; Life Assn of Scotland
		Lucas Industries
		Metal Box; Savoy Hotel
Left in 1977		
Lord Croham (Sir Douglas Allen)	Head of Civil Service	Bank of England

Left in 1977	Final Department	Where they went
Sir Roy Denman	Cabinet Office	European Commission (Director General for External Affairs)
Sir Denis Dobson	Lord Chancellor's Office	Advisory Council on Public Records
Alan Lord	Treasury	Dunlop
Sir Bryan Hopkin	Treasury	University College, Cardiff
Sir Derek Mitchell	Treasury	Guinness Mahon
Sir Arthur Peterson	Home Office	Mersey Docks Board
Sir Ronald Radford	Customs & Excise	EEC – Customs Co-operation Council
Sir Norman Skelhorn	Director of Public Prosecutions	Recorder of the Crown Court
Sir Peter Thornton	Trade	Courtaulds Hill Samuel Rolls Royce

Eleven Permanent Secretaries went unambiguously into private industry or commerce. Two of these, however (Sir John Cuckney and Lord Rothschild), were not career civil servants. This leaves nine career civil servants who left for private industry. (The Civil Service Department says ten Permanent Secretaries had obtained official permission to take up such jobs during this period. One of them, Sir Norman Price, did not take up his industry appointment, but went to Luxemburg instead to work for the European Court of Auditors.)

Getting the figures right, however, does not dispose of Sedgemore's more fundamental point that 'there is a merry-go-round of jobs between industry, top civil servants and quangos'. Indeed, had Sedgemore included quangos and international organizations in his calculations, then a clear majority of departing Permanent Secretaries take up posts that depend on the patronage of either industry or Whitehall.

There are, in the nature of things, no written rules about who qualifies for a quango appointment and who does not. There are, however, rules about business appointments. These were last revised in 1975. According to the preamble to these rules:

It is in the public interest that people with experience of public administration should be able to move into business and industry, and that the possibility of such movement should not be frustrated by public concern over a particular appointment. It is also no less important that whenever a Crown servant accepts a particular business appointment he should not be open to any suspicion or impropriety.

The critical rule states:

All officers of the rank of Under Secretary (or, in the Diplomatic Service, Counsellors) and above, and of the equivalent ranks in HM Forces, are required to obtain the assent of the Government before accepting within 2 years of resignation or retirement offers of employment in business and other bodies:
(a) which are in contractual relationships with the Government;
(b) which are in receipt of subsidies or their equivalent from the Government;
(c) in which the Government is a shareholder;
(d) which are in receipt from the Government of loans, guarantees or other forms of capital assistance; or
(e) with which Services, or Departments or branches of Government are, as a matter of course, in a special relationship.[23]

The wording of that rule is so wide that in practice it includes almost every British company of any size. As a consequence the rule, far from defining the line that separates acceptable from unacceptable appointments, leaves the matter up to the discretion of the Government. In the case of Permanent Secretaries the exercise of this discretion rests with the head of the Civil Service, the Prime Minister, and a small advisory committee appointed by the Prime Minister. Most requests from Deputy Secretaries and below are handled within the Civil Service, without involving ministers.

Between 1974 and 1977, thirty-two Under Secretaries and above received permission to take jobs in private industry.[24] The CSD does not say how many civil servants are refused permission, although occasional examples have come to light. In January 1979 James Callaghan stopped Sir Freddie Kearns, who had recently resigned as Second Permanent Secretary at the Ministry of Agriculture, from taking up a post as consultant to the National Farmers' Union. Callaghan told Kearns he had to wait until a year had elapsed.[25] Three months later, however, Callaghan relented. He told Kearns he could go to the NFU – straight after the general election.

A more graphic example is provided by Richard Crossman.

In November 1969 Crossman was Secretary of State for Social Services; his Permanent Secretary was Sir Clifford Jarrett. Crossman's diary entry for 16 November records:

> I have received a top secret letter from him, all covered up in envelopes, saying that when he retires he wants to be given leave to accept a job he has been offered as President of the Corporation of Society of Pension Consultants. . . . He has got a letter from William Armstrong . . . saying that if I concur it would technically be perfectly respectable. Well, here we are in the middle of a battle royal with the whole of the private pension interests, including the pension consultants, and he has been talking with them about this forthcoming job. I am sure there is nothing dishonest about it . . . but it seems to me that if my top civil servant has without my knowledge been talking to the pension consultants about a job with them, in any other country that would be thought to be an improper relationship.[26]

Eventually the issue was taken to the Prime Minister, Harold Wilson. Armstrong argued that

> according to the precedent set in the last three or four years, if we refused Clifford this we would have to change all the rules and protocols on the retirement of Permanent Secretaries. So William then had to get down to the job of seeing Clifford and telling him that although there were plenty of precedents for what he wanted to do, the Prime Minister had decided that the precedents are wrong and the rules must be changed.[27]

In the event, a year after retiring, Jarrett became chairman of the Tobacco Research Council, and a member of the Dover Harbour Board. And the revisions to the rules that this episode provoked have done nothing to stem the flow of Permanent Secretaries to private business. What the rules do prevent is the specific corruption of individuals by companies: it would be almost impossible for a senior civil servant to secure a Government contract for a particular company in return for a job on retirement. In that sense, the rules discourage blatant bribery. But the wider, and more subtle, point is that retiring senior civil servants are increasingly marketable to private business: subsidies, investment grants, government contracts, the industrial strategy and so on, all increase the need for large companies to understand how Whitehall works. And who better than recently retired Permanent and Deputy Secretaries to tell them?

The official view, enshrined in the rules, is that this interchange is a good thing and should even be encouraged, providing that individual corruption is avoided. Is that enough? According to one disenchanted Labour minister:

> Twenty years ago it was the exception for retiring civil servants to go to jobs in industry or finance. Now it's almost the exception not to. It is not so much specific corruption as atmospheric pollution. People trim their sails expecting jobs. They are sometimes useful to their employers, knowing their way round Whitehall. I don't mind that. It's the way they drink together, play golf, or go shooting beforehand. Nothing is ever said directly; but the civil servants know what to expect.[28]

Like so many aspects of the Civil Service this charge cannot be substantiated or refuted by hard evidence, as the essence of the argument lies in the subtleties and nuances of relations between senior civil servants and leading businessmen. Yet the combination of the early retirement age, the increasing tendency of civil servants to take up business appointments, and the absence of retired civil servants from (say) Oxfam, The Child Poverty Action Group, and the trade union movement, all suggest a bias towards established business values. Sedgemore's numbers may be wrong, but his central argument remains unanswered.

PART THREE
WHO ARE THE MASTERS NOW?

MANDARINS AND MINISTERS

'The constitutional position is both crystal clear and entirely sufficient. Officials propose, Ministers dispose. Officials execute.'
(*Times* leading article,
15 February 1977)

IT IS EASY ENOUGH to ask whether the civil servants or the politicians more often win the daily battles and skirmishes in Whitehall and Westminster. But there is no easy answer. Indeed, some would argue that even to raise such a question betrays a complete failure to understand the workings of the central machinery of government. After all, the civil servants are there to serve their political masters. So the civil servants give advice, the politicians make decisions and the civil servants carry them out – no pitched battles there. It is all a cooperative enterprise to find the most effective way of implementing ministerial and government policies; and it is clearly recognized on all sides that the last word is with the ministers who are themselves responsible to Parliament.

The quotation at the head of this chapter is, in *The Times*'s view, a statement both of the traditional concept of ministerial responsibility and also of the contemporary reality. Certainly, the concept of ministerial responsibility is an essential ingredient of our whole system of parliamentary democracy. MPs are elected by the voters; ministers are responsible to Parliament; and the officials serve ministers. Thus, by a clear, if indirect route, civil servants are *our* servants.

But what if power does not reside exclusively in the hands of the directly elected representatives of the people? What if non-elected civil servants can, and often do, thwart or modify the will of ministers and Parliament by devising and operating policies of their own? How can that be squared with parliamentary democracy and ministerial responsibility? Yet perhaps today there has to be at least some bureaucratic power. The solution of (and, indeed, the understanding of) the complex economic, social and technological problems of our day, not only needs an expertise which politicians do not usually possess, but also requires a much longer period of gestation and continuous application than the frequent changes of ministers and governments make possible. So, perhaps, it is inevitable that civil servants should have much more power and influence than our traditional democratic theory would allow.

Two former Prime Ministers, however (Edward Heath and Sir Harold Wilson), seem to reject this. Both recently re-emphasized that the traditional view of the relationship between ministers and civil servants was still the correct one. When Heath gave evidence in February 1977 to the House of Commons Expenditure Committee which was then investigating the Civil Service he said of his time in office:

> I would say quite clearly and definitely that the civil servants were under ministerial control. I have absolutely no doubt about it. In my ministerial life this has always been the case. What is more, I believe that civil servants like to be under ministerial control. There is nothing they dislike more than to have a minister whom they feel is weak, who does not know his mind and who wants to leave it to them. That is not their mentality or their approach. On the occasions when I have seen it happen they disliked it intensely and quite obviously disliked it. What they like is to have a minister who knows the policy he wants to pursue, *who will take advice on the consequences of it, and how it can be implemented,* who will carry sufficient weight in cabinet to see it through and who will also have sufficient influence with the Chancellor of the Exchequer to get it financed.[1]

Sir Harold Wilson, appearing in the same month before the same MPs, said:

> I have always taken the view that Attlee took years ago; that if a minister cannot control his civil servants, he ought to go. . . . I do

not think any minister should, or can, shelter behind civil servants and say 'My civil servants won't let me do it'.[2]

We are presented, then, with an idyllic picture of a cooperative enterprise dedicated to finding the most effective way of implementing ministerial and government policies, painted by two men with wide and long experience of running the government machine, both of whom worked their way up the ministerial ladder before viewing the scene from Number 10.

Yet there is an alternative view which must also be considered. For one thing, two earlier chapters of this book demonstrate that the traditional model of policy-making hardly fits the facts as far as the implementation of the Fulton Report is concerned.[3] Indeed it might well be said that what actually happened after the Fulton Report shows the insidious operation of civil service power at its most triumphant. Not only did civil servants successfully block the key Fulton proposals, but whilst doing so, they actually had the audacity to claim they carried out most of them.

The Fulton Committee was not directly concerned with Civil Service power; but it recognized that many of its recommendations would inevitably increase Whitehall's grip. The idea of a more professional Civil Service is inseparable from the idea of greater authority and influence. So Fulton attempted to balance this with other proposals to keep that power in check. The Civil Service College, for example, should have had a largely independent governing body, as opposed to the weak advisory council which eventually emerged. Traditional and ingrained Civil Service attitudes were to be challenged and countered by the late entry of experienced people from outside the Service to posts at any level (and particularly at the most senior levels) where their qualifications and experience could be expected to make a substantial contribution to policy-making. Fulton also thought that each minister should be able to appoint from outside the Service, and on a temporary basis, all the advisers and experts he believed he needed; these outsiders Fulton emphasized should be members of the powerful 'official' committees (i.e. committees of civil servants which meet without ministers being present) which have such a major impact on policy-making. Other outsiders, Fulton believed, should be involved in the appointment of top civil servants. It should also be made easier for a new minister to change his private staff – and even to get rid of a Permanent Secretary found to be too rigid or tired.

Most of these recommendations – as we have seen – were either ignored, distorted, or watered down. Instead, the Civil Service has acted to preserve, and even strengthen, the citadels of its power – where minister and official interract. For those Fulton recommendations that were adopted were those that, potentially at least, strengthened the power and position of the traditional Administrative Class; while those that have not been adopted are the ones that provided for at least some countervailing pressures.

The fate of one of those intended 'countervailing pressures' is worth considering in more depth. This was the proposal that each major department should have a Planning Unit headed by a Senior Policy Adviser. The way this was rejected is a real illustration of Civil Service determination and even dissimulation, in the cause of preventing any possible weakening of its position vis-à-vis ministers.

This proposal had two main objectives. The first was to improve long-range policy planning. So a special unit needed to be set up consisting not of generalists burdened with the problems of day-to-day administration, but of specialists and experts in the Department's main field of activity. The unit was to be headed by a Senior Policy Adviser who would also be a specialist and who would have direct access to the Minister. The second objective was that it would break the monopoly, held by generalist Permanent, Deputy and Under Secretaries, over the departmental advice received by Ministers.

Perhaps it is not surprising that this reform was blocked. What is particularly illuminating, though, is how it was blocked. First, according to the CSD's checklist for the English Committee, the idea of a Senior Policy Adviser could not be:

> reconciled with the requirements of accountability and organizational effectiveness which Fulton highlighted. It has generally been judged that the main aim of the recommendation can better be achieved by strengthening the machinery for planning without changing the existing accountabilities of Permanent Secretaries in

the field of policy advice. This should ensure that a minister has adequate policy advice available to him from his service officials, and that his department is fully alert to outside advice and opinion.[4]

Secondly, the CSD's checklist completely misrepresents the purpose of the Fulton-type Planning Unit. Fulton said that 'research is the indispensable basis of proper planning' and the main task of the unit should be to: 'identify and study the problems and needs of the future and the possible means to meet them; it should also be its function to see that day-to-day policy decisions are taken with as full a recognition as possible of their likely implications for the future.'[5] The CSD's checklist, though, asserts that: 'Fulton proposals for Planning Units seem to be concerned only . . . with the review of departmental policies to analyse their costs and benefits.'[6] And it goes on to imply that departments already had, under different guises, planning units which were much better than Fulton was proposing.

One of the units the CSD had in mind was the one I* found in the Department of Education and Science when I was Minister of State there from October 1974 to January 1976. It was called the 'Departmental Planning Organization'. It consisted of three high-level Committees composed almost entirely of top-level generalist civil servants who were all almost totally immersed in day-to-day operational and administrative questions. Thus the chief members of these committees were the Permanent Secretary, the Deputy Secretaries and the Under Secretaries who headed the different operational branches (e.g. the Under-Secretary heading the Universities Branch and the Under-Secretaries heading the various Higher and Further Education branches). This was the very opposite of what Fulton had in mind.

These three Committees were serviced by a body called the Planning Unit. This, too, was the very antithesis of the Fulton recommendation. It had fourteen members, almost entirely generalist civil servants doing a two- to three-year stint in the unit. There was a not a specialist among them, none of the

---

* Lord Crowther-Hunt

experts that were the essence of the Fulton proposal – no educational psychologists or sociologists, no counterparts of professors of education, for example. And to cap it all, it is worth noting that during the fifteen months I was in the Department no fewer than three different individuals in succession were moved into this Planning Unit to fill the Under Secretary job at the head of it.

If this whole Planning Organization was typical of the existing planning arrangements in departments which the CSD checklist implied were better than Fulton, it would at least have been more honest if the CSD's checklist had pointed out that this was indeed the very opposite of what Fulton had proposed. It was, in fact, the status quo that Fulton believed must be changed. And it was very much criticized (on Fulton-type grounds) by the Organization for Economic Cooperation and Development when they investigated DES Planning in 1975.[7]

More generally, the Civil Service skilfully downgraded the role of special advisers. In Labour's 1964-70 Government a number of advisers such as Thomas Balogh at 10 Downing Street and Christopher Foster at the Ministry of Transport managed to insert themselves with some effect into the advice-and-decision process. Senior civil servants were seldom amused, as the Crossman Diaries illustrate, with the pitched battles fought between Balogh and the then Cabinet Secretary, Sir Burke Trend.

During the 1970-74 Heath Government special advisers were used much less, but the return of Labour in March 1974 revived the threat, as Whitehall saw it, of ministers acquiring a separate channel of advice and – more important – information not controlled by the Permanent and Deputy Secretaries. Not that the Wilson Government did much in the way of appointing the 'men and women of standing and experience' that Fulton had in mind. But even with the younger, former 'chocolate soldiers', whom a number of Ministers brought in with them, the Civil Service took good care to keep them out of the crucial deliberations of the 'official' committees. Thus, soon after Wilson returned to Number Ten, Sir William Armstrong, in his final weeks as Head of the Civil Service, put his view:

We had to decide what to do with these advisers. They were mostly young, private-office types. That meant they could see anything the minister saw, but not until it had been sent to him. They could not sit on official committees or see official papers, just as the minister did not see official committee papers. They became involved at a later stage in the process.*

Wilson agreed. The predictable result was that most advisers – themselves usually far removed from the notion of a Senior Policy adviser – were shunted off into the relatively harmless pursuit of keeping ministers' lines open to Transport House and Labour MPs. Most advisers were, crucially, kept away from the very documents and discussions that would have allowed them to marshal information and advise *in time* to affect policy decisions. Treasury officials speak with some pride of how they neutralized the impact of two evidently talented advisers to Denis Healey as Chancellor of the Exchequer – Adrian Ham and Derek Scott.

The Conservative victory in May 1979 led to Margaret Thatcher reversing Labour's tendency to expand the number, if not influence, of special advisers. At the time Thatcher's move was widely thought to represent a change in the process of government. In fact it was little more than an acceptance of the realities of influence and power.

By such means, civil servants continue to take advantage of the traditional Whitehall machine to strengthen their position vis-à-vis ministers. But the machine itself is also evolving; and the mandarins are exploiting some of these new developments to add still further to their power at the expense of ministers.

There are, it must be said, some immediate difficulties in establishing this two-pronged thesis about the growth of civil service power. For one thing, it is extremely difficult to measure power in any meaningful way. Of course, ministers have the theoretical and ultimate power to tell their civil servants what to do. But day-to-day government is not normally conducted on the basis of ministers giving orders and civil servants obeying.

---

* Interview with Peter Kellner

And even in so far as it is carried on in this way, then civil servants advise ministers on the orders they should give them. For the most part, though, decisions simply emerge as a result of discussions between ministers and civil servants – and those discussions take place in the context of parliamentary and outside pressures and loyalties. It is not easy to measure the power relationship between ministers and civil servants in that sort of environment.

There is a further difficulty, too, in measuring power. In our seamless web of government, it is never easy to identify the moment and place at which crucial decisions are taken, let alone who takes them. Take devolution, for example. This was the problem I came into government to handle as Harold Wilson's Constitutional Adviser in March 1974, after serving for four years as a member of the Commission on the Constitution, which produced a whole series of devolution recommendations in 1973. In September 1974 the Labour Government produced a White Paper committing itself to a broad but quite specific scheme of devolution for Scotland and Wales. In November 1975, in a second White Paper, it elaborated those schemes in much more detail. During the whole of that period I was present at virtually all the ministerial discussions on devolution; and up to September 1974 I was at virtually all the civil service interdepartmental discussions as well. But out of this whole range of meetings and discussions, some formal and some informal, it is impossible for me to point to a particular meeting and say that *there* the crucial decision or decisions were taken. Indeed, there are only two generalizations I can make with confidence. The first is that the two meetings of the cabinet which approved the September and November White Papers were certainly *not* the occasions when crucial decisions about devolution were taken. For the most part, they were merely rubber-stamping meetings for all that had gone before. The second is that most civil servants were fundamentally opposed to devolution, and so, for that matter, were most ministers. The point is that when it is so difficult to be certain when and where crucial decisions are taken, it makes it even more difficult to decide whether ministers or civil servants have the more powerful voice.

One major disadvantage for ministers is that the average ministerial tenure in a particular department is woefully short; for example, since 1945, we have had *fifteen* Chancellors of the Exchequer – which means that, on average, each chancellor has had about two-and-a-half years seeking to run the Treasury. (Denis Healey's five-year tenure is by some margin a post-war record.) During the same period, by way of contrast, West German finance ministers have averaged nearly twice as long in the job. Given the enormous complexities of managing a modern economy, it must have been extremely difficult for an average chancellor in his two-and-a-half years to counter the Treasury view in any coherently rational way, bearing in mind the fact that his first year must be largely spent being initiated into the manifold complexities of his new job; bearing in mind, too, the long time-scale required both for the formulation and implementation of most policies and the subsequent period which has to elapse before their impact can properly be assessed. No wonder one Permanent Secretary at the Treasury who served under three post-war chancellors recently estimated, in an incautious moment, that seventy-five per cent of the time, successive chancellors accepted uncritically the advice he gave them.

The Department of Education and Science is another example of the same pernicious practice of ministerial musical chairs. Since 1944 there have been twenty ministers of education – which, on average, means rather less than two years each. This rapid turnover of ministers is not confined to the top departmental ministers. When I moved into the department as Minister of State in October 1974, I was number two to Reg Prentice. I had responsibility for the whole of further and higher education in England and Wales including the universities. I stayed in the job only fifteen months, which was not long enough to develop and see through any major new policies, even though it was soon abundantly clear to me that our overall strategies in this area needed fundamental reappraisal. The fact that Reg Prentice was replaced by a new Secretary of State after I had been there eight months enabled the Civil Service to fight back against some of the new initiatives I had got under way with Reg Prentice's blessing. Yet my stay was just about par for the course. My immediate predecessor had been in the job only six months and my four predecessors in Wilson's government of 1964 to 1970 had lasted, on average, seventeen months each. So, with Secretaries of State for Education averaging, since 1944, just under two years each, and with Ministers of State in recent years averaging less than seventeen months, where can you really expect the balance of power between ministers and their officials, to lie – particularly when at the time I left, the Permanent Secretary had been there for six years and, like the Deputy Secretaries, had spent the major part of his career in the department?

There is a another small but important aspect of this ministerial musical-chairs game which still further undermines ministerial power: there is not usually much personal ministerial handover. This is obviously difficult, if not impossible, when one government replaces another; under one of our meticulously-observed constitutional conventions an incoming minister is precluded from access to the papers and files of his predecessor. So whatever losing battles civil servants may have been fighting, they can then start afresh from a new position of strength. Even when the change is between colleagues in the same administration, normally there is still not much of a personal ministerial handover – perhaps a morning at the most – and often not even that. This is partly because the outgoing minister is either so anxious to get on with the new ministerial job to which he is being promoted, or because he is so despondent at getting the sack. More important, though, is the fact that any meaningful handover from minister to minister of the extremely wide range of departmental issues would take weeks rather than hours. So it is left to the permanent civil servants to do a gradual day-by-day handover. This inevitably gives them the opportunity to reopen the fight on issues they may have been losing (or, indeed, had lost) under the previous minister. The one thing you can be certain of here is that they will have implemented with alacrity, and without further consultation, all those decisions of the former minister where he had accepted their advice. Everything else will be proceeding at a much more leisurely pace.

The balance of power is tilted further against ministers by the inexorable Whitehall and parliamentary annual timetable of events, which means that urgent decisions cannot wait until a new minister has played himself in. For example, when I moved to the Department of Education in October 1974, the annual round in the public expenditure survey was already well advanced at the civil service level. It could hardly be held up to enable me to give adequate consideration to whether, in my view, the proposed departmental apportionment of expenditure over the next five years between schools on the one hand, and higher and further education on the other, was correct. In any case, there was not much anyone could do about the next two years, given the existing pattern of expenditure. Equally, when, within a month or two of taking office, I was faced with proposals from officials about the breakdown of capital expenditure on the future building programme as between the universities and the polytechnics, the urgency of the need for ministerial approval precluded any possibility of a fundamental appraisal of possible alternatives – though I sought to set that in hand for the following year's round. In other words, in your first year you have to say 'yes' to many proposals because you lack the time and knowledge to say 'no'.

In some respects the ministerial musical chairs resembles the rapid movement of civil servants – something, as we have seen, that prevents them properly mastering their job. But there are two important differences. The rapid movement of civil servants is frequently movement between very different jobs but within the same department. Moreover a new Under-Secretary, say, inherits the experience, the staff and, most important, the files of his team; and when he meets the Minister he will, because of his own lack of knowledge in depth, be flanked by the relevant Assistant Secretary and Principal. So, as a team, they are in a strong position to out-gun the Minister and to expound the departmental line. By way of contrast the Minister may be armed by little more than the party manifesto and some research done by party officials. So when ministers and mandarins disagree it is not an equal contest between two temporary incumbents, but an unequal match between a temporary minister and the permanence of the accumulated experience and policy of the department itself.

On top of everything else ministers have an excessive, though sometimes unnecessary, burden of work. Besides dealing with major policy questions it was, for example, my job to decide whether Brighton College of Education should merge with the University of Sussex or with Brighton Polytechnic; whether the Church of England should have a few hundred more teacher-training places in their colleges than the departmental officials wanted; and whether Kidderminster College of Further Education should run its proposed diploma course in art and design in conjunction with Wolverhampton Polytechnic (as Kidderminster wanted) or with Birmingham Polytechnic, as my departmental officials were trying to insist.

I also found myself signing about 300 letters a month on individual cases, with perhaps two to three hours a day being absorbed on individual or executive casework of some kind or other. The initial drafting of letters was done by my officials but I always felt that where the department was rejecting a specific individual complaint or what appeared to be a legitimate and reasonable request from a particular local authority, I had to be absolutely certain that there really was no possibility of a more accommodating answer. I was, after all, often the last point of appeal. But it took a lot of time. If you say 'yes' to your officials' proposals in the ceaseless flow of files into your in-tray, it can all be relatively quick and straightforward; all you have to do is read their final summary of the issue and then sign the letter they have prepared. But if you want to reject or modify what they propose, then you have to spend a lot of time mastering all facets of the particular case, and in subsequent to-ing and fro-ing between yourself and your officials.

Ministers in the House of Commons have a much greater burden of work than those in the House of Lords. For one thing the House of Lords keeps civilized hours, rarely going on much later than 7 or 8 pm. In contrast the House of Commons usually keeps ministers at least in easy reach of Westminster until shortly after 10 pm; and sometimes much later. For example, in the 1975-6 session of Parliament only 3 per cent of the Commons sittings ended by 10.00 pm – 53 per cent went on until between 10.00 pm and midnight, 26 per cent until between midnight and 2.00 am and no less than 17 per cent until after 2.00 am. The impact of this on ministerial power was neatly underlined by the cabinet minister (renowned for having both a real command over his department and also for being a tough fighter for his point of view in the Cabinet and Cabinet Committees) who told me at a 9.00 am Ministerial Committee meeting after an all-night session in the House, that he would have to rely entirely on the departmental brief in his overnight box because he had had no time, and anyway was too weary, to give any real thought to the problem in hand.

A vivid picture of the demands on a minister's time is given in a recent analysis by Tony Benn, then Secretary of State for Energy, of the way he spent 1977. During that time he:

(a) Fulfilled fifty public engagements in his constituency, made twelve general speeches in Bristol, held sixteen constituency surgeries, and handled more than 1,000 personal cases.

(b) Attended four General Management Committee meetings of the Bristol South East Labour Party; attended twenty ward meetings, and five Labour Group meetings to discuss policy.

(c) Attended twelve meetings of the Parliamentary Labour Party, and made fourteen speeches to various sub-group meetings of MPs.

(d) Dealt in parliament with three Energy Bills, produced fifty-four statutory instruments; presented thirty-three explanatory memoranda to the House re European Community Energy matters; answered fifty-one oral questions and 171 written questions; had 154 meetings with non-governmental groups; produced 1,821 ministerial minutes on papers taken home in the official red box; made 133 appointments to various bodies, etc.

(e) Attended forty-two Cabinet meetings and 106 Cabinet Committee meetings; submitted four Cabinet papers and forty-five Cabinet Committee papers; received 1,750 Cabinet papers covering the whole range of government policies.

(f) Made nineteen visits abroad, and received in his office thirty-two Foreign Ministers and Ambassadors.

(g) In the first half of 1977 presided over the Energy Council of the European Community. This involved taking the chair at six Council meetings and having sundry other official meetings on European Energy questions.

(h) Attended fifteen meetings of the Labour Party National Executive and sixty-two committee meetings.

(i) Made eighty speeches up and down the country, gave eighty-three radio interviews, fifty-seven television interviews, gave thirty-four press conferences, wrote sixteen articles, had thirty interviews with individual journalists, and received or answered 1,000 letters which did not involve constituency casework or ministerial work.[8]

That is a killing and intolerable burden of work by any standards – and there must have been occasions when even the inexhaustible Mr Benn accepted on trust recommendations from his civil servants without being able to give them the thoughtful scrutiny that might otherwise have been the case. Now Benn is in many ways no ordinary cabinet minister. His devotion to Labour Party duties outside government business has not always been appreciated by his colleagues. But the general picture of a minister hemmed in by political demands outside his department is by no means unusual. An analysis of the working weeks of fifty ministers – covering the 1964-70 Wilson administration and the 1970-74 Heath administration – found that ministers spent a minimum of sixty hours each week (excluding weekends) working; of this at least forty-five hours each were spent in cabinet and cabinet committee meetings, Parliament, interviews and discussions with people outside the department, formal receptions and lunches, official visits, and constituency responsibilities.[9] In other words, every minister has a strenuous full-time job as politician and as ambassador for his department *before* he can deal with the direct task of running his department – reading departmental papers, considering official advice, discussing and deciding policy options with colleagues and officials inside his ministry. No wonder most ministers prefer short briefing papers with clear advice on all but a few issues. If a minister accepts his officials' advice and he is challenged, he at least knows he can go back and get all the supporting evidence he wants. But if he strikes out in a direction of his own choosing, he can all too easily find himself alone and lost. Few ministers are prepared to copy the response attributed to Ernest Bevin to one policy proposal prepared by his officials: 'You have given me ten good reasons why I should do what you say. You are very clever fellows. Go away and give me ten good reasons why I should do the opposite.'

The ministerial musical chairs game; the enormously increased complexity of business which departments now handle; and the vastly increased burden of work that ministers individually and collectively have to shoulder: all this gives added power to the recommendations which come to ministers from committees of civil servants. It is a perfectly normal and traditional process of government that, before issues are ripe for ministerial decisions, they should be fully investigated and considered by committees of departmental officials. This was, naturally enough, what happened as far as devolution was concerned. Under Mr Heath's government some half-dozen or so interdepartmental committees of officials (with no ministers present) were beavering away on different aspects of the devolution recommendations which had been made by the Commission on the Constitution. When Wilson replaced Heath as Prime Minister, in March 1974, the work of those committees was already well advanced, so they went on to complete their recommendations and judgments. The change of government did not make much difference to what they produced. As Wilson's Constitutional Adviser, I was classified as a senior civil servant, so I joined in the deliberations of those committees and was present at their meetings. Convinced as I was of the need for a substantial degree of devolution I got the committee to widen the range of options they were considering. I think I was also able to make them appreciate more fully what was actually involved in the different schemes of devolution recommended in both the majority and minority reports of the Commission on the Constitution. But I do not think I was able to affect significantly their recommendations and judgments, with most of which I basically disagreed. The essential point is that, for months, these committees were meeting to assess devolution issues and, in the end, they produced reports and recommendations for ministers, in the early summer of 1974, all pointing in a particular direction.

On the surface, the reports seemed to be in-depth studies and purely objective; in my view, however, they were neither purely objective nor in any real sense fundamental – though this could be apparent only to specialized experts in the subject and certainly was not apparent to most of the extremely busy ministers who had to consider them. Most ministers, in fact, certainly could not challenge these reports – or even agree with them – on the basis of a detailed and realistic understanding of the issues involved. It has to be borne in mind, too, that all the ministers were being separately briefed by their own departmental civil servants to accept, in effect, the analyses of these interdepartmental civil service committees. And this has to be set in the context of the fact that all the ministers concerned were so exceptionally busy with departmental or other business that they barely had time to read the mass of devolution documentation, let alone consider it carefully and fundamentally. Further, before the September 1974 White Paper which committed the government to broad but specific schemes of devolution for Scotland and Wales, ministers had collectively had only two or three meetings at most, lasting altogether a mere handful of hours, to consider a Civil Service presentation which had taken months to prepare and well over 1,000 civil service man-hours in interdepartmental committee meetings alone to hammer out – to say nothing of the time these officials had spent working on the issues in their own departments. It was a forbiddingly unequal balance of power. And so it is with all the other issues where interdepartmental committees of civil servants are matched against interdepartmental committees of ministers.

There is a similar balance of power as far as purely departmental committees of officials and their ministers are concerned. The Department of Education and Science is a good example of this. The three main policy committees were exclusively composed of high-ranking departmental officials. I found it extraordinary that ministers were never present at any of their meetings, nor even normally saw the minutes of their meetings. It was even resented by officials if, as a minister, you tried to find out what they were actually discussing before they were ready to serve up specific recommendations. This, of course, could be justified on the basis of saving the time of busy ministers; but clearly, education ministers would have been making a more serious contribution to policy-making by taking at least an occasional part in the work of these committees rather than being faced with having to make quick decisions in the space of hours – and sometimes even minutes – on the basis of recommendations that civil servants had been chewing over for months among themselves.

In recent years, there has been a new Whitehall development which has given added form and power to these committees of officials. It is the system of programme analysis and review – PAR, as it is called in the jargon of the trade. It is simply a quasi-scientific means of subjecting a particular programme, problem or policy to a particularly rigorous scrutiny, with special emphasis on a cost-benefit approach. Mr Heath's cabinet decided, for example, to do a PAR on the contributions made by various government programmes to the preparation of young people for the world of work – starting with careers education and vocational guidance in schools, taking in training and further education for the sixteen- to nineteen-year-old group, and including satisfactory placement in employment. For over two years a group of interdepartmental officials made an intensive study of the problems involved. But no ministers were ever present at their meetings. Nor were there any meetings of ministers during this time to review the progress of the work or to give the officials particular guidance in the light of the problems they were uncovering or illuminating. When, as Minister of State in Higher and Further Education, I became aware, quite by chance, that this study was in progress, my attempts to get immediate access to the papers were politely side-stepped with the promise that I should shortly have before me a draft of the final report. Eventually, the report was circulated to the ministers of the departments most closely concerned for them to accept, reject or modify the PAR proposals. Now, the report had already been agreed by officials in the departments concerned, and the Treasury and the Central Policy Review Staff officials had been closely associated with the progress of the work from its inception. But ministers had *not* been associated with the progress of the work over these years; so, inevitably, it was enormously difficult to challenge the recommendations in any meaningful or substantial way. And since the normal practice is that PAR reports are never published, the basic evidence and advice on which ministers then reach major policy decisions is not subjected to public scrutiny. So here we have the power of civil servants that comes from years of confidential interdepartmental work and study, still further compounded by the cloak of secrecy.

A further factor in tilting the balance more in favour of civil servants has been the emergence of giant departments. The Department of the Environment, created in 1970, consisted of over 38,000 civil servants – with nearly 100 of them at under-secretary level or above – and this vast establishment was controlled, in theory, by only four ministers. But though the giant departments have crystallized the problem of ministerial control, they are, in fact, largely symptomatic of the general twentieth-century trend. In 1900, we had 50,000 civil servants controlled by about 60 ministers. Today, we have some 700,000 civil servants with just over 100 ministers. With civil servants multiplying at over seven times the rate of ministers, this must in itself have the natural tendency to tilt the balance of Whitehall power more in favour of civil servants and away from ministers.

Membership of the Common Market gives still further advantages to the Civil Service. First, it is adding very considerably to the all-too-heavy burden of ministerial work. Ministers now increasingly have to consider major policy questions in the context of Europe, which means regular visits to Brussels and consultations with their European counter-parts. The busier ministers are, the more they tend to depend on their officials. But there is a second factor here which increases that dependence still further. Because the European dimension is a complicated one involving the harmonization of a whole range of national policies, there has to be an enormous amount of preparatory discussions between British civil ser-vants and their European counterparts both in Brussels and in the countries of the different member states before ministers meet to take decisions. When, after all these international bureaucratic to-ings and fro-ings, a British minister is then advised by his civil servants, often at the last moment before the crucial ministerial meeting, on what line to take at that meeting, it is obviously very difficult indeed to reject or modify that advice.

The civil service has, in recent years, been able to absorb or neutralize a whole series of rival power centres which might otherwise have weakened its power monopoly. This is at once an illustration of the extent of its power as well as being an example of the way that potential power is being still further increased. Four examples will suffice to indicate these octopus characteristics of our mandarins.

1. When potentially rival power centres have been set up within the Whitehall machine, the civil service establishment has quickly succeeded in absorbing or neutralizing them. Thus, in 1964, the Department of Economic Affairs was set up with a substantial contingent of 'outsiders' to act as a counterweight to the Treasury. It took the Treasury just five years to get it abolished. A similar fate is befalling the Central Policy Review Staff. This much-needed adjunct to government was set up by Heath in 1970. Serving the Prime Minister and the Cabinet directly, it was partly intended as a countervailing force to departmental or interdepartmental official advice that was coming to ministers collectively. Since it included a significant proportion of outsiders on its staff (indeed, under Lord Rothschild it was run by an outsider), it was expected to bring a broader and more independent view to ministers collectively than that hitherto produced by the traditional Whitehall machine. But what is happening to it? It is now being absorbed by the traditional machine. It is no longer run by an outsider. It no longer has any significant outsiders on its staff. In fact it is now not infrequently brought in at the top level as an allegedly quasi-independent body to give added support to any crucial civil service recommendations which the Whitehall mandarins feel ministers might otherwise be bold enough to reject. This certainly was what happened as far

as devolution was concerned.

2. When potentially rival power centres are set up outside Whitehall, the Civil Service quickly sets out to neutralize them. The creation of the office of the Ombudsman in 1967 is perhaps the best example of this. Here was an organization specifically designed to protect the individual from the Whitehall bureaucrats. But the Civil Service up to 1979 succeeded in ensuring that the Ombudsman himself was always one of themselves – a retired civil servant; his entire staff, now some ninety individuals, have been, and still are, all civil servants on temporary secondments from their parent departments. No doubt the Civil Service would seek to justify this on the principle of 'set a thief to catch a thief', but to many of us it is as if a Regional Crime Squad was headed by a retired convict and staffed by career burglars.

Another example of the same sort of Civil Service take-over of an apparently 'outside' power centre is the University Grants Committee. By intention, it is a body of independent academics to advise the Secretary of State for Education about the universities and it is there to act as a bulwark between the universities and the government, so maintaining the independence of the universities. But what has happened to it? One might well have thought that the universities themselves would have appointed the twenty or so academics who are the members of the UGC. Not so. The civil servants in the Department of Education advise the Minister of Education on which academics shall be appointed; for the most part they are academic second liners lacking the weight and authority of their respective Vice-Chancellors. Secondly, the 120 or so full-time members of the UGC's permanent staff are virtually all civil servants on temporary loan for a two to three year period from the Department of Education; and they are even posted by that Department between the Department and the UGC in the same way that the Department moves its officials round between its own individual branches. As if all this were not enough to ensure adequate departmental oversight of the workings of the UGC, when the twenty or so members of the UGC have their regular monthly meeting they almost invariably meet in the presence of senior officials from the Department of Education –

the Permanent Secretary and the Deputy Secretary, for example.

3. Civil Servants usually manage to dominate any apparently independent 'outside' advisory committees a department might set up. A good example of this was the Department of Education's Advisory Committee for the Training and Supply of Teachers. It was serviced by the Department's officials. They provided the information and papers on which it worked and senior departmental officials were present at its meetings. But ministers were not normally there. I caused something of a stir by being present at one meeting to initiate face-to-face discussions on an issue on which I wanted the committee's views. And I insisted on being present because I believed my officials would otherwise introduce the question in a way which might slant the subsequent advice I received. If, on this occasion, I was trying to use this advisory committee to back me in a particular battle I was having with my officials, it is equally true that, for the most part, officials viewed it and sought to use it as a device for reinforcing the advice that they themselves were directly and separately giving their ministers. And if they are present much more often than ministers, they are much more likely to succeed.

4. The most recent example of the octopus qualities of the Civil Service was devolution. Here were two Acts of Parliament which sought to set up separate assemblies and governments for Scotland and Wales. But these separate assemblies and governments were not to have their own independent staffs. Their officials were to be members of 'Her Majesty's Home Civil Service' which meant that their basic loyalties would have been to Whitehall (which would have had the last word in transfers and certainly in promotion as far as the upper echelons were concerned). And as if this were not enough, the Westminster government would have had its own offices and directly employed staff in Scotland and Wales so Whitehall could keep a close watch on all that would have been happening there. The intended Whitehall embrace could not have gone much further. The frigid response of Scottish and Welsh voters did at least prevent such questionable plans from being implemented.

Much of this chapter so far has been drawing attention to

various features and developments in the Whitehall machinery of government which could greatly strengthen the mandarins against the ministers. But has it turned out like that? There is a strong temptation to believe that the bureaucrats more regularly thwart their ministers than act as their obedient servants – to believe, too, that when there seems to be a cooperative harmony between ministers and their civil servants, it is, in reality, the mandarins, as a result of their superior, subtle and devious cleverness, who mostly prevail even though their ministers may believe quite the opposite. After all, if developments in the operation of the Whitehall machine have given potential advantages to the civil servants rather than the politicians, it would be a strange lot of bureaucrats that did not convert the potential into the actual.

The most recent testimony to this is to be found in the Report of the English Committee published in September 1977. The relevant chapter starts by putting what purports to be the Civil Service point of view: 'All civil servants naturally say that they exist solely to serve the Government and that they take their policy instructions *automatically* from Ministers.'[10] This is an inaccurate summary of what civil servants told the Committee (no civil servant has ever said that he takes his instructions *'automatically'* from Ministers); nevertheless, the Report immediately casts doubts on the statement by saying: 'They could scarcely be expected to give your subcommittee evidence other than to this effect.'[11] And then, without specifically accepting evidence to the contrary, the Committee rather implies that it agrees with a different point of view: 'many who have been, or who are, ministers believe that ministers do not always get the service which it is claimed they get'. Indeed, they (i.e. ministers and former ministers) say:

> they find on coming into office that some departments have firmly held policy views and that it is very difficult to change these views. When they are changed, the department will often try and reinstate its own policies through the passage of time and the erosion of ministers' political will. Many departments are large and it is not difficult to push forward policies without a minister's knowledge. Further, it is often said to be extremely difficult to launch a new policy initiative which is not to the liking of the

department. Delay and obstruction are said to be among the tactics used, together with briefing ministers in other departments to oppose the initiative in Cabinet and Cabinet committee. The workload on ministers is immense and procrastination and repetition of the difficulties of a policy would be tactics that ministers would have difficulty in overcoming.[12]

Without actually accepting all this as proven truth, the English Reports says 'there can be no justification for any of [these] practices'.[13] So it gives its blessing to the system of bringing in a 'limited number of special advisers (though not as now limited to two per Cabinet Minister) . . . *Only with the assistance of such advisers can ministers maintain a level of political control over an increasing Civil Service.*'[14]

Here, then, are innuendoes that ministers are losing out in the Whitehall power struggle – but no actual proof. And this, indeed, is the main problem. Any number of assertions can be made about the growth of civil service power – but they remain assertions no matter who is making them.

We find the most vivid of these assertions made by people like Brian Sedgemore and Lord Balogh. Sedgemore, for example, tried to get the English Committee (of which he was a member) to include in its Report his view that the role that Civil Servants have invented for themselves:

is that of governing the country. They see themselves . . . as politicians writ large. . . . They justify this role to themselves and to others by reference to their superior intellect and by the difficulties, real or imagined, of ministers deciding or being told about the very large number of important decisions which have to be taken. They can and do relegate ministers to the second division (appropriately enough they call their own union the First Division) through a variety of devices. These include delay, which is a potent one when governments are in a minority situation or coming to the end of their political life; preclosing options through official committees which parallel both cabinet sub-committees and a host of other ministerial committees; interpreting minutes and policy decisions in ways not wholly intended; slanting statistics; giving ministers insufficient time to take decisions; taking advantage of Cabinet splits and politically divided ministerial teams; and even going behind ministers' backs to other ministries and other ministers, including the Prime Minister. In doing all these things they act in what they conceive to be the public good. Some would say they perceive that good in the interest of their own class.[15]

Lord Balogh makes similar points. On the power of interdepartmental official committees he says:

> Most decisions of any importance involve more than one ministry. First they go to one interdepartmental committee at Assistant Secretary/Under Secretary level. Then they go to an official committee of Permanent Secretaries chaired by the head of the Treasury or the Cabinet Office. Usually some compromise is reached there before it comes to ministers. For a cabinet minister to reverse a document that has been through these stages requires the intellect of a Newton and the thrust of an Alexander the Great combined with a Napoleon. Such people are seldom met.[16]

Balogh also makes the familiar points about civil servants keeping information from ministers and trying to rush them into important decisions when there is insufficient time to consider the papers before them:

> The question is whether and when you get papers, especially interdepartmental papers. Sometimes you get complicated papers which require a decision within twenty-four hours or even on the same day at a committee meeting. Sometimes you query something being done in the department and the office says 'the Cabinet has decided it'. You then ask for the Cabinet minutes, and they say you can't have them, 'they are confidential'. Occasionally there's a row and it goes to the Secretary of State. Sometimes you get your way. But after a while you say 'Oh . . . it' before you start.[17]

Balogh, there, is particularly viewing the scene from the perspective of a number two minister in a Department – the Minister of State level – and certainly that is not an easy level from which to operate. There is your relationship with your ministerial boss, who may want to cut you down to size if there seems to be any danger of your building up a more attractive public image than the minister himself. And then there is the delicate relationship between yourself and the top civil servant. As number two minister it would be most unusual for you to chair a meeting at which the Permanent Secretary was present. That would be *infra dig* as far as the Permanent Secretary was concerned. Nor, if you wanted a talk with the Permanent Secretary, would you 'send' for him, Of *you* wanted to see *him* it would be arranged by the two private offices that you would go to his office at a convenient time; and if he wanted to see you, then it would be arranged for him to call on you at a convenient time. You would normally call Deputy Secretaries and below to your office. But only the number 1 minister would 'send' for the Permanent Secretary. From a Minister of State's point of view what this means in practice is that the civil servants can go behind your back to your minister and undermine you. And if there was any division between yourself and the top civil servants this would be fully exploited if the civil servants believed that your personal relationship with the Secretary of State was in any way 'shaky'.

In this broad area of relationships between ministers themselves and between ministers and their civil servants, and between civil servants themselves, the rules of the game give civil servants a very considerable advantage. For one thing civil servants undoubtedly spend much more time talking to each other without ministers being present than vice-versa. Comparatively speaking, it is rare for ministers to have formal or informal sessions together without civil servants being present or, at the very least, knowing about it. This is one reason why the minister's private office is so important. The handful of staff there are civil servants first, second and third. And, though they will often give very loyal service to a minister, an important part of their job is to ensure that the minister observes all the Whitehall conventions, and to ensure that action is taken, or not taken (as the case may be) on any commitments or promises the minister may make. So, as we saw in Chapter 8, they have to be privy to all the Minister's activities; naturally enough, therefore, ministers tend to feel civil servants know everything they are doing – but they are certain they do not know all their civil servants are doing.

Dr Jeremy Bray, the Labour MP for Motherwell, recently gave a telling example of what can arise from this general state of affairs. He was describing an incident which took place while he was Minister of State in the Department of Power in the mid-1960s:

Wanting an independent view on oil, I had fixed a lunch with Dr Peter Odell . . . Dr Odell has continued his interest in oil and is now an adviser to the Department of Energy. Hearing of this lunch date, Mr Pitblado (the Department's Permanent Secretary) went to the Minister and objected that I was having lunch with undesirable characters. Dick Marsh quite properly told him that I would have lunch with whomever I liked.[18]

This not infrequent occurrence is possible because Ministers' diaries and engagements are, as a matter of routine, circulated to top civil servants, but most Ministers do not have any similar information about their top officials' engagements (except perhaps they may see the Permanent Secretary's diary).

In this web of criss-crossing relationships clearly the question of loyalties is of crucial importance. Lord Balogh put it like this:

In the private office they pretend to be loyal; but the Minister does not control the career of his private office officials. They are high-flyers: they know they must be Assistant Secretaries by the time they are thirty-five, and Under-Secretaries by the age of forty — otherwise they are not going to make it. And their fate is in the hands of senior civil servants.[19]

There Balogh is making a particularly important point. Annual reports and promotions are entirely in the hands of senior civil servants. They have infinitely more impact on a subordinate's career than the extremely rare ministerial interventions. So, when it is a question of loyalties, any civil servant knows where his bread is buttered and how to get at the jam.

In this context, there is a strong temptation to take at face value the Civil Service's own description (no doubt inadvertent) of the duties of what used to be the Administrative Class. In its written evidence to the Fulton Committee the Treasury (which then ran the Civil Service) said that the duties of the Administrative Class *'include the formulation of policy*, the coordinating and improvement of Government machinery and the general administration and control of public departments' (emphasis added). Not, be it noted, 'to assist in the formulation of policy'; no, it is their job apparently to do the formulating. True, the next sentence of the passage quoted above adds: 'Members of this class form the majority of those civil servants responsible for directly advising ministers.'[20] But what that addition in this context would mean is that civil servants having formulated policy then advise ministers accordingly!

The constant theme of Crossman's diaries is his war of attrition with the Whitehall bureaucrats. Like other critics of civil service power, his main aim is concentrated on the official committees:

> In addition to the Cabinet committees which only ministers normally attend, there is a full network of official committees; and the work of the ministers is therefore strictly and completely paralleled at the official level. This means that very often the whole job is pre-cooked in the official committees to a point from which it is difficult to reach any other conclusion than that already determined by officials in advance; so if agreement is reached at the lower level of a Cabinet Committee, only formal approval is needed from the full Cabinet. This is the way in which Whitehall ensures that the Cabinet system is relatively harmless.[21]

He also makes what has now become in effect the regular critics' view of a Minister's Private Office:

> The Private Office is the heart of the Ministry . . . John Delafons [his Private Secretary] is superb. Personally we don't know each other much better than we did on the first day. But he is learning a lot from me . . . and he really does try to get my ideas across to the Department. Nevertheless, I have got to face it that his main job is to get across to me what the Department wants. The Private Office is the Department's way of keeping a watch on me, of making sure I run along the lines they want me to run on, of dividing my time and getting the Department's policies and attitudes brought to my notice.[22]

Crossman is particularly good at describing how much most of the Ministers, except himself, are run by their civil servants. Thus he describes how on Monday 1 April 1968 he chaired a Cabinet Committee on policy for the fish industry:

> On Friday night in my box I found an enormous document which I worked through during the weekend – the report of a working party [presumably composed of civil servants] which has been sitting for two years . . . As soon as we got down to the meeting Fred Peart [then Minister of Agriculture, Fisheries and Food]

started reading his brief aloud . . . After five or six minutes I interrupted with a question and he replied happily that he would answer that when he'd finished all he had to say. I knew then that he had to read his brief aloud because that was all he knew, so I let him read to the end.[23]

Crossman then relates how he started 'cross-examining Fred' in a way which made it clear that he was reluctant to support the main recommendation Peart was making, and which, in effect, came from the working party report. At this point, according to Crossman, Edmund Dell (who was representing DEA in the absence of Peter Shore) entered the fray completely opposing all that Peart was recommending:

Fred Peart was dumbfounded and looked across the table at Edmund Dell and said, 'But your officials have agreed the report and recommendations with my officials.' 'Yes,' said Edmund Dell, 'my officials may have agreed but I have just given the view I am representing at this Ministerial meeting today.'[24]

And so, apparently, Dick Crossman and Edmund Dell triumphed over the interdepartmental official recommendations which the luckless Fred Peart had been presenting. This sort of ministerial victory over the civil servants is in effect the main theme of the Crossman story. Contrary to what is generally believed, what Crossman is mostly saying is that of course civil servants have some power, often a lot; of course they think they know what is best for the country; of course they mostly resent outsiders getting between the ministers and themselves; of course, on occasions, they seek to win their battles by their monopoly of information; but . . . and the 'but' is that ministers as clever as Crossman usually prevail in the end, even if lesser (and perhaps the majority of) mortals succumb to the civil service embrace.

A rather different view is portrayed by Joe Haines[25] and Lady Falkender[26] who give evidence of downright sabotage and attempted sabotage by civil servants. But even in this version the Prime Minister, assisted by his devoted entourage, usually wins through in the end.

Dr Jeremy Bray, though, comes nearest to proving a case of civil service sabotage. In the Rhodesia debate on 7 November

1978, Dr Bray asserted that: 'Instead of seeking means of implementing Government policy (i.e. sanctions against Rhodesia) the Ministry of Power officials advised the oil companies on how they could best undermine the Foreign Secretary's [George Brown's] plans.'[27]

Bray's experience as a junior minister in the Ministry of Power during the first year after UDI means that he must be taken seriously; and his specific allegations quoted in Chapter 7 have not been refuted.[28] Yet it is worth observing that the Bingham Report itself paints a more complex picture. For example, Shell and BP executives took part in two crucial meetings in January 1967. At first George Brown told the oil companies he wanted oil sanctions to work, and suggested restricting supplies to Mozambique. (Most of Rhodesia's oil then came through Mozambique.) At the second meeting, Ministry of Power officials agreed with Shell and BP that such a restriction would be impracticable – and that they had advised the Foreign Office of this. Bingham concludes: 'Clearly, there were differences between the two departments.'

By implication, Bingham means the *officials* as well as ministers in the two departments; and it is clear from the story told by Bingham that Ministry of Power officials held a number of detailed talks with the oil companies at different times, leading to the oil companies surviving a difficult period in their sales to southern Africa. It is also clear that some of the most important facts of that time were not supplied to the Cabinet. But the evidence in the Bingham Report suggests that at least the Commonwealth Secretary, George Thomson, approved some of the most controversial agreements with the oil companies: if civil servants did help the oil companies, the timidity and acquiescence of some of the most closely involved ministers was in large measure responsible.

It is significant that most of the assertions about the extent to which ministers are actually overborne by their civil servants comes not from ministers themselves, who are, like Crossman, for the most part, proud of their victories against stiffer opposition than they expected, but from number two ministers (e.g. Ministers of State and below) and from political advisers like Lord Balogh, Robert Neild and myself. Because they cannot always get what they want they tend to produce some sort of conspiracy theory and thus blame the civil servants whom in the last analysis they have not got the authority to over-ride. This, no doubt, is why a Conservative MP, a former Minister of State, could tell one of the authors:

> Briefs always arrived late. Complaints were useless. There was always an explanation. Perhaps some crucial information couldn't be obtained till the last minute. It was not, they maintained, the well-known ploy of keeping ministers uninformed until the last minute. Often I would get the box at midnight and find I was due to be at a Cabinet committee at nine the next morning on a subject I knew nothing about. I would be there instead of X (another junior minister) whose subject it was, even though he might be available. The next morning he might be at another meeting instead of me. Switching ministers in this way was common. There was never any notice of cabinet committees; and the Permanent Secretary decided who went to them. Another ploy was for our officials to brief rival ministers. Ideally they wanted people at cabinet meetings who knew nothing except what was in their briefs. And if I did go to a meeting on something I was familiar with, I would find other ministers displaying oddly similar arguments, all worked out in my department.

If a Minister of State has to put up with a situation like that, then he ought not to *be* a Minister of State. Still, lack of ultimate authority does tend to make Ministers of State feel much more at the mercy of officials than they would be if they had the power to issue orders which had to be obeyed. The situation is even worse for political advisers who have no status or authority at all. They are simply not in the departmental chain of command and however close to ministers they are, they can often be side-tracked.

The evidence about the power of the civil service that comes from ex-junior ministers or political advisers has, then, to be seen in its proper context. They may well believe they are nearer to the engine room than the skipper on the bridge, and therefore know more of what is really going on in the department. But the top minister sees all the problems in a broader context than his juniors or advisers; he has ministers in other departments and in the Cabinet to contend with. And it needs to be recognized that the minister at the head of a department does have the real power of command, as far as that department is concerned, whenever he chooses to use it.

What does all this add up to? Clearly we cannot necessarily accept at face value the assertions of junior ministers and political advisers. Clearly, too, Crossman's revealing diaries are not so much about civil servants thwarting ministers, as about Crossman, the boss minister, triumphing over much stronger opposition than he had expected. So, are we then driven to accept that the actual position today is still the traditional one which *The Times* summed up as, 'Officials propose, Ministers dispose. Officials execute'?

In reality the relationship between ministers and their top civil servants is much too subtle to be expressed in a simple generalization. We have to start with the recognition that for the most part civil servants do seem to change course when the electorate throws out one party and gives a majority to the opposition instead. This is where the party manifestos are so important – 'the battering ram of change', as Dick Crossman called them. Manifestos are carefully studied by every department during the general election campaign period. This is to find out what the commitments of an incoming government will be as far as each department is concerned and to get some clue about priorities. It may also be that during this period departments get additional information on what the Opposition has in mind – since there is now a convention under which contacts between a shadow minister and the appropriate Permanent Secretary may be authorized at this time. And if they are not authorized it is almost certain that there will be some contacts between some senior civil servants and some shadow ministers. In any event by the time the election campaign is over each department will have two sets of briefs ready – so that it is poised to service an incoming government of either party. The briefs cover the general situation facing the department and the implications of that situation for the incoming government's objectives. In addition the changes to which the incoming (or continuing) departmental minister is committed by the party manifesto will have been costed – and there will be broad indications of how those policies can be achieved.

That does not necessarily mean, of course, that all will be plain sailing for the new minister, if change there has been. It is difficult to change the policy direction of any large-scale organization, be it a government department, a business firm or a university. Old attitudes and policies almost inevitably linger on, particularly if they are not specifically referred to in the relevant party manifesto. Prior to the 1979 election a Permanent Secretary at the head of one of the largest departments told one of the authors:

> It takes about eighteen months for a change of direction to percolate down – for all Assistant Secretaries and Under Secretaries to get the message and alter their style of thinking. My job, of course, is to get a quick grasp of the attitudes of the new minister to percolate down and reflect these in the way we run the department . . . You must not underrate the ingrained attitudes of Under Secretaries and Assistant Secretaries. They are now used to a Labour government; if a Tory government were elected tomorrow they would take some time to adjust.

That period of adjustment is longer with minor changes in the administration of existing departmental policies and in the mass of individual ministerial case work that arises from these policies. During this time the department and its ministers will primarily be focussing on the one or two major changes the incoming ministers are committed to.

But the simple point to make in this connection is that the department *will* be changing directions as far as the major policies are concerned. Dick Crossman used to say that if the new departmental minister concentrated on one or two major policies, then these can be implemented whatever opposition the department may mount against them. In total, this can in fact amount to a massive amount of change; and it is certainly often more than parliament, as at present organized, can satisfactorily handle in a four- or five-year period.

So successive governments do make major changes of direction and policies. And this is testimony to the fact that either civil servants have been cooperating fully with ministers or that ministers have successfully overcome them. Perhaps one of the best recent examples of this is the last Labour Government's devolution policy. In spite of the fact that the great majority of civil servants were opposed to devolution (and so were most ministers), nevertheless, the schemes for major changes in the government of Scotland and Wales did emerge from the government machine. Despite their imperfections they represented the triumph of a handful of ministers both over their colleagues and over the government machine as a whole. No doubt some will argue that during the course of this long struggle in Whitehall civil servants managed to flaw these schemes in the hope that parliament or the people in the end would reject them as unworkable. That conspiracy theory could be further bolstered by the fact that the Constitution Unit in the Cabinet Office, which was in charge of the whole operation, was led by a Permanent Secretary, Sir John Garlick, who was basically opposed to devolution, as were many of his staff. So, too, were the great majority of civil servants on the various official committees concerned with devolution. Clearly, all this did not help the devolution cause. But my own belief, having seen a lot of this operation from the inside, is that ministers could have remedied most of the much-criticized defects in the schemes if they had really wanted to and been determined enough. The hostility of civil servants, therefore, simply reflected the hostility of most ministers and of parliament. But in the end, ministers believed, reluctantly, that they had to march down the devolution road for narrowly political reasons (i.e. to bolster Labour's position in Scotland) and so civil servants, perhaps rather more reluctantly, marched with them. It took the March 1979 referenda to halt the process.

Of course, as devolution shows, what eventually emerges from a government committed to important changes by its election manifesto may not be (and perhaps often is not) quite what the ardent advocates of that particular change were hoping for. Now if this happens over a wide enough area, does it follow that ministers have been defeated by their civil servants – or at best have produced an honourable draw?

Again, even to ask such a question betrays a major failure to understand the whole decision-making process. For the most part any new government will not have worked out its policies in sufficient detail to be able to implement them at once. Whatever advisory committees it may set up in opposition to help it, these hardly ever begin to match the full resources and information which government departments can command. So inevitably each proposal has to be processed through the government machine. That involves discussion with other ministers and their departments, and particularly with the Treasury if the plan involves more expenditure. Here it will become a question of economic priorities. There will have to be discussions, too, with outside bodies who are interested in the new proposals or basically affected by them, and here concessions may have to be made to produce the voluntary acquiescence of those involved. So the minister will be at the centre of a web of often conflicting pressures – from civil servants, other ministers, MPs generally, his own party inside and outside parliament, outside interests or pressure groups and so on. In this web of pressures, policies are refined and modified, sometimes even rejected, compromises have to be made, public opinion satisfied. So when policies eventually emerge from the government machine it is hardly ever possible to determine relative responsibilities for what has or has not happened. Neither individual ministers nor ministers collectively are really free agents at any point in the decision-making process.

But in this whole process civil servants have five very considerable advantages. First, besides being part of the pressures themselves, they are also the crucial channel through which most of the other pressures must eventually be canalized. Secondly, civil servants collectively have much more time than individual ministers, and also a greater command and control or information. Thirdly, many decisions are not regarded as sufficiently important or controversial to engage ministerial attention. Indeed, in a complex society, many second-line decisions must be taken by officials rather than politicians. But, as officials themselves control the process and the information, they largely *define* which kind of decisions should not go to ministers, as well as taking the decisions themselves. The fact that many of these decisions are then countersigned by ministers does not negate the point: if any minister called for the papers on each decision he had to sign, it would take him a month to get through each day's work.

Fourthly, ministers are very dependent indeed on their civil servants in processing a Bill through Parliament. And they are very dependent on them, too, in all their other dealings with Parliament. Without full cooperation from their civil servants here, ministers would not be able to cope with the wide-ranging debates and questions which are the regular fare of the Parliamentary struggle. So ministers and their civil servants are inextricably bound together as they face Parliament.

The fifth and final factor which inevitably puts the civil servants in a very powerful and influential position indeed is that they have a virtual monopoly of the drafting process. Ministers confront problems on the basis of papers written by officials. When committees or ministers meet it is civil servants who draft the minutes. This is perhaps seen in sharpest relief at Cabinet level. The papers and briefs ministers have before them have been almost entirely drafted by civil servants. Decisions at least appear to be made when the Prime Minister sums up at the end of a discussion on a particular item. By the very nature of the case that summing up cannot be fully detailed or comprehensive. Indeed, there will often be parts of the summing-up that seem to be deliberately vague perhaps to convince opposing ministers that some sort of compromise has emerged which all can accept. Yet no verbatim record is taken of the meeting or the summing-up. There are no shorthand writers present and no tape-recording is made. So the Secretary to the Cabinet and the other civil servants present have to rely on their longhand notes and memories when they begin to put into writing what appears to have been decided. And, extraordinary as it may seem, the draft minutes are not normally cleared with the Prime Minister before they are circulated. So what the Cabinet has decided is what the civil servants say it has decided on the basis of the papers they have drafted.

The civil servants are, of course, extraordinarily skilled in their powerful drafting and recording roles. They are the master of the nuance which is so crucial a feature in the Whitehall decision making process. They know more about nuances than any busy minister can possibly be conscious of.

And at the end of the day the sum of the nuances may well add up to major policy changes or modifications.

The exact balance between ministerial and civil service power will very much depend on what is being decided, the political circumstances surrounding it, and the relative abilities of civil servants and ministers. This last point is crucial. Certainly a minister with much less ability than his top civil service advisers will inevitably not be able to make much personal impact on this complex decision-making process. The balance of ability can often, in the end, determine the balance of power.

10

CIVIL SERVANTS AND PARLIAMENT

A CENTURY AGO, IN *The English Constitution*, Walter Bagehot distinguished between the 'dignified' and the 'efficient' parts of the constitution. The House of Commons, he said, had its 'dignified aspect'; but this was 'altogether secondary to its efficient use'. The source of its 'efficient use' was the ultimate independence of sufficient MPs from the ties of strict party discipline. They constituted 'a deliberate assembly of moderate and judicious men' whose power, though by no means total, provided an important foil to the executive.[1]

Richard Crossman, in his introduction to Bagehot's work, pungently observed how greatly things had changed by the early 1960s:

> Parliamentary control becomes a fiction with the disappearance of that solid centre of independent and independent-minded members, on which Bagehot relied to ensure that party government was always 'mild'. Once the party leadership runs a modern machine and can discipline its MPs, government control of Parliament and its business becomes absolute. The Commons, which in Bagehot's day had a real collective life and a general will, is split into two sectarian armies – the Cabinet with its phalanx of supporters, and the Shadow Cabinet also with its phalanx.[2]

When Crossman wrote that passage (and for a decade afterwards) one of the two main parties had a majority in the Commons; the whip system ensured that, except on very rare occasions, the majority could be used to support every major policy the Cabinet proposed. The two 1974 elections, with the upsurge in Liberal and Scottish Nationalist support, made simple Cabinet dominance of the Commons more difficult. After by-election defeats wiped out Labour's slim overall majority of October 1974, Commons votes occasionally over-turned major Cabinet proposals – sometimes with a few backbench Labour MPs supporting the opposition. (An impor-tant example was a Commons vote at the end of 1978 to oppose sanctions against employers who violated the Government pay policy: one of the contributory factors in the Government's defeat was that it sought to rely on administrative measures to penalize companies, and had thereby sought to impose its policy without the prior approval of Parliament. Some of the outcry was as much against the Government's methods as against its intentions.)

These set-piece occasions have created the illusion of a swing back to the authority of the Commons. In fact the surrender of executive power has been very limited. First, it has happened only on selected (if important) occasions. Second, on those occasions, MPs have only had a limited choice of pre-packaged options: they have played little or no part in the *creation* of the policy options from which they make their choice. (A rare exception was when two left-wing labour MPs, Jeff Rooker and Audrey Wise, supported by the Conservatives, obtained a majority in the Commons Finance Committee in 1977 to index-link personal tax allowances, against the wishes of the Govern-ment. The Labour whips ensured that they were not selected for membership of the Finance Committee in 1978.) Third, there has been no indication that the special conditions created when the government had no overall majority are being repeated in the (more normal) circumstances of a return to majority government following the Conservative victory in May 1979.

There is a fourth component to the illusion, more complex than the other three, but also arguably more important. It is that much of the power of the executive, and especially of the Civil Service, flows from a mastery and manipulation of detail that is denied to outsiders. Most decisions ratified by Parlia-ment, however ideologically pure in their origins, concern detail. There is more of it than MPs can sensibly handle: by the mid-1970s, legislation and statutory instruments were being shovelled into the Parliamentary fender at the rate of 11,000 pages a year – more than double the rate of twenty years earlier.[3] Or, to take a dipstick to another part of the government engine, Edward du Cann, then Chairman of the Commons Public Accounts Committee, expressed his despair, at the very height of Labour's minority administration, over the lack of control by MPs of government expenditure. He told MPs on the Procedure Committee, which was seeking ways to make the Commons more effective, that expenditure needed to be brought under MPs' command. He had the following exchange with Enoch Powell:

> *Powell:* 'I do not quite understand when you say it is not under command. There is no expenditure which is not covered by a vote of the House.'
> *Du Cann:* 'No, of course not, but the position is, as I think Mr Powell knows better than any of us here – he has studied the subject more deeply and spoken more passionately about it than any of us – that over the years we have connived at a situation where government expenditure has grown inexorably and hugely. It is the largest inflationary force in the economy. The country at large is contemptuous of our inability to command in our own House. It is perfectly true that we write every cheque, but we very rarely stand back and have a clear look at what we are doing and seeing whether or not we are doing the things which are correct, seeing that we are spending every penny wisely. It is that I complain of.'[4]

Du Cann's formulation of the problem was specifically Conservative in its implied criticism of the level of Government spending. But the underlying problem that his committee has consistently faced is not so narrowly political, in that it concerns value for money, whatever the overall relationship between public and private expenditure. That does not mean the only worthwhile areas for detailed parliamentary scrutiny are those that are bipartisan; but the admitted weakness of the Public Accounts Committee, where the discipline of party whips is largely irrelevant, does suggest that the impotence of MPs goes considerably deeper than the level required to sustain the authority of their party leadership.

In February 1972 the Labour MP John Mackintosh reported a rare Whitehall admission of its true feelings towards MPs. In a Commons debate on the Common Market he said:

> Representing two agricultural counties, I recall going round before the annual price review collecting information from my farmers. I studied the statistics and prepared a memorandum on what I thought ought to be done in farming policy for the coming year. I wrote to my Rt Hon. Friend the Member for Workington [Fred Peart], who was then Minister of Agriculture, Fisheries and Food, asking whether I could see him. I hope he will not mind if I quote his reply, which I have always treasured: 'Thank you for your letter and I am, of course, always glad to see backbenchers, particularly those with agricultural constituencies. However, as it is agricultural broad pricing and policy questions that you wish to discuss, I must point out that I am engaged with the NFU [National Farmers Union] and the Treasury in the annual price review and it would be quite inappropriate for me to listen to, or be influenced by the views of a Member of Parliament on such a matter.'[5]

Nor did Mackintosh achieve enthusiastic help from Whitehall when he channelled his efforts into the Commons Agriculture Committee. In 1967 the committee arranged to visit Brussels to investigate Common Market agriculture policies: 'The Foreign Office, on the instructions of George Brown, rang our poor little clerk at Heathrow and said did we realize that we were not authorized as a committee to board the plane. While he was talking, we just got on the plane and went.'[6]

Yet Parliament cannot be ignored altogether, at least not publicly. In July 1973, when he was still head of the Civil Service, Sir William Armstrong was questioned in a 'mock' Parliamentary inquiry on Granada TV by Michael Foot:

> *Foot:* 'In view of the absolutely vast increase in government powers and government business . . . don't you think it's rather remarkable that such a ramshackle institution as the House of Commons keeps any control at all – if you think it does keep any control?'
> *Armstrong:* 'Oh, it certainly exercises some control, certainly a very great influence. Things are quite different when Parliament's not sitting. In a recess, especially the long summer recess, the feel in Whitehall is quite different – a certain slackness sets in.'

Foot: 'You mean you've got a feeling that somebody's got an eye on you after all?'
Armstrong: 'That's right.'[7]

But what does 'having an eye' on Whitehall amount to? According to Nicholas Ridley, a Conservative critic of the Civil Service,

To Whitehall, Parliament is slightly frightening and unpredictable . . . something to be survived, weathered, rather than listened to or placated. Rather than the elected assembly of the nation, whose views and anxieties they want to accept, Parliament is a hostile ordeal which can occasionally mar their plans.[8]

If Ridley is right – and he wrote that in 1973, when the Conservatives had a working majority in the Commons – then the apparent revival of Parliamentary control over the executive since 1974 has been purely a question of scale: minority governments merely have their plans 'marred' by the Commons a little more often.

There are two principal ways in which MPs can, in theory, keep senior civil servants on their guard. The first is through the use of Parliamentary Questions (PQs); the second is through the cross-examination of officials in select committees. PQs, as we have seen, are formally answered by ministers, but ministers rely heavily on briefs supplied (typically) by Assistant and Under Secretaries. PQs certainly need to be weathered: and the highly formalized system of both oral and written questions-and-answers gives great scope for evasion. Oral questions – notably to the Prime Minister on Tuesdays and Thursdays – fit well into Bagehot's description of 'the lyrical function of Parliament. . . . It pours out in characteristic words the characteristic heart of the nation.'[9] Nobody any longer equates question-time with systematic control of the executive, though it may occasionally provide a random test of a minister's mental and verbal agility. In the words of Professor Bernard Crick, question-time is 'a modest little trip-wire'.

Written PQs, when drafted with precision, may elicit more information. But the right of MPs to probe any part of the government machine is far from absolute. Apart from the opportunities for departments to evade questions, or to plead that a particular piece of information would be too expensive to obtain, there are about 100 subjects that MPs are forbidden to ask about. These range from obvious security issues, through general subjects that governments do not want to discuss, down to particular topics where disclosure might simply demonstrate executive incompetence. Successive administrations have refused to answer questions about rent for government offices, telephone tapping, Cabinet Committees, the cost of the hot line, air near-miss inquiries, trade statistics for Scotland, details of export licences, advice from economic planning councils, contracts for the Forestry Commission, forecasts for future trends in incomes, forecasts for changes in food prices, the names of non-medicinal and cosmetic products containing hexachlorophane, the number of successful and unsuccessful prosecutions against chief constables since 1945, details of government contracts with manufacturing companies (including those contracts for building Concorde), the report of an inquiry into government building standards, and a report on the Central Office of Information and departmental information services.[10]

In 1977 a request for a copy of the Head of the Civil Service's guidance to departments on open government (see next chapter) was stalled on the grounds that MPs were prohibited from obtaining information about internal government administration. In this instance the MP, Jeff Rooker, eventually persuaded the government to publish the letter by recourse to the debates on devolution legislation: as the government intended some openness in the Scottish and Welsh administrations, the guidance given in Whitehall should be published to indicate to MPs more precisely what the government had in mind. It was, as Rooker says, an absurd rigmarole for getting some straightforward information – on open government, of all things!

The second device that, in principle, should allow MPs to control the executive is the select committee system. In their modern form select committees date back to 1956 when the Nationalized Industries Committee was set up: a group of MPs who would take evidence about nationalized industries, examine witnesses, and produce occasional reports. (Select committees are separate from standing committees, which examine and revise legislation.) In the 1950s and early 1960s select committees were widely regarded as the weapon that would seize back power from the executive. No longer would an ignorant Commons, whipped into party line, provide the government of the day with a reliable, unquestioning majority for any proposal it cared to put before it: select committees, the hope was, would prise open the doors of government sufficiently to give MPs greater access to the information and ideas and arguments that lay behind government decisions. Expertise was what MPs lacked in their fight with Whitehall: expertise was what select committees would provide.

One of the characteristics of select committees has been the increasing frequency with which civil servants have given evidence. This, indeed, has been regarded as one of the breakthroughs that the select committee system has made: civil servants defending in detail, against critical questioning, the policies and practices of their department. While, in theory, the Secretary of State remains the person answerable to Parliament, often only civil servants are capable of handling the kind of detail that proper supervision of the executive requires. Hence the delegated authority to civil servants to speak to departmental policy.

That, anyway, is the idea. A case study demonstrates how difficult it can be to make it work in practice. In February 1976 the Government published its annual white paper on public expenditure. As part of the select committee process, the white paper was examined by the general sub-committee of the Expenditure Committee. The Expenditure Committee had been set up in 1970 (superseding the Estimates Committee) with the remit to monitor future spending plans – in contrast with the longer-established Public Accounts Committee, whose job has historically been to monitor the propriety and efficiency of public spending *after* it has taken place.

The Expenditure Committee received startling advice about the white paper from the committee's adviser, a young Cambridge economist, Terry Ward. Ward's careful academic analysis of the white paper's economic arguments was punctuated with phrases such as: 'this claim does not stand up to examination . . . no evidence that anything remotely approaching this scale has ever occurred before . . . that is obviously implausible.'[11] The stage was set for what should have been a perfect example of the legislature testing the quality of the advice given to ministers by Treasury officials. The white paper involved future spending plans, so anything badly wrong could be changed. The MPs were receiving at least some expert advice, so had some chance to debate in detail with the four Treasury officials who came to give evidence – a Deputy Secretary, Fred Jones, and three Under Secretaries, John Anson, Hans Liesner and Patricia Brown. If MPs and civil servants were ever to engage in a rational public debate on future policy thinking, that opportunity came on 26 February 1976, when seven MPs and the four officials met.

To the outside observer one thing immediately distinguished the officials from the MPs. The officials, sitting along a narrow table facing a horse-shoe table, each had thick loose-leaf files containing vast numbers of statistical tables. The MPs, facing them from round the horse-shoe, had just a few pieces of paper each, with some of the questions they wanted to ask. This was, perhaps, reasonable assuming that the Treasury team did not know what was going to be asked, and wanted to be prepared for all eventualities. Yet the remarkable thing was that *not one single new figure* was provided at the meeting.

Early on, Fred Jones said, 'May I say straight away that we shall not be able to give precise assumptions about the inflation rate, interest rates and borrowing requirement underlying the debt interest figures.'[12] The reason for this refusal was the need to preserve secrecy. But without revealing these assumptions it was impossible to assess the debt interest figure (rising to £7,500 million a year): it had to be taken on trust. On other points the Treasury team seemed unable to lay their hands on the precise information that MPs wanted, even though the questions arose directly from Ward's paper. In other words, it would have been possible, even prudent, to anticipate these questions, but the Treasury officials apparently failed to do so. Thus:

How much of Britain's debt interest was owed by central Government, how much by local government, and how much was owed abroad? 'I do not have that information with me. I think it is extremely difficult.'[13]

How rapid was the anticipated growth in private investment from 1975 to 1979? 'I have not got to hand the figure for fixed investment from 1975.'[14]

What assumptions were made about the growth in imports and exports between 1975 and 1979? (The white paper had only given figures for the trade balance, which was impossible to assess without knowing the separate import and export figures that led to it.) 'I am sorry to say that I cannot give you the figures from 1975 because I do not have them available.'[15]

What projection was assumed in the white paper for the level of tax allowances to home owners? 'I cannot give you a projection.'[16]

The figure for unemployment was then 1.3 million. Did the Government consider it a reasonable assumption that it would rise to at least 1.5 million before reaching its peak? 'We are not in a position to answer that.'[17]

The MPs were not satisfied with these answers, or by the defence of the Chief Secretary to the Treasury, Joel Barnett, that the absence of some details from the white paper was because 'Ministers . . . felt we were in danger of overloading the public mind with the volume of paper.'[18]

The impotence of MPs was demonstrated by what happened next. The white paper was rejected by Parliament, with a combination of Conservative and left-wing Labour MPs voting against the Government. The Government's response was to call for a vote of confidence – which it won – and then carry on applying (and amending) the policies of the white paper as if nothing had happened. A few weeks later the Expenditure Committee delivered its own sharp verdict – that the information given by the Government was inadequate, and its economic projections were absurd – yet, in the short term its strictures went unheeded. The 1977 white paper contained even fewer details than the 1976 one.

In the longer term the Expenditure Committee has had some impact: by 1979, the amount and variety of information contained in the annual expenditure white paper had increased to take account of some of the Committee's criticisms. But on the fundamental issues of economic analysis and forecast, the Treasury remained as tight-lipped as ever.

In September 1976 senior civil servants were issued with detailed guidance by the CSD on what they should and should not say to select committees. The Memorandum of Guidance, running to 6,000 words, carefully reflects the formal constitutional position that ministers are in charge:

> Officials appearing before Select Comittees do so on behalf of their ministers. It is accordingly government policy that it is for ministers to decide which officials shall give evidence to Select Committees on their behalf. . . . If, however, a Select Committee summoned by name any other official to appear before them, and insisted on their right to do so, it would be for the ministers to decide what course to follow. The formal constitutional position is that although a committee's power under their terms of reference to summon persons and papers is normally unqualified, such a summons is effectively binding only if backed by an Order of the House.[19]

In other words there would be considerable difficulties for a Select Committee trying to get (say) a specific Assistant Secretary to answer questions about policy details, if the department were against it. The committee would have to obtain the support of the House of Commons as a whole and any majority government could use the party whip system to seek to overturn a Select Committee's wishes. The fuss caused when the Nationalized Industries Committee attempted – and finally succeeded – to extract information from a reluctant British Steel Corporation in January 1978 showed how cumbersome the task of summoning 'persons and papers' can be. In practice, Select Committees accept unquestioningly whichever officials, if any, a department chooses to put before them.

The guidance to officials appears to sanction a relaxed, even forthcoming attitude to the provision of information to Select Committees:

> The general principle to be followed is that it is the duty of officials to be as helpful as possible to committees, and that any withholding of information should be limited to reservations that are

necessary in the interests of good government or to safeguard national security. Departments should, therefore, be as forthcoming as they can (within the limits set out in this note) when requested to provide information whether in writing or orally.[20]

Any thoughts that the parenthetical qualification is some mere technicality to be lodged in the back of the mind is quickly dispelled. A few lines later comes the first hint that the mentality of closed government still reigns:

> Once information has been supplied to a Committee it becomes 'evidence' . . . . *The risk of publication* (whether authorized by a committee or not) must be taken into account in deciding what it is prudent to make available *even within authorized categories*.[21] [emphasis added].

If the general idea were to be helpful, the logical formulation would have been to talk about the *opportunity* of publication, rather than the risk; and the rider that the 'risk' relates even beyond the 'limits set out in this note' suggests a strong bias towards caution and reticence.

Then we come on to the limits themselves. They seem to cover everything, including government-owned kitchen sinks. Apart from the obvious (though at the borderline debatable) restrictions governing national security, the guidance to officials is, in effect, to stop MPs discovering anything of use about what is going on inside Whitehall: 'Committees' requests for information should not be met regardless of cost or of diversion of effort from more important matters.'[22] (As it is up to ministers, rather than MPs, to arbitrate on what constitutes 'more important matters' the executive's opportunity for dissembling on difficult topics is considerable.)

> In order to preserve the collective responsibility of ministers, the advice given to ministers by their departments should not be disclosed, nor should information about interdepartmental exchanges on policy issues, about the level at which decisions were taken or the manner in which a minister has consulted his colleagues. Information should not be given about Cabinet committees or their discussions, nor should the methods by which a subject is being reviewed, e.g. by the Central Policy Review Staff or under PAR (Programme Analysis and Review), be disclosed.[23]

This extraordinary no-go area might be consistent with the rhetoric of open government if it applied only to sensitive subjects known to be under active debate by Cabinet ministers. But the guidance makes it clear that, however technical the subject, civil servants should not go beyond *already published information*: 'It may be that information about the methods being used for the examination of policy has been made public, for instance in reply to Parliamentary Questions, and Committees might ask further questions. Officials should confine themselves to what has already been made public.'[24] For specialists who might be tempted to wax eloquently about their own subject there is a special warning:

> A Select Committee may invite specialist (as opposed to administrative) civil servants to discuss the professional or technical issues underlying controversial policies. This raises particular problems which are clearly exemplified in the case of economists who may be asked to appear before the Expenditure Committee . . . Where economic advisers to the government appear as official witnesses, they may find themselves in the difficulty that their own judgment of the professional issues has, or might easily appear to have, implications critical of the government's policies. It is not open to them to explain the advice which they have given to the government on such a matter, or would give if asked by the government. They cannot therefore go beyond:
> (a) Explaining the economic reasoning which, in the government's view, justifies their policy . . .
> (b) Explaining the state of knowledge and opinion of a subject among professional economists, presenting a fair balance of views and referring . . . to *the public evidence* of the government's view[25] [emphasis added].

But what if there is no such public evidence? 'The witness . . . should refer to the political nature of the issue and suggest . . . that the questioning be addressed, or referred to ministers.'[26]

The paragraph that, perhaps, reveals most about the true attitude of the Civil Service towards openness concerns departmental committees that contain outside members. The paragraph starts with an observation of the – to Whitehall, regrettable – obvious:

> While Select Committees should not press for internal advice to

ministers to be revealed, they are less likely to accept without argument a refusal to reveal a report from a departmental Committee containing outside members, and even less likely to accept a refusal in the case of a wholly external Committee.[27]

So how should departments avoid friction? Refusing to say anything could cause trouble. Publishing everything would be too radical. The trick that the guidance suggests is to try not to let on to MPs that some of these Committees or their reports exist, so that MPs do not think up the awkward questions in the first place: 'These implications [of MPs asking questions about the work of Committees that contain outsiders] need to be taken into account in deciding *how much publicity* should be given to the establishment of Committees of this kind'[28] (emphasis added).

Another problem for civil servants is that MPs might request 'documents relating to the internal administration of a department.' Here the guidance to civil servants delicately side-steps the issue of whether MPs have the right to know how, in detail, the structure of a Department operates. It suggests keeping certain kinds of information out of MPs' hands, under the guise of offering to be helpful:

Detailed information is contained in departmental directories and organization charts. These are, however, generally restricted to official use, or contain much extraneous information unlikely to be of interest or value to Select Committees. It would therefore usually be more appropriate to offer specially prepared papers describing the organization of the Department or particular parts of it.[29]

When the Procedure Committee published its report in July 1978 it drew attention to this range of restrictions on the questions that civil servants were advised to answer. In particular the MPs on the Committee disliked the way the principle of Cabinet and ministerial responsibility had been stretched to embrace almost every aspect of government work that might attract attention:

We are aware of the long-standing convention which prevents the disclosure by Ministers or civil servants of the existence, composition or terms of reference of Cabinet committees, or the identity of their Chairmen . . . We are disturbed, however, by the extension of these conventions to all questions of departmental or inter-departmental organization which, if consistently and uniformly applied, would debar Members and committees from access to information about the organization of the government service which is essential for any attempt properly to scrutinize the administration and expenditure of government departments. We recommend that select committees should regard any refusal to provide information of this kind – unless fully and adequately explained by ministers and justified to the satisfaction of the committee concerned – as a matter of serious concern which should be brought to the attention of the House.[30]

The Procedure Committee's central proposal for monitoring the executive was to abolish the existing 'subject' committees that had developed *ad hoc* over twenty years, and replace them with twelve new Select Committees, each shadowing one or more government departments. 'Single ministry' committees would include Agriculture, Defence, and Energy. 'Multiple ministry' committees would include one for Industry and Employment; another – the Treasury Committee – would shadow the Treasury, the Civil Service Department and the Ombudsman.[31] (The Public Accounts Committee, not strictly part of the Select Committee system, would remain independent.)

Changing the structure alone would, however, achieve little, except a more consistent coverage of Whitehall activities. The principal reason why Select Committees have achieved little is that they have lacked information, expertise and motivation. Without information MPs lack the opportunity to find out what is really happening. Without expertise they have little chance to analyse what information they do get, or to make sense of the policy options. Without motivation they are unlikely to go to the bother of challenging the executive and risking the wrath of their party whips.

We have already seen some of the ground rules that allow civil servants to conceal information, and the modest proposals that the Procedure Committee made for lifting the curtain an inch or two. On expertise, the Procedure Committee drew attention to the scarcity of staff and part-time advisers who help MPs on Select Committees. In 1977 the Committee Office consisted of fifty-six full time staff, of whom twenty-seven were in secretarial, clerical or executive grades. Between them they serviced twenty 'operating units' (that is, Committees and Sub-Committees).[32] The Procedure Committee observed that its new proposed Committee structure would not

> be able to undertake the full range of tasks proposed for them without rather more substantial permanent staff resources than those at present available . . . We suggest that an investigative select committee should expect to have at its disposal at least one Clerk, one executive or clerical officer, and one secretary.[33]

To this modest complement, the Procedure Committee suggested adding more outside experts. (In 1977 there were thirty part-time advisers and a handful of full-time advisers.) In reaching this conclusion the Committee overrode the arguments of the Clerk of the House, the chief paid official working to MPs on Select Committees:

> The view of the Clerk of the House was that it was doubtful if the value of select committee reports 'would be enhanced if they became reports of specialists which had received the formal endorsement of a Committee'. This view was supported by a number of witnesses. We disagree with them. If the new select committees which we propose are to call ministers and civil servants to account, to examine the purposes and results of expenditure programmes and to analyse the objectives and strategies behind the policies of departments, they will require full-time expert staffs.
>
> We recommend that the present restriction on the appointment of part-time specialist advisers 'for the purposes of particular inquiries' should be removed, and that all select committees should in future be free to appoint whatever advisers they wish for the purposes of their work . . . We recommend that the scales of fees for advisers should in future be laid down by the [House of Commons] Commission, and not, as at present, by the Treasury.[34]

(The Treasury's scale fees for part-time advisers, as for outside lecturers at the Civil Service College, have long been a source of discontent among recipients.)

The committee might have added, but did not, that MPs need more time to examine witnesses. At present a civil servant or minister generally needs to block just two or three questions from one MP at a time before the chairman insists on moving on to the next MP – and the next topic.

Even if all these proposals were carried out in full, the balance of advantage would still be overwhelmingly with Whitehall. The Select Committees would still have fewer than one hundred, and possibly fewer than fifty, senior staff and paid advisers, while ministers have 2,000 officials of Assistant Secretary rank and above to advise them, with at least as many Principals and specialists on tap to handle detailed problems.

Information and expertise are the necessary conditions for select committees to become more effective, but they are far from sufficient. The core of the problem is motivation: the motivation to make select committees in themselves tougher, and the motivation then to take their conclusions to the House of Commons as a whole and win votes there, if necessary against the advice of party whips. Until now Select Committees have seldom been able to win the difficult arguments on the floor of the House; and this has denied them any substantial sanctions against people or institutions who do not wish to be forthcoming. In 1968, for example, the Nationalized Industries Committee wanted to examine the Bank of England. As Roy Jenkins, the Chancellor of the Exchequer, opposed the idea, the matter had to be debated by the Commons as a whole. According to John Mackintosh, 'There was a debate in the House in which everyone who spoke, from whatever party, was for it; but as soon as the bell rang they turned out from the bar or wherever they'd been hiding, and filed through the "no" lobby.'[35]

The motivation of MPs to challenge the executive systematically, thoroughly and determinedly is probably the most difficult reform of all to accomplish. Of 635 MPs, about 100 are in the Government, and therefore part of the executive. Another 50 to 100, say, in the governing party, entertain hopes of appointment to government posts; and since appointment is entirely by patronage, there is a considerable incentive not to rock the boat. Equally, 150 to 200 MPs on the opposition benches have hopes of varying plausibility that after an election they will become ministers; so while they are keen to expose the weaknesses of a current government, they still have some incentive not to make life intrinsically more difficult for Whitehall as such. So for about half of the MPs in the Commons there is a personal interest in allowing Whitehall to maintain at least some of its privileges. That does not mean that every actual or potential minister is reduced by these pressures to a quivering unquestioning jelly: but it does mean that the mainstream career structure for MPs of high or moderate talent lies inside the executive, and therefore the general incentive for them is to retain the power of the executive.

That still leaves 250 to 350 MPs outside the executive career net. Many of these have outside interests (especially, though not wholly, among Conservatives), and do not take a close interest in the detail of government anyway; some are time-servers who equally show no interest in detailed scrutiny; some are principally concerned with specific causes (notably in recent years most of the Scottish Nationalist, Welsh Nationalist and Ulster MPs).

The most interesting group of MPs who have in the past opposed the expansion of the investigatory select committee system has been the 'pure' Parliamentarians. In recent times the two most noted members of this group have been Michael Foot and Enoch Powell. In 1973 John Mackintosh, speaking in a Granada TV debate, reca led one of the great controversies of the 1964-70 Labour Government:

> I remember once listening to Michael Foot making an attack on the Labour Government's policy of keeping troops East of Suez, a brilliant attack I thought, [though] without being disrespectful a little insubstantial in places. And I remember saying to him, wouldn't it have been a good idea if we'd had a Defence Committee which could have discovered the cost of the bases East of Suez. We could have heard the generals and the admirals on how effective they thought our forces were, and heard about our treaty commitments, and discovered a little of the thinking behind it. And Michael said to me, 'No, it wouldn't have helped me at all'. He said, 'I only find facts confuse my arguments.'[36]

Foot was then, of course, a backbench MP. Later, Leader of the House, he had to respond to the Procedure Committee's proposals for reform. While not explicitly rejecting the proposals, he couched his argument in terms of the damage powerful select committees might do to the supremacy of the House of Commons as a whole:

> I believe that access to the Chamber by an individual member, throughout his whole career, is the supreme attribute of the House of Commons. . . . I believe that if that attribute is broken, injured or impaired, great injury will be done to the House. . . . The proposal is for a range of Select Committees which are supposed to deal with the major question of the disbalance between the Executive and the legislature. That is not a minor matter; it is a proposal for dealing with a major question. If these Committees, applied to each Department, are to rectify such a disbalance, they will have a predominance in our parliamentary affairs which will be different from anything that we have previously experienced.[37]

Enoch Powell's record on the subject closely follows Foot's. In the 1973 TV debate Powell said:

> If I hated the House of Commons as much as I love it . . . I would take Hon Members and I would stuff them with information as one stuffs a goose to produce *paté de foie gras*. They should have information until it was coming out of their ears, because they would be quite unable . . . to get together in the lobbies, to meet, to talk to one another.[38]

As both Foot and Powell are noted for their rhetorical abilities it is tempting to read into their arguments a special pleading for the survival of their own rare talents. But there is a deeper argument about the Chamber of the House. Powell touched on it in his Commons speech in February 1979 on the Procedure Committee's report:

> The House is not just a corporation, and simply to talk about the House vis-à-vis the Government is a totally inadequate description. The House comprises parties and, for most of the purposes of the House, its partisan character overrides its corporate character. If it did not, we could not be the continual, living and flexible expression of the will of those whom we represent.

According to this view – and it can be heard on the Labour left as well as on the Conservative and ex-Conservative right – the unitary nature of British government needs to be preserved, with the power of MPs flowing from their organization into parties within Parliament, rather than from cross-party alliances that might be set up within Select Committees. Their argument against powerful Select Committees is that they would lead to more bipartisan politics, and also to a greater separation of powers between the executive and the legislature. Both developments, the argument runs, would weaken the role of political parties to develop coherent programmes, present them to voters, and then implement them in Parliament. The danger perceived in select committees with teeth is that they could frustrate the implementation of party programmes: they would turn into devices for filibustering.

Against this stand two groups that for differing reasons support strengthened select committees. Some, mainly Conservative, feel that there is too much Government, and want it checked; others, mainly Labour, feel that the greatest obstacle to radical change is Whitehall, and feel that greater scrutiny of the executive (especially when there is a Labour government) could *accelerate* change. Whereas the former group lump ministers and officials together and want to check both, the latter group wants to prise ministers away from the suffocating embrace of their Permanent and Deputy Secretaries, and give them back their political virility.

Both groups, however, are relatively small, at least as far as enthusiasts for select committees are concerned. In the 1974-79 Parliament they included the Conservative MPs Edward du Cann (chairman of the Public Accounts Committee), Sir David Renton (acting chairman of the Procedure Committee) and Kenneth Baker; and the Labour MPs Michael English (chairman of the General Sub-Committee of the Expenditure Committee), John Garrett (a former management consultant who had advised the Fulton Committee) and Brian Sedgemore. One of the ways their ranks might be swelled would be if select committees had sufficient power to provide some rival to ministerial office in the career ambitions of able MPs. The Procedure Committee dangled its toe in the water and concluded:

> We regard this as wholly desirable, and believe that the work of select committees, and in particular of their chairmen, should be

recognized by the House. We recommend that consideration should be given to the payment of a modest additional salary to the chairmen of select committees, perhaps on the same level as the salaries of parliamentary under-secretaries in the Government. . . . We believe that [this] would be both desirable for its own sake, and could also provide some element of a career opportunity in the House not wholly in the gift of the party Leaders.[39]

Although the Procedure Committee's proposals were modest – perhaps *because* they were modest – they secured general assent from MPs who spoke in the two-day debate on the report in February 1979. Norman St John Stevas, the shadow Leader of the House, promised that a Conservative government would implement most of the reforms. Three months later, however, when Margaret Thatcher became Prime Minister, the new government started to draw their teeth (see chapter 12).

The Public Accounts Committee stands in a special category of its own. It has on paper semi-authority over a staff of more than 600 – the men and women who comprise the Exchequer and Audit Department. Since 1972 they have not counted as civil servants, although the regulation of salaries and recruitment methods are determined by the Treasury; and the head of the E & AD, the Comptroller and Auditor General, is generally an ex-Treasury civil servant. The essential task of the E & AD is simply stated: to audit the books of government departments, and prepare assessments for the Public Accounts Committee (PAC). In his reports to the PAC the Comptroller and Auditor General draws attention to any overspending or mis-spending that appears to have occurred. The PAC then questions senior civil servants in each department, and subsequently delivers its own verdict on each department's performance.

The ground rules on the auditing of government departments were established in 1866, when their combined expenditure was less than £100 million. Apart from minor amendments in the Exchequer and Audit Departments Act of 1921, the rules have remained unchanged, even though the auditing task has grown immensely. Until recently the work of the E & AD and of the PAC was widely respected, with only isolated critics pointing out their shortcomings. Since Edward du Cann became chairman of the PAC in 1974*, however, the criticisms have grown, not least because du Cann himself has regularly publicized his own misgivings about the opportunities of the PAC to do more than uncover occasional detailed lapses in the past behaviour of departments. The criticisms have centred on two main issues: the independence of the E & AD, and its professionalism.

According to Dr Leslie Normanton, the author of the standard work, *The Accountability and Audit of Governments,*[40]

> The idea that the reform of 1866 created a state audit wholly as the servant of Parliament was from the outset a serious oversimplification. The 1866 Act mentioned the words 'Parliament' or 'House of Commons' 28 times, whereas 'the Treasury' appeared 68 times. The Treasury reserved to itself detailed powers; it was responsible for deciding which departments would submit accounts to the Comptroller and Auditor General, and the manner in which accounts were to be kept.[41]

One result is that about half of all public expenditure sanctioned by Parliament is not audited at all by the E & AD – for example, nationalized industries, the National Enterprise Board, local authorities and universities all escape its grasp, as do the proliferating 'fringe' bodies or Quangos that are funded by the Government but have semi-independent status.

On the quality of accounts presented to Parliament, Lord Armstrong told the English Committee when it was examining the Civil Service:

> I have never seen a form of accounts, whether it is those presented to Parliament or those presented to the public at large under the Companies Act, that was of the slightest use for management purposes at all. . . . We were developing our own form of management accounting which was quite different from what we gave Parliament. We give to Parliament a combination of what Parliament wants and what ministers are willing to let it have, which is a funny thing.[42]

This means, for example, that it is often impossible to discover what a particular government function – like running Britain's

---

*Du Cann was succeeded by Labour MP Joel Barnett in 1979.

prisons – costs, especially if the function involves more than one department (as the prison service does).

At least as serious as these formal obstacles to the assessment of departments' financial performance has been the historically low grade of E & AD staff that the Treasury has provided for. The pay and career structure within the E & AD parallels that of the executive grades in the mainstream Civil Service, with the result that their staff are nearly always of inferior status – and often greatly inferior status – to the civil servants whose record they are examining. As late as 1969 the E & AD contained only ten university graduates, and a further ten with a professional qualification: almost all other members of the staff had joined as school-leavers.[43] Recently, as with the recruitment of Executive Officers, recruitment has shifted towards graduates, and new E & AD staff are encouraged to obtain professional qualifications. It is, however, still difficult to argue with Normanton's conclusion that the status of E & AD staff has for sixty years been 'unquestioningly the lowest of any major country in the western world. The controllers, save for their chief, the C and AG, were (and were seen to be) less than the controlled.'[44]

Since 1969 the position has started to improve: between 1970 and 1976 fifty-six graduates were recruited to junior auditing grades (although only one of these had a professional qualification in accountancy).[45] By 1976 graduates formed a majority of recruits. However, according to Normanton,

> Despite this new stir at the bottom of the seniority list, it remains true that Britain's state auditors are second-class citizens in the Civil Service. . . . It is symbolic of this permanent inferiority of status that the E and AD Office List of January 1977 shows only one person out of the total of 651 whose name had appeared in a Civil Honours List, one solitary OBE. . . . Honours in the Civil Service go with rank and assumed importance; the historic British assumption about its state auditors is obvious.[46]

In contrast, the office of the Comptroller General of the United States insists on a highly professional staff. Although the US economy is far larger than Britain's, the *federal* bureaucracy is comparable in size with Britain's Civil Service (chiefly because more functions in the US are carried out by individual states or by the private sector). But in comparison with the E & AG's handful of professionally qualified staff, Washington's Comptroller General employed in 1975: 2,556 professional accountants, 531 management specialists, 126 attorneys, 103 mathematicians, 36 engineers, 37 computer scientists, 177 economists and other social scientists, 36 personnel management experts and 186 other professionally qualified staff.[47]

Both the English Committee and the Procedure Committee pointed out the relative weakness of the E & AD compared with Washington's General Accounting Office, run by their Comptroller General. Sir Douglas Henley, Britain's G and AG, commented on this point when he replied to the strictures of the English Committee:

> Although much of the GAO's activity is of a similar type to that which E & AD carries out, they go a good deal further into analyses of policy execution and of policy alternatives. These wider types of study are no doubt found valuable by Congress in the very different constitutional situation in the United States. For a national audit institution to provide in effect a second opinion on a very wide range of Governmental policies, projects, services and programmes requires a large number of administrators and other specialists if the job is to be effectively done, and the GAO employs about 5,300 staff, of whom only about half are accountants. I doubt whether this approach would be a cost-effective use of skilled and scarce resources in this country.[48]

Henley's essential defence is that the E & AD performs a limited function well. By its nature this is a difficult proposition to test directly: in general, defects in government spending that the E & AD fails to detect remain undetected by anyone else. On a few occasions, however, events make it necessary to re-examine work the E & AD has done – and it has been found wanting. The most startling example in recent years suggests that the E & AD might well have done better if it did have more staff with professional qualifications and the seniority to monitor government spending with greater authority. It concerns the disastrous record of property speculation in the early 1970s by the Crown Agents, leading to losses of more than £200 million. A Committee of Inquiry headed by Judge E. S. Fay found that a contributory factor was that the E & AD permitted the Crown Agents to hide its failures by delays and the use of inadequate accounting standards:

> The accounts, as audited by the E & AD, fell short of [the required] standards. The principal shortcoming was as regards delay. . . . The statutory requirement that the E & AD should make their examination 'with as little delay as possible' was lost sight of. . . . Some of the delay may have been due to inadequate audit staff allocated to the Crown Agents. More important in our view was the apparent lack of concern over the delay on the part of the E & AD higher directing staff, and the failure to report it as a departure from the accounting standards prescribed by the Treasury.[49]

In 1969 Hubert Long, a Deputy Secretary at the E & AD, had reported critically on a new Crown Agent venture called Finvest. Subsequently, however,

> the most significant impression that we gained of the part played by the E & AD in the rise and fall of the Crown Agents as bankers and investors was that they never recaptured the spirit of alertness and perceptive inquiry so clearly shown in Mr Long's report on Finvest to the Treasury in October 1969. . . .
> Finally we must notice the apparent indifference of the E & AD to the failures of the Crown Agents' internal accounting system. . . . A contributory factor [to the Crown Agents' losses] lies in the apparent omission by the E & AD to perform for the Crown Agents the recognized auditor's function of advising management of defects and weaknesses of their financial system, a matter they might also have included in their reports to the Treasury.[50]

If the E & AD fails on such a major task, it is legitimate to ask how often 'minor' lapses (involving tens rather than hundreds of millions of pounds) go undetected. The experience of Leslie Chapman, the former Southern Regional Director of the Property Services Agency, suggests that the E & AD is not always as tough as it should be at controlling government waste. When Chapman's plans for saving money were approved by ministers of both parties, and instructions given to officials to implement similar cost-saving schemes in other regions, the E & AD did indeed discover that the other regions had patchy records. But it never reported to the PAC *why* and *how* instructions were blocked; nor did it uncover a falsehood in the explanation given by Sir Robert Cox, the chief executive of the PSA, when Cox was questioned by the PAC. Cox had said that the Southern Region's exceptional cost-cutting performance was helped by the 'substantial redeployment of military resources' away from the Region.[51] This was not true. But the E & AD did not detect the mistake, which meant that the MPs on the Public Accounts Committee lacked the ammunition to deal with Cox's reply. To the embarrassment of both the E & AD and the PAC, the mistake was uncovered only after extensive inquiries started by the *Sunday Times*[52] and pursued by Granada TV's *World in Action*.[53] These led Cox not only to admit the error – but to release files to the E & AD showing that his evidence was *known* to be defective for more than a year before press and TV inquiries forced it out into the open.[54]

The recent record of the Public Accounts Committee, and the Exchequer and Audit Department, suggests two broad conclusions. The first is that the ability of MPs to scrutinize Whitehall is crucially affected by the quality of the information presented to MPs (and then, of course, by the determination of MPs to act on it). The E & AD has a record of uncovering various lapses in government spending programmes: but the lapses of the E & AD itself have started to give rise for concern.

The second lesson is that the E & AD's defence of itself depends on a recognition of its limited role. Henley's statement to the English Committee that to monitor policy decisions, and not just past spending practice, 'requires a large number of administrators and other specialists [sic] if the job is to be effectively done', can be turned on its head: if 600 full-time E & AD officials cannot perform this function, how can 635 MPs do so on their own when they have so many other calls on their time?

Parliament evidently lacks the means to scrutinize the executive; but at present it also lacks the will. Although implementation of the Procedure Committee's recommendations would go some way towards providing the former, they make only a limited contribution to reviving the latter. Parliament's impotence is the handmaiden of closed government: but it is as much the fault of timid MPs as of reticent civil servants.

11

CIVIL SERVANTS AND SECRECY

ON THEIR APPOINTMENT civil servants are required to 'sign the Official Secrets Act'. In practical terms, civil servants sign a declaration whose contents, taken at face value, prevent them from telling anyone else almost anything about their work:

> . . . I am aware that I should not divulge any information gained by me as a result of my appointment to any unauthorized person, either orally or in writing, without the previous official sanction in writing of the Department appointing me, to which written application should be made and two copies of the proposed publication to be forwarded. I understand also that I am liable to be prosecuted if I publish without official sanction any information I may acquire in the course of my tenure of an official appointment (unless it has already officially been made public) or retain without official sanction any sketch, plan, model, article, note or official documents which are no longer needed for my official duties, and that these provisions apply not only during the period of my appointment but also after my appointment has ceased . . .

The debates of the past decade about reforming the Official Secrets Act have merged two distinct, though related, issues. The first is: how can an effective law be devised to protect real secrets? The second is: should the public, as of right, have access to more government information? Because these issues have become hopelessly tangled, neither has been resolved.

The confusion stems from the nature of the Official Secrets Act itself. Originally passed in a day in 1911 at the height of public (or, to be more precise, politicians') hysteria about German spies, it incorporated the notorious 'catch-all' provisions of Section 2, which covers the points that are drawn to the attention of new civil servants when they 'sign' the Act. As a result, the Act lurks in the background of many episodes where the activities of Whitehall are leaked to the Press, even though there is no question of national security being involved. As it happens, the courts have not taken too kindly to the government using the Act to mount prosecutions against journalists or their informants: in the two most celebrated cases of recent years, the editor of the *Sunday Telegraph* and Jonathan Aitken (now a Conservative MP) were acquitted of *receiving* secret information, and the three defendants in the 'ABC' trial – Crispin Aubrey, John Berry and Duncan Campbell – received trivial punishment for attempting to bring into the open the activities of the Government's Communications Headquarters at Cheltenham (two were discharged, and one given a suspended sentence). The real impact of the Act lies in the environment of secrecy that it creates inside Whitehall. The fact that tens of thousands of people each year 'sign' the Act has almost nothing to do with national security; it has a great deal to do with indoctrinating civil servants into the culture of closed government.

In 1972 a committee appointed by Edward Heath and chaired by Lord Franks proposed a more limited law than the Official Secrets Act, so that transmitting and receiving trivial government information should no longer be a criminal offence. Franks wanted the new law designed 'so that criminal sanctions are retained only to protect what is of real importance'.[1] Yet this idea, as one of Harold Wilson's entourage quickly observed when the Labour leadership was assessing its attitude to the Franks Committee, was viciously double-edged. On the one hand Section 2 was certainly effective in discouraging openness by civil servants. On the other hand, it was so all-embracing that, when it came to the test, it was difficult to use effectively against people who were merely trying to shine a torch on the inner workings of government. A new law, apparently more sensible, might actually make many prosecutions easier. 'We would be taking away a blunderbuss,' Wilson's aide said angrily, 'and giving them an Armalite rifle.'

Rifle or blunderbuss, Franks's proposals addressed themselves only to the specific issue of Section 2, and the essentially negative question of what should be a criminal offence. The more positive question of open government – what *rights* should the public enjoy in having access to government files? – was barely raised at this stage. This half of the debate crept into the public arena, barely noticed, in 1974. That summer a Transport House sub-committee published a discussion paper, 'People and the Media', which floated the idea of greater public access, as of right, to official information. By the October general election the idea had been incorporated into the Labour Party manifesto: 'Labour believes that the process of government should be more open to the public. We shall replace the Official Secrets Act by a measure to put the burden on the public authorities to justify withholding information.'

The manifesto pledge was almost naïve in its optimism, for the prospect of seriously open government does not just put the shivers up many leading civil servants – it also frightens most ministers. It is an attack on the essence, on the *mystery*, of executive power. Two groups of opponents need to be identified. One group, consisting of most senior civil servants and some ministers, have seen no real case for altering Section 2. James Callaghan told the Franks Committee: 'I would be inclined to leave it alone as it is . . . I see no reason why one should alter things for the sake of it.'[2]

For this group the advantage of an unwieldy but all-embracing Act that provides a general deterrent to civil servants from divulging what they know, outweighs the disadvantage that prosecutions are difficult to mount. The second group, consisting of Ministry of Defence and some Home Office officials, would trade in the general deterrence for the chance to mount more successful prosecutions. But they would still draw the definition of what constitutes a secret sufficiently wide to prevent any real kind of open government.

For a while, however, there seemed to be a chance of carrying out Labour's manifesto pledge in some form. The Home Secretary of the time, Roy Jenkins, had a reputation for libertarian instincts. An official committee on open government was set up – MISC 89, meaning that it was the eighty-ninth *ad hoc* committee Harold Wilson set up after returning to

Downing Street in March 1974. One of Jenkins's first acts was to visit Washington, where America's Freedom of Information Act might provide an example for Britain to follow.

Jenkins's visit to Washington in January 1975, with Sir Arthur Peterson, his Permanent Secretary, and Anthony Lester, his special adviser, could scarcely have taken place at a worse time. The Freedom of Information Act had only recently been strengthened, over an attempted veto by President Ford, and against the wishes of the Justice Department. Although it was too early to tell, a number of officials in the American administration informed Jenkins and his colleagues that the newly amended Act would be expensive to administer, and employ many extra civil servants. And because the new Act was so young, its supporters did not yet have evidence to counter the Justice Department's assertions. Jenkins returned to London and announced his fears that a British Freedom of Information Act would be 'costly, cumbersome and legalistic'.[3]

For some months MISC 89 carried on spasmodically reviewing the Official Secrets Act, but also seeing if other, simpler, ways could be found of offering more open government. Civil servants in the Home Office and the Civil Service Department found it difficult to provide enthusiastic briefs for ministers they had already persuaded to be half-hearted. Yet to avoid backtracking too instantly on the October 1974 Labour manifesto pledge, the 1975 Queen's speech still offered 'proposals to amend the Official Secrets Act and to liberalize the practices relating to official information'. But MISC 89 had reached no firm conclusions by the time Harold Wilson resigned as Prime Minister in April 1976 and James Callaghan took over.

Callaghan's first instinct was to implement the views he had given to the Franks Committee. He ordered all work on open government to stop. Two months later he was forced to change his mind, when *New Society* carried a spectacular leak of cabinet minutes relating to a row over child benefits.[4] The leak raised in an acute form the problem of leaving Section 2 unreformed. The author of the article in *New Society* was Frank Field, the director of the Child Poverty Action Group. In theory he could have been prosecuted, but everyone knew that the prosecution of Field alone would probably fail. Callaghan instructed Sir Douglas Allen, as Head of the Civil Service, to conduct 'an urgent inquiry' to discover who in Whitehall had leaked to Field. Not surprisingly, Allen failed. The episode persuaded Callaghan, and a number of senior civil servants, that the general deterrent of Section 2 was no longer adequate. A more specific law was needed that would make it easier to prosecute the purveyors of real secrets – which, naturally, included cabinet minutes. Callaghan instructed the cabinet committee (reclassified as GEN 29) and officials to prepare proposals for amending Section 2.

In September Merlyn Rees succeeded Jenkins as Home Secretary. Soon afterwards Rees received from Sir Arthur Peterson a blueprint for amending Section 2 – but doing nothing about open government. In November 1976 Rees outlined the Government's new thinking to MPs. He concluded that 'the blunderbuss is replaced by the armalite rifle – we shall get to the point'.[5] The criticism of Franks four years earlier had been translated into a term of approval.

As officials from the Home Office, Cabinet Office and Civil Service Department wrestled with drafts of a white paper to give flesh to the Government's new policy, Callaghan attempted to deflect some of the pressure from the 'open government' critics of his retreat from Labour's 1974 manifesto pledge. On November 24 1976 he told MPs:

> When the Government make major policy studies, it will be our policy to publish as much as possible of the factual and analytical material which is used as the background to these studies. This will include material used in the programme analysis reviews [PARs: policy reviews that take place within departments] unless – and I must make the condition – there is some good reason, of which I fear we must be the judge, to the contrary.[6]

It took more than seven months for Callaghan's announcement to be translated into a directive from Sir Douglas Allen to Heads of Departments. Allen's letter of 6 July 1977, is published in full as Appendix 4. The crucial sentences are:

> In the past it has normally been assumed that background material relating to policy studies and reports would *not* be published unless

the responsible Minister or Ministers decided otherwise. Henceforth the working assumption should be that such material *will* be published unless they decide that it should *not* be. (Allen's emphasis)

Later in the letter, Allen showed that it was not his intention to open up government processes in any substantial way. For example, while repeating Callaghan's promise to make available some of the material used in PARs, 'It is not the intention to depart from the present practice of not disclosing PARs nor identifying them publicly; any question of releasing PAR material in circumstances not covered by a Ministerial decision should be referred to the Treasury.'

Towards the end of the letter, Allen indicated that one purpose of the exercise was to avoid pressure for greater openness:

There are many who would have wanted the Government to go much further (on the lines of the formidably burdensome Freedom of Information Act in the USA). Our prospects of being able to avoid such an expensive development here could well depend on whether we can show that the Prime Minister's statement has reality and results.

Two useful tests came in the spring and summer of 1978. First, the publication of the white paper responding to the English Committee's criticisms of the Civil Service prompted Peter Hennessy of *The Times* to ask for the background papers in accordance with the terms of Allen's letter. There were no such background papers, Hennessy was told: it was not 'that kind of white paper'.[7] Then, in July 1978, came the white paper on the reform of the Official Secrets Act. Again Hennessy asked for the relevant background papers. Again he was told there were none that could be divulged. *The Times*'s leading article next day was unusually bitter:

The putative Official Information Bill might be easier to swallow if the Government had not demonstrated so blatantly yesterday that it cannot be relied on for the voluntary disclosure of more information under the Prime Minister's open government policy announced last year . . . Those with a taste for irony can only exult when a White Paper on the reform of secrecy fails to achieve the minimal openness laid down under existing guidelines. There are two possible interpretations of this dereliction. If the Franks report of 1972 is, as the Home Office claims, the background material for ministerial decision, that suggests a strange indolence on the part of latter-day civil servants. What have Sir John Hunt and Mr William McIndoe of the Cabinet Office, Mr Neil Cairncross, Mr Anthony Brennan and Mr Anthony Langdon of the Home Office, Mr John Moore and Mr Alan Duke of the Civil Service Department been doing with their admirable talents the past two years in servicing GEN 29? The second interpretation is that they have deliberately flouted [Sir Douglas Allen's] instructions and have not prepared policy briefs in the way intended.[8]

The failure to produce background papers – or, rather, the assertion that the Franks report *was* the background paper – made it impossible to assess the evidence that led to the conclusions of the official secrets white paper. For example, despite the child benefits leak, the white paper was more liberal than Franks on the disclosure of Cabinet minutes:

> The Franks committee also recommended . . . that the criminal offence should apply to Cabinet and Cabinet committee documents, . . . irrespective of subject matter or security classification. The purpose of this recommendation was to safeguard the collective responsibility of the Cabinet; and it was limited to the communication of the actual document or information based on the document in a verbatim or virtually verbatim form. The Government attaches major importance to the security of Cabinet and Cabinet committee documents. For the generality of these documents, however, the great majority of which deal with home and economic affairs, the Government considers that it is enough to rely on special distribution and handling procedures, on the sanctions of Civil Service discipline and on the judgment of ministers. It is therefore proposed that Cabinet and Cabinet committee documents should be protected by criminal sanctions only if they fall into one of the specific categories of information to be so protected.[9]

How did the government reach this conclusion? Did it accept the advice of officials or overturn it? What arguments and evidence were given? The same questions arise over the white paper's attitude to open government, culminating in the open admission of a retreat from Labour's 1974 manifesto. After summarizing American and Swedish policies of giving the public the right of access to large areas of government information, the white paper concluded:

> Legislation on these lines would completely change the nature of the Government's obligations: instead of accepting a declared obligation to make more information available, operating on a voluntary and discretionary basis, the Government would be under a statutory duty to disclose all and any information that might be demanded unless it was specifically exempted from doing so . . . This is a matter on which the Government has come to no conclusion and has an open mind. The Government recognizes that its proposals do not go as far as the Labour Party manifesto of October 1974 . . .[10]

The tone of those two passages provides some clues about why ministers and civil servants refused to provide background papers. They did not like the idea of legislating for open government; they wanted a new criminal law that would be effective; but the mystery of the executive could best be preserved by administrative rather than legal measures – 'the special distribution and handling procedures'.

The last point is often ignored in debates about open government. While the Official Secrets Act has become the symbol of closed government, the executive's real defence is a culture that makes a great deal of information simply inaccessible. Far from modifying the position, the white paper underlined it. The most important consequence of this is that even if more background *facts* are gradually disclosed following the Allen letter of July 1977, the *processes and arguments* that determine government policy are explicitly to be kept secret. As on most open government issues, ministers and civil servants stand together. Allen's letter makes it clear that 'background material' must be kept separate from official advice to ministers:

> When policy studies are being undertaken in future, the background material should as far as possible be written in a form which would permit it to be published separately, with the minimum of alteration, once a ministerial decision to do so has been taken. It will generally assist ministers to reach their decisions on publications if they can see an identifiable *separate part of the report appropriately written for this purpose* (emphasis added).

271

This accords with the tradition that facts are neutral, advice is confidential, and the two are separate. Quite apart from any fundamental doubts about the validity of this idea, the practical result is to give officials the most obvious loophole: anything they do not want published they define as 'advice', leaving relatively harmless material for publication. The fact that Peter Hennessy came away empty-handed after asking for the background material to the white paper on the Civil Service and on the Official Secrets Act, suggests that the loophole has been stretched to take articulated lorry-fuls of private 'advice'.

The Civil Service's capacity to impede reform is admitted even by Lord Armstrong. In November 1978 he was asked by BBC TV about the prospects for a Freedom of Information Act, similar to that in the United States. (The American Act provided much of the inspiration for a private member's Official Information Bill introduced in Parliament at the end of 1978 by the Liberal MP, Clement Freud.) Armstrong said:

> I don't think I would say that I'm against it. But I think it would be very doubtful whether it would do what its protagonists think it will do. Let's suppose that it goes as I believe it does in America, that the public has a right to documents. All right we won't – when I say we I mean the Civil Service – just won't create documents, until we're ready to. It's perfectly easy as you conduct things in conversation and make yourself aide memoires; the word 'aide memoire' and the word 'memorandum' mean a piece of paper which is not a document. That's how they came into existence. The real thing is the conversation. My memory is fallible: I've made myself a little note. There is no reason why you should see that.[11]

Behind the wall that guards their privacy, civil servants would be allowed to protect the mystery of their operations. This is how William Plowden, as a former high-flyer Under Secretary, explained the private world of senior civil servants on the same BBC TV programme:

> They develop like any kind of closed profession, a culture and a language of their own. They communicate with each other in terms that they understand; phrases like 'at the end of the day', 'ball's in your court', 'a sticky wicket' largely used inside the Civil Service.

And I think the sorts of arguments they use are phrased in terms which they recognize and which convey their meaning to each other, but which wouldn't carry so much conviction with an outside audience . . . The thing about the language of Whitehall is that it makes it unnecessary very often to carry arguments right through to the end, because so many assumptions are shared. It's not so much the language as the culture really. So many assumptions are shared that one doesn't need to argue every point out in detail in the way you would if you were trying to persuade a hostile or certainly critical outside audience.[12]

The 'assumptions' that Plowden speaks of are varied: sometimes they are broad and fundamental (the belief, for example, that government intervention in almost every national problem is a good thing); sometimes they are specific (such as the Treasury's long-standing embrace of rigid incomes policies, and dislike of import controls and monetarist economic theories). The privacy of these assumptions does not in itself invalidate them. What matters is that the duty 'to persuade a hostile or certainly critical outside audience' is avoided.

The combination of Armstrong's 'aide memoires' and Plowden's 'shared assumptions' would make the private world of Whitehall difficult to penetrate even with enthusiastic ministerial help. What underpins the mystery of the executive with bomb-proof foundations is the active help of successive political leaders in concealing the processes of policy-formation. All governments have concealed the existence and membership of Cabinet Committees (of ministers) and of the Official Committees (of civil servants) that prepare the ground for ministers. In February 1978 Callaghan sent a private minute to cabinet ministers outlining his reasons. The text, leaked to the *New Statesman*, is a candid statement of the politician's case for mounting a joint picket with the mandarins at the gates of open government:

Consistently with the practice of all former Prime Ministers I have always refused to publish details of Cabinet Committees or to answer Questions in the House about them . . . I accept that the present convention has certain disadvantages for us. In particular non-disclosure makes it difficult to answer charges that the Government's policies are not properly co-ordinated. For example, the Select Committee on Overseas Development has recommended the establishment of a Cabinet Committee to co-ordinate political, trade and aid policies towards the developing world largely because the ODM were not able to disclose that such a committee (RD) already exists . . .

It is important therefore to understand the reasons for the current practice of non-disclosure . . . The existence of some [committees] could not be disclosed on security grounds: others are set up to do a particular job and are then wound up . . . Publication would almost inevitably lead to pressures for both more and larger Committees, and for disclosure of information about their activities . . . Disclosure [of the *ad hoc* 'GEN' committees] would often reveal that very sensitive subjects were under consideration or that we had something in train about which we were not ready to make an announcement. Disclosure of the main standing Committees would thus give a partial picture only.

Moreover having gone as far as this I do not believe that it would be possible for me to hold the line and refuse to answer any further questions about the composition and activities of the Committees. At the minimum we would be under pressure to reveal the names of the Chairmen. This would make it harder for me to make changes: and it would have implications for the responsibilities of Departmental Ministers since Select Committees would try to summon the Chairmen of Cabinet Committees to give evidence in addition to the responsible Ministers. I should also be under continuing pressure to say that a committee was considering a particular subject (and it would often be a GEN group): and there would be questions about when the Committees were meeting, the work they were doing, whether particular Ministers are on them, the details of under-pinning Official Committees, etc.

I have therefore decided that we should not change our stance on this matter. The present convention is long established and provides a basis on which we can stand. Any departure from it would be more likely to whet appetites than to satisfy them. I ask my colleagues therefore to rest on the position that the way in which we co-ordinate our decisions is a matter internal to Government and not to answer questions about the Cabinet Committee system.[13]

Callaghan's minute placed two things beyond doubt. The first is that, despite a public policy of more open government, the processes of decision-making would remain concealed. The second is that the mysteries of executive power depend crucially on the formal secrecy of ministerial and official power structures: disclose that, Callaghan says in effect, and you have to disclose everything. The culture, and conversations, and aide memoires all contribute to the private power of senior civil servants: but they are protected by a rigid and explicit wall of secrecy that shields them from public examination.

Speaking to civil servants about open government is sometimes like speaking to house-owners about immigration: it's not me, it's what the neighbours would think. Thus, according to one very senior Cabinet Office man sketching in the arguments over Cabinet Committee secrecy:

> I would not mind if the membership of Cabinet Committees were made public, but successive Prime Ministers have strongly taken the view that it would be wrong to reveal them. There are lots of myths about this, people thinking decisions get taken in secret and so on. The real reason is that the system would be much more difficult to operate if it were done in public. The farmers might say, why don't we have a Cabinet Committee of our own? Another group might say, why isn't this minister on the Committee – the Education Secretary, for example, as education policy could affect the issue. On left-right issues there might be arguments about the balance of the committee.[14]

It is an interesting argument. The pivotal word is 'difficult': public (including Parliamentary) scrutiny of the Cabinet Committee system would make things more *difficult* – not necessarily produce worse decisions, or diminish democracy, but cause inconvenience. The implication is that in an open system the Prime Minister would be unable to fight off public pressure with rational argument. If there is a good reason why the Education Secretary is not on such-and-such a committee, why not say so? If the farmers' interests are well catered for by the Ministry of Agriculture and by existing economic committees, why not explain this?

The unspoken heart of the argument for closed government is that private debate among civil servants and ministers produces more *rational* policies, freed from public pressure, which is assumed to be irrational. Wise men, cogitating quietly on the nation's problems, will produce 'right' answers, if they are shielded from the hubbub of the political marketplace. But once exposed to pressure groups and vested interests and newspapers that will get it all wrong, who knows what absurdities will result?

Various secondary arguments are deployed to make an essential contempt for democratic debate more palatable. In the course of one interview, a senior official of the CSD involved in monitoring the response of Government departments to Sir Douglas Allen's letter on background papers, deployed the following arguments:

> There are some people who want to get at the papers just to get at the titillating stuff, who think politics is all about intrigue and that sort of thing . . .
> There would be an upsurge in sensational journalism. For example, if all Public Health Inspectors' findings were made public, a restaurant which was quite innocently doing something wrong – and was happy to correct things once it was pointed out – might quite unfairly be branded as a filthy restaurant . . .
> If you sit Mr Begin and Mr Sadat down to negotiate, and broadcast to the world everything they say, then do not expect peace to come to the Middle East.[15]

As in many bad arguments there is a good argument struggling to get out. The good argument is that – quite apart from military secrets – certain kinds of government information are properly kept confidential. In a mixed economy any Government will have access to commercial confidences; in a society where money markets are allowed to function with some freedom, some aspects of monetary policy cannot easily be anticipated in public. That argument, however, is about specifics, not about the generality of closed government. The fact that examples lie readily to hand where most reasonable people would concede the Government's right to secrecy does not invalidate the *principle* of open government – just as the laws of libel and contempt should not invalidate the *principle* of free speech: nearly all rules have their exceptions.

The central argument of both civil servants and ministers, however, does not concern the sensible exceptions. It concerns the character of policy-making, of government administration, and of democratic debate. The essence of Callaghan's minute, and of the ideas that circulate in the Cabinet Office and the CSD, is that closed government is better government. The odd thing is that they provide little if any evidence for this hypothesis. On the contrary, a number of instances of closed government that have come to light suggest it can actually encourage bad policy-making and bad administration.

Five recent examples of questionable decision-making behind closed doors are:

1. Concorde. In the 1960s, when the important decisions were being taken, there was no effective opportunity to challenge publicly the Government's false optimism about its prospects. And because there were no adequate outside checks, the internal system of checks and balances – with the Treasury supposed to act as a questioning foil to departmental enthusiasm – was allowed to fail unnoticed. Professor David Henderson, chief economist at the Ministry of Aviation from 1965 to 1967, recently said: 'Even now we don't know whose opinions counted at what stage, what figures were accepted on what evidence at what stage, what outside checks were made. How can one justify that? How can we pretend to be trying to learn lessons from experience?' Henderson was asked whether outside, independent checks were ever made on the economics of Concorde: 'Not that I'm aware of . . . It offends the British administrator's sense of what is orderly. [The Treasury] can question the departments, it can disbelieve them, but it has no independent checks.'[16]

2. Oil sanctions. When Thomas Bingham QC inquired in 1977 and 1978 into the breaking of oil sanctions against Rhodesia he found that a secret decision was taken in 1968, involving the Commonwealth Secretary, George (now Lord) Thomson, civil servants, and oil companies, to allow the oil companies to help arrange for oil to reach Rhodesia. The crux of the decision was a 'swap' arrangement, whereby the French oil company Total sent oil into Rhodesia on behalf of the British companies Shell and BP. The details were negotiated between the oil companies and Alan Gregory, an Assistant Secretary at the Ministry of Power. The arrangement allowed ministers to say that no *British* oil was reaching Rhodesia, although Parliament was never told what decisions had been reached. Following the report of the Bingham inquiry, evidence emerged that not even the full Cabinet was ever told of the swap arrangement: and

the Prime Minister of the day, Harold Wilson, has denied knowing of its essential details. According to Wilson, the minute of the relevant meeting with the oil companies was indeed sent to No. 10. But:

> It was not circulated to the Cabinet either by the Foreign Office or by No. 10 . . . There is no record of my seeing it . . . It would have been inconceivable for my Cabinet colleagues, myself, the Attorney-General or the officials to have connived at any action brought to our notice constituting a body blow to our sanctions policy.[17]

3. Child benefits. In May 1976 the Labour Cabinet decided to defer a scheme to end family tax allowances and replace them with cash child benefits. Since tax allowances went to the father, while child benefit payments would be received by the mother, the move was designed specifically to help women. Barbara Castle, as Secretary for Social Services, enthusiastically piloted the legislation through Parliament. In April 1976, however, Callaghan became Prime Minister and replaced her with David Ennals. A few weeks later, caught between Treasury caution and pay policy fears (if the take-home pay of husbands suddenly fell with the switch to payment to wives), the Cabinet deferred the scheme. A month later *New Society* published the Cabinet minutes of the crucial meeting: these showed that a decisive argument was the reported opposition of the TUC to the child benefit scheme. In fact the TUC had been told the day before by Denis Healey that the problem was *Cabinet* reluctance: this was the main reason why the TUC went cool on the scheme. In other words, Healey deceived both the TUC and the Cabinet about the other's true beliefs, and so persuaded both to acquiesce in a change of policy. Only the leak of the Cabinet minutes, and the subsequent checking by the *Sunday Times* of TUC records, revealed how Treasury officials, through Healey, overturned both Labour and TUC policy.[18] In the event the full child benefit scheme was delayed two years: had it not been for the *New Society* leak, the delay might arguably have been longer.

4. Education planning. In 1975 the Education Arts and Home Office Sub-Committee of the Commons Expenditure

Committee asked to see certain internal planning papers drawn up within the Department of Education and Science. In accordance with their rules for responding to select committees (see Chapter 10), the Department's officials refused. These documents were supplied, however, to the international Organization for Economic Co-operation and Development. The OECD then published a highly critical study of the DES's planning, based on the papers that MPs had not been allowed to see. The OECD condemned the DES's planning approach as merely 'identifying existing trends' and then seeking to cater for them as best it could in the future – whereas the OECD argued that educational planning should be more positive, and consider the objectives of educational policy. The OECD concluded that in the DES 'there is no attempt at a new identification and formulation of educational goals in a world where the traditional canons of knowledge, values, attitudes and skills are continually questioned.'[19]

The OECD also criticized the DES for its lack of openness. This, it said, had two serious consequences:

One is that in certain cases policy is less likely to be understood and therefore less likely to be whole-heartedly accepted when the processes that lead up to it are guarded as arcane secrets. The second is that goals and priorities, once established, may go on being taken for granted and hence escape the regular scrutiny which may be necessary for an appropriate re-alignment of policy.[20]

5. Tax relief and public schools. Labour's October 1974 election manifesto promised to 'withdraw tax relief and charitable status from public schools'. The promise was not implemented, and Sir William Pile, Permanent Secretary at the Department of Education until 1976, played a part in the process. In October 1975 he briefed Fred Mulley, the Education Secretary, on 'technical problems to which at present nobody knows the answers'. Pile's minute, dated 9 October, is a gem for connoisseurs of civil service delaying tactics:

First, the term 'public schools' has no definable meaning . . . There are substantial problems of definition involved in discriminating between one kind of school and another. Secondly, there is at the root of the matter the problem that charitable status is not enjoyed by the schools as such but by the institutions which provide them . . . Thirdly, any progress in relation to the withdrawal of tax reliefs is critically dependent upon finding ways of redefining charities or discriminating between charities . . . Treasury Ministers are satisfied that it is not practicable to discriminate between policies and covenants intended to finance school fees and other policies and covenants. Last, an independent school provided by a charity enjoys a 50% relief from rates on the school site . . . The withdrawal would involve legislation and the question of discriminating between one kind of school and another would of course have to be faced.

Pile concluded that immediate responsibility for action 'lies primarily not with you but with the Home Secretary, the Chancellor of the Exchequer and the Secretary of State for the Environment . . . I cannot think of anything that we ourselves can usefully do in the interim.'

One possible course Mulley might have taken was not suggested: enlist the help of tax and education experts outside Government who were sympathetic to its policies. It would have been remarkable if widening the debate would not have prompted any suggestion as to how Pile's 'technical problems' might be overcome. Yet Mulley's officials were pressing the very opposite tactic. When Joan Lestor, a junior minister in the department, was preparing to speak at a Cambridge Union debate, an Assistant Secretary, M. W. Hodges, prepared the following advice:

In the light of the Government's legal advice, it would appear inadvisable for Miss Lestor to suggest any date by which *charitable status,* as such, might be expected to be withdrawn from the public schools. It would be advisable to speak rather in terms of the *fiscal benefits* associated with charitable status – a fine distinction, perhaps, to the ears of a lay audience, and indeed one which may be lost on them; if so, so much the better.

Those examples are, in detail, very different: but there is one important factor. In each case the decisions that were taken reflected not so much wise, rational men arriving at considered judgments, as ordinary frail mortals using closed government to hide their inadequacies. As Lord Armstrong – again candid in retirement – described Whitehall's obsession with secrecy: 'It obviously is comfortable, convenient, and one has to say it allows mistakes to be covered up.' Asked whether it also allowed incompetence to be covered up, Armstrong replied, 'Of course it does.'[21]

The obsession is not just with the making of policy, but with its execution. The Department of Health and Social Security's guidance to social security officers on the administration of supplementary benefits consisted in the past of a number of secret 'codes' – thick, loose-leafed books indicating how to handle various contingencies. Only when leaked copies started to circulate did claimants' groups find out how to help certain people – and discover that some social security officers were paying less than they should. The fact that immigration officers at London Airport were performing highly distasteful 'virginity tests' on some prospective immigrants did not come to light until it was revealed in the *Guardian* in February 1979: the publicity instantly forced the Home Secretary, Merlyn Rees, to ban the practice. A host of information that Government inspectors discover about anything from invalid cars to unhygienic ships is designated confidential. In the case of unhygienic ships, the irony was that similar US information about British ships was released under the Freedom of Information Act, and formed the basis of a report in the *Sunday Times* in 1977. And the leaking of Government information about invalid cars to Adam Raphael, first on the *Guardian* and later when he moved to the *Observer,* eventually forced the Government to revise its policy.

The axiom that information is power, allied to Lord Acton's dictum that power corrupts, can be usefully welded into the notion that secrecy corrupts. Far from producing more rational government, the evidence suggests that secrecy produces more manipulative and arbitrary government. Officials are often ill-informed about the real world; ministers are often inadequately briefed and advised by officials; Parliament often receives too little information too late from ministers. Our political traditions have produced a subtle but deep-rooted system of information-rationing; and like all rationing schemes, it creates a black market where information, often of poor quality, is traded in the shadows between civil servants and industrialists (or trade union leaders or academics), and between ministers and lobby journalists. Whenever a battle takes place in Whitehall over a policy decision, hints are dropped, kites are flown, friends are warned. The art is to be discreet.

One of the most frequent responses to the Fulton Committee's charge that the Civil Service is based on the 'obsolete' cult of the generalist is to say that administration is itself a highly professional activity. In one important sense that is true: manipulating information and the processes of Government are skills that successful mandarins have developed to a high degree. And, as we have seen, they have developed them largely with the support of ministers.

The closed world of British government will not be easy to open up: the refusal to disclose the membership of Cabinet and Official Committees means we are denied access to the basic geography of power; the privacy of civil servants' advice to ministers prevents outsiders understanding *how* policy decisions are reached; the absence of an effective Freedom of Information Act allows arbitrary administration to carry on unchecked by the Press or Parliament, or even on occasion by ministers; Britain's political career structure sucks able MPs – potentially often the best adversaries of the executive – into government jobs, so that they then tend to see their interests in preserving the mysteries of executive power; the Civil Service career structure equally, but using different mechanisms, preserves the private culture of closed government.

Each component of secrecy reinforces the others; and together they allow the defects of the Civil Service observed by Fulton and others to flourish unreformed. That is why occasional leaks of Whitehall documents – like a memorandum by Sir Douglas Wass of the Treasury on industrial policy to the *Guardian* in 1979; the Cabinet minutes on child benefits, to *New Society* in 1976; or detailed proposals to cut back Britain's rail network, to the *Sunday Times* in 1972 – provoke something close to panic, with official inquiries and police surveillance, and threats of prosecution under the Official Secrets Act. It is not an irrational response. Ministers and civil servants perceive in such leaks (as opposed to the muffled lobby briefings that more regularly fill newspaper columns) a threat to the mainspring of their authority. They are right. For that very reason the reforms that are most urgently needed – if the other faults are also to stand some chance of being corrected – are those that open Whitehall up to public scrutiny.

12

POSTSCRIPT: 'THE BIGGEST PRESSURE GROUP'

THE ARRIVAL OF A NEW GOVERNMENT provides an occasion for one of Whitehall's precisely formulated rituals. New ministers sign the Official Secrets Act. They then receive a discreet briefing from MI5 on how to avoid unfriendly spies. They are told which telephone to use for regular official business, which to use for private or party business, and which to use for Top Secret conversations. (It is called a Pickwick.) They receive a catalogue of instructions from their officials on how to behave on everything from the security of cabinet minutes to the answering of Parliamentary Questions.

Even while ministers are absorbing this, and meeting their new Permanent Secretary and getting to know their private office staff, the red boxes start arriving. *The* Government may have changed: but *government*—the web of rules, regulations and decisions that embrace national life—must carry on with as little disruption and as much continuity as possible. The red boxes, stuffed with documents, transmit departmental papers up and cabinet papers down to each minister. Unless he is careful his office becomes a prison. Richard Crossman, in his first diary entry after becoming a minister in October 1964, wrote of 'the sense of being isolated from the world. Every time I walk down those great steps into the open air outside the Ministry I breathe again and I feel I've entered real life again.'[1]

Perhaps the most significant rule of all is that no minister may see the papers from the previous administration. The logic of this rule is straightforward. Officials, the argument runs, must be free to give ministers candid advice which may include, for example, tactical ploys for confounding the opposition. It would be intolerable for that advice to be shown to these opponents after they win an election and enter office with their own policies. Such disclosure would embarrass the civil servants who must work with their new masters; it could also perturb the outgoing ministers to have their more private deliberations revealed to their political rivals. It is a conspiracy of silence that no one dare break: you ignore the skeletons in your predecessor's cupboard and trust that your own skeletons will be similarly respected.

So a new minister arrives with his manifesto promises and a jumble of ideas from his party's research department, but little more. He cannot discover whether some of his ideas have been considered before, or with what result if they have been considered. The body of experience and knowledge that builds up in a department does not expand in a political vacuum—it develops in conjunction with the problems and pressures and ambitions of each government. To be denied access to the papers of the last government is to be denied the right to understand the evolution of the department itself.

What new ministers can do is ask questions to get information. When Michael Heseltine became Secretary of State for the Environment after the Conservative victory in May 1979, he could seek all kinds of information on housing finance; what he could not do was ask for the papers of the detailed (and expensive) housing finance review of his Labour predecessors, Anthony Crosland and Peter Shore.

Such problems do not matter to ministers who care little for detail. But it has become increasingly clear in recent years that radical changes in policy require not just ideological commitment but a mastery of detail. Access to departmental information and experience is a vital component of the relationship between ministers—especially new ministers—and their officials. Ministers may have the will, but the mandarins have the files.

Margaret Thatcher came to power with a radical programme—radical not least in her intention to reverse the long-term trend towards a larger public sector. A central feature of this strategy is a diminution in the role of the bureaucracy. Thatcher's problem parallels those faced by the Fulton reformers: how to engage the commitment of a government machine that is both the agent and the object of change. It is a difficult trick made no easier by the knowledge that civil servants, in the words of Richard Wilding, a Deputy Secretary at the CSD, must not only serve their current ministers but also 'be able to be the wholly loyal and effective servants of the Minister of the next administration who reverses [their policies].' Wilding explains how it is done:

> We must, I think, distinguish energy from commitment. It is absolutely necessary to pursue today's policy with energy; it is almost equally necessary, in order to survive, to withhold from it the last ounce of commitment. At the same time, however, I believe that it *is* possible to care, and to care passionately, to throw in the last ounce of commitment, for the idea of service itself; and to invest that commitment in our particular institution, the Civil Service itself, with all its manifest imperfections.[2]

For a radical government the implications of Wilding's statement are fearful; for 'that last ounce of commitment' is likely to be denied to ministers, *especially* when they confront the bureaucracy itself. It is difficult to see how this obstacle may be removed, without some reform in the system of government.

In the early months of her administration Thatcher showed no inclination to meet this challenge, despite coming to office with a healthy scepticism of Whitehall's enthusiasm for radical change—and despite mounting evidence in the first few months that it would be no easy task to 'curb the bureaucrats'. Heseltine stated the problem with remarkable candour after seven months at the Department of the Environment:

> Central and local bureaucracies have developed their own momentum. In May I was told that there were 52,122 people in my Department. How could I know what they all do each day? How could I take decisions, or reach informed judgements, on relative priorities? I had general advice on every policy issue—but no analysis of how each part of the machine operated, why it operated in that way, and how much it cost. I do not know. Nobody knows.
> Because political leadership lacks such detailed information it is at the mercy of pressure groups. And the biggest pressure group comprises those administering a department or a local authority. If

options are called for, the usual response is to submit the least attractive in political terms, the easiest to achieve in administrative terms, and with the minimum effect on those putting them forward. Because the Minister or councillor does not know what is going on elsewhere, he cannot devise alternatives. If you do not know what people are doing, how much it costs and why they are doing it, how can there be an informed debate?[3]

Heseltine's attitude is not dissimilar to that of Leslie Chapman revealed in his book *Your Disobedient Servant.* Indeed, during the 1979 election campaign Thatcher brandished Chapman's book in the face of anyone who asked her how she planned to cut government spending without cutting deep into the services government provided. Soon after becoming Prime Minister Thatcher attempted to enlist Chapman into her campaign to reduce waste in the Civil Service. She failed— principally because, in the event, she was unwilling to translate her radical rhetoric into a practical programme to fight 'the biggest pressure group' head on.

Chapman's contacts with the Conservative leadership dated back to the spring of 1977, shortly after the original *Sunday Times* article on his own cost-saving work (see page 15). Sir Keith Joseph, then director of the Conservative Centre for Policy Studies, engaged in a lengthy dialogue: 'As one of those responsible for Conservative Policy I plainly have much to learn from you', Joseph wrote in his opening letter.[4] At Joseph's request Chapman prepared a memorandum suggesting how the number of civil servants could be reduced by 50,000 to 100,000—saving between £1,000 and £2,000 million in public expenditure—*without any reduction in the functions of government.* Chapman's proposals included:

● Changes in the rules for dealing with sick and inefficient civil servants to make it possible to terminate quickly unsatisfactory service.

● More vigorous extension of Line-Manager concept. This would help to get away from diffused responsibility and management by default which is now prevalent.

● Exchequer and Audit Department needs to be strengthened by: sharp increase in numbers—probably from 500 to 1,500; taking over staff inspectorate role from CSD; widening terms of reference so that as of right they can inquire into anything involving economies.

● The Official Secrets Act needs revision along the lines of the USA National Security Council Directive of 1972 which proscribes the use of classification to conceal inefficiency or administrative error, or to prevent embarrassment to persons or departments . . .[5]

Chapman amplified these points in his book, a copy of which he sent to Joseph in May 1978. Joseph replied: 'I had already bought one which I have now finished reading and marking—in practically every case with an enthusiastic tick . . . I am, today, writing to Mrs Thatcher who heard you on the radio and spoke to me enthusiastically about what you were saying . . .'[6] Three months later, after further talks, Joseph wrote: 'By using cash limits *together with the techniques described in your book*, we shall seek to reduce public spending as is necessary if we are to reduce borrowing and to reduce direct taxation' (emphasis added).[7]

When the Conservatives came to power, however, none of Chapman's proposals were tried. Thatcher appointed Sir Derek Rayner, the Joint Managing Director of Marks and Spencer, to conduct a waste-cutting exercise, working with one Principal in each department. He asked Chapman to help, but Chapman declined:

I do not believe that the scale of effort, the techniques, or the organization which you intend to use begin to match either the size or the nature of the problems you are tackling. Equally, I do not think that by any test, your suggestion that my contribution to all this should consist of one address to the individuals in the Departments who would be carrying out the investigations, bears any relationship to the 'sharp-edged job' which was the phrase you used more than once in this connection during our discussion.[8]

Chapman subsequently had a long discussion with Thatcher. He told the Prime Minister that he thought her strategy for eliminating waste would fail. Not surprisingly, their ways parted.

Instead of pursuing Chapman's ideas, as Joseph had indicated, the Government launched a two-stage exercise to reduce civil service manning levels, supplementing the work done by Rayner. In May 1979 it announced a three-month freeze on all but the most essential recruitment. This reduced the number of civil servants by 20,000, though in an arbitrary and uneven manner—posts with a low turnover, such as senior administrative jobs, were reduced by less than those with a high turnover, such as clerical staff. In the Treasury—an awkward building with long corridors—there was for a time a shortage of messengers, and Under-Secretaries complained that they themselves had to spend time carrying urgent papers round to their colleagues.

The recruitment freeze was a stop-gap arrangement while the second phase of the exercise got under way. Between June and September each department drew up options for cutting their staff costs by ten, fifteen and twenty per cent. These options were then discussed between individual ministers and Lord Soames, the Lord President of the Council and minister in charge of the Civil Service. (Some of the more detailed negotiations were conducted by Paul Channon, the Minister of State at the Civil Service Department, and by Richard Wilding.)

Wilding made it clear during the summer that the purpose of the exercise was chiefly to reduce the role of government rather than to eliminate waste. He wrote privately to each department to say he had promised the civil service unions 'that this [is] genuinely an exercise to reduce functions and not to reduce staff while leaving functions intact'.[9] The end result, however, echoed Heseltine's complaint about options which officials put forward. Thus the Ministry of Agriculture proposed reducing the levels of inspection of horticultural produce; the Department of Education suggested doing less work on health and safety in schools; and the Department of Energy came up with the idea of adopting 'a minimal role on energy conservation'.[10]

Not surprisingly only a few Government functions were eliminated by the review. In December Lord Soames announced 'savings in Civil Service staff costs of about £212 million, most of which will be achieved by the financial year 1982-83 . . . In terms of staff numbers, the savings total some 40,000.'[11] According to Channon, 'these are the largest savings announced by any minister in charge of the Civil Service in the last 25 years'.[12] True though that was, 40,000 represented a reduction of just 5.5 per cent over three years, or barely half the minimum option of ten per cent that each minister was asked to explore.

Even that figure inflated the extent to which functions were to be eliminated. Around 10,000 of the cuts would involve industrial civil servants—that is, a cut of 3,000 to 4,000 a year. This is actually less than the steady trend of 5,000 fewer jobs a year *consistently since the mid-1950s.* And some of the proposed cuts would save the Government no money: the Department of Transport, as part of its contribution to the cuts, announced that it would sell off its heavy goods vehicle testing stations, employing one thousand staff, to the private sector. Yet these stations are self-financing; and past governments have decided against selling them off because of the risks of corruption.

Some of the functions are being cut in the limited sense that they are being subcontracted out of the Civil Service, but must still be paid for. The Post Office is to take over much of the work of issuing road tax discs; the Ministry of Defence said it would put some of its cleaning and catering work out to private contract. In both cases the stated intention was to save money by having the work done more efficiently; but in the case of private contractors part of the lower cost is liable to be achieved through the payment of lower wages. (Some Conservative ministers have acknowledged this point, but argue that Civil Service pay rates are sometimes higher than the market rate for the job.)

Finally, some of the cuts involve no reduction of functions at all, but instead vague promises to do the same work in a more streamlined way. The Home Office announced 'improved efficiency generally and miscellaneous savings', but was unable to explain this statement to reporters seeking details. The Department of Employment promised 'administrative improvements in Unemployment Benefit Offices'. The Department of Health and Social Security said it would introduce 'measures to improve efficiency and simplify procedures in social security administration'.[13] This DHSS statement was a deliberately unspecific interim proposal while a longer-term review of the department's operations was mounted. Yet the very fact that substantial cuts could not be announced in December represented a defeat for the wishes of Patrick Jenkin, the Social Services Secretary, in a minute he sent to Sir Patrick Nairne, his Permanent Secretary, in June 1979. In stressing the need for 'immediate cuts in staff costs, responding to the Cabinet decisions on the Lord President's proposals', Jenkin wrote:

> You have made it abundantly clear to me, both in written briefs and in discussion, that significant cuts have already been made in the Department over the last three years, and that there is little fat left. It will not be enough though simply to trim the tasks on which the Department is engaged; something a good deal more radical is called for . . . Central Government is in any case trying to do too much in the field of social policy. We must be much readier to resist the pressures from Parliament and outside . . . Please do not hesitate to think boldly. My colleagues in the Department and I must look to you and your colleagues to identify the options for staff savings, taking account of this guidance and of the policy priorities of the Government.

Whatever proposals finally emerge from the DHSS review—in which Jenkin tacitly admitted the weakness of ministerial control—they cannot provide the 'immediate cuts in staff costs' that Jenkin sought.

Overall, the clear elimination of functions occupied only about half the savings that Soames announced—measures like the abolition of the Metrication Board, the end of administering exchange control, and the closure of some diplomatic missions abroad. (The exercise embraced the Foreign Office as well as the Home Civil Service.) Over a three-year period, that is equivalent to a cut of barely one per cent a year. And on the evidence of past exercises few if any senior administrative posts will go.

It is, nevertheless, a programme for cutting rather than expanding the Civil Service steadily over a period of years. The gradient may be gentle, but it does point downwards. Also, Channon insisted when the announcement of the 40,000 job cuts was made that more would follow. Channon was an interesting choice as the minister to supervise the process. In 1970, when he was a junior minister at the Department of the Environment, he saw Leslie Chapman's work at first hand. He was sufficiently impressed to announce that up to £30 million a year (£100 million at today's prices) could be saved nationally on the maintenance of government property. He instructed his officials to adopt Chapman's practices 'as a matter of urgency'. They did not, and the defeat rankled Channon. After he arrived at the CSD he was determined to succeed where before he had failed.

In one aspect of her administration Mrs Thatcher showed few signs of even attempting radical change. Her ministers made very little progress towards more open government. When Peter Hennessy of *The Times* sought background papers from each government department on the ten, fifteen, and twenty per cent options for reducing civil service costs, only the Civil Service Department, Customs and Excise, and the Stationery Office responded in accordance with the general directive first issued by Sir Douglas Allen in 1977 (see Appendix Four) and broadly reaffirmed by Thatcher in June 1979.[14] Other departments gave either very limited information or none at all; some refused to reply. The Ministry of Agriculture said: 'The options were purely hypothetical, the decision has been made, and that is the end of the matter.' The Home Office, 'after careful consideration . . . has decided that it is unable to let you have the information you have requested'. And so on. Hennessy concluded: 'If [Whitehall] cannot be open about its own routine internal affairs, what can it be expected to divulge?'[15]

One exception to this tight-lipped approach came from Thatcher herself just three weeks after becoming Prime Minister. Mike Thomas, a backbench Labour MP, asked if the Prime Minister 'will now answer questions on the membership and terms of reference of cabinet committees'. No previous Prime Minister had ever given any information on cabinet committees, for reasons spelt out by Callaghan in 1978 (see pages 273-4). Thatcher, however, raised the veil a little way in a written answer:

I have established four standing committees of the Cabinet: a defence and overseas policy committee and an economic strategy committee, both under my chairmanship; a home and social affairs committee under the chairmanship of my Right Hon. friend the Home Secretary [William Whitelaw]; and a legislation committee under the chairmanship of the Lord Chancellor [Lord Hailsham]. Attendance at these committees will vary according to the subject under discussion. Where appropriate, sub-committees of the standing committees will be established. Membership, and the terms of reference of the standing committees or their sub-committees, will remain confidential.[16]

In that reply Thatcher said little that was useful in unravelling the processes of government; and she ruled out providing the kind of information that would help outsiders understand what was going on. Yet the very fact that she gave any information at all was significant. Whatever her intentions about holding the line on giving further details, she has accepted that the subject of cabinet committees is no longer taboo. As Callaghan's own minute on the subject observed, any departure from the 'long established convention' of saying nothing 'would be more likely to whet appetites than to satisfy them'.

The other noteworthy step towards reducing the secrecy of government came from Patrick Jenkin. In November 1979 the Social Services Secretary announced that the A-code—the confidential manual used by social security officials to assess supplementary benefits—would disappear. Instead there would be a published list of what could and could not be claimed. Jenkin said: 'We attach very considerable importance to the fact that the system will no longer be shrouded in secrecy. People will be able to see what their entitlement is and will be able to judge whether they are getting it.'[17]

Such open-mindedness did not extend to the Government's intentions to reform the Official Secrets Act. In October 1979 the Government published a Protection of Official Information Bill, to replace Section Two of the old Act (see pages 264-5). Some measure of the bill's character can be gained from an observation of one of Callaghan's closest aides that it was almost identical to a draft bill prepared by Home Office officials under the last Labour government and rejected even by Callaghan for being too restrictive. The bill defined five categories where the transmission of information would continue to be criminal offences: information on defence and international relations where disclosure 'would be likely to cause serious injury to the interests of the nation or endanger the safety of a citizen of the United Kingdom and Colonies'; security and intelligence; the enforcement of criminal law and the prevention of prison escapes; telephone tapping and the interception of mail; confidential information received from foreign governments, international organizations, nationalized industries, companies and individuals.[18]

Some Government ministers said that the bill was more liberal than the 1972 Franks Committee, notably on the grounds that cabinet documents were not automatically covered. Against this there were two broad strands of criticism —not only from the Government's political opponents but also from some Conservative MPs. The scope of the bill itself was attacked: why should newspapers and other media not be free to report on, say, telephone tapping or the Government's relationships with nationalized industries and private contractors, if abuse is suspected? More important, however, was the bill's definition of what a prosecution would need to establish to send a defendant to prison. It would require a certificate by a government minister 'that at the time of the alleged offence unauthorized disclosure of the information or article would have been likely to cause serious injury to the interests of the nation'.[19] The minister's decision would be final, for a certificate of any threat of serious injury 'shall be conclusive evidence of that fact'.[20] So a defendant's attempt to prove that his or her actions were not harmful, or were even helpful to the national interest, would be doomed to fail. As a *Times* leading article observed, 'No court can go behind that certificate however patently misguided it might be.'[21]

The bill also empowered any civil servant who could be deemed a 'responsible authority' to classify information whose disclosure could harm the national interest. The bill did not define the status or level of civil servants who would have this power; nor did it specify the chain of accountability for exercising it.

Less than three weeks after the bill was published it was mortally wounded. Andrew Boyle's book, *The Climate of Treason,* gave clues to the identity of the 'fourth man'—a Russian agent working inside British intelligence in the 1940s alongside Guy Burgess, Donald Maclean and Kim Philby. On 15 November the Prime Minister confirmed that the fourth man was Sir Anthony Blunt. One side-effect of the kerfuffle that followed was a realization that had the new bill been law it would have prevented the publication of Boyle's book, and hence the public unmasking of Blunt. While some of Thatcher's security advisers would undoubtedly have approved of this state of affairs, it was untenable as a public posture. The Government had little choice but to withdraw the bill.

The culture of secrecy, however, has survived, even if the Protection of Official Information Bill has not. Caution on open government is not generally surprising when a Conservative administration is in office; but this time it is significant. A radical government, of the right or of the left, needs all the allies it can find if it is to overcome the natural inclination of many people and institutions, and Whitehall most of all, to defend their past ways of working from change. Secrecy aids the conservatism (with a small 'c') of the bureaucracy by allowing it to conceal its assumptions and practices and policies from public, and sometimes even ministerial, scrutiny. Opening up government in general, and the Civil Service in particular, will tend to transfer power from insiders to outsiders. When a radical government is in power it is apt to find itself first isolated and then imprisoned by the insiders of the machine it thinks it controls. The Government's true friends are the outsiders—its backbench MPs and its supporters in the country. They need to know as much as possible about what is happening in their name if they are to be much help.

Powerful select committees can also help a radical government, for much the same reason that greater freedom of information does; for while such committees arm opposition MPs, they also arm the Government's MPs with the ammunition to fire at any laggardly bureaucrats. And Government MPs are in a majority in committees, as they are in the House of Commons as a whole. But powerful committees, as we saw in Chapter Ten, are not what Parliament has traditionally allowed.

When the Conservatives came to power they arrived with Norman St John Stevas's promise to implement the main proposals of the Procedure Committee (see page 258) to reform the select committee system. The principal structural change was carried out: fourteen new committees were established to shadow government departments—broadly, the twelve proposed by the Procedure Committee, together with one each for Scottish and Welsh affairs. But when the new committees started sitting in December 1979 they had none of the extra power or authority that was needed to make them more effective. They had no extra power to summon ministers or obtain information from them; they had no extra staff to service and advise them; their chairmen received no salary. In the early weeks of their operation there were no signs that the new committees would have any greater success than the old ones in rattling the executive—although their potential for becoming a series of powerful and expert adversaries remains.

Nor have there been any signs of the Civil Service transforming its system for recruiting high-flyers (see Chapter Six). Following criticisms from the Expenditure Committee in 1977, together with requests for fuller analysis of the statistical biases towards public school, Oxbridge, and arts graduates, the Civil Service Commission mounted its own inquiry, chaired by the first Commissioner, Dr Fergus Allen. This reported in December 1979.[22] Early on the report criticized the way the MPs reached their conclusions:

> The problem for the Civil Service Commission is that the critics tend not to look. Members of the Expenditure Committee, for instance, did not take up the invitation offered them to visit CSSB and observe the selectors at work. And what they said in their Eleventh Report, without benefit of this experience, may well have had the effect of further entrenching the myth that AT selection is unfairly biased in favour of the independent school—and Oxbridge—educated arts graduate.

And later:

> The Expenditure Committee recommended that consideration should be given to widening the membership of the Final Selection Boards. Though we say so with respect, the Expenditure Committee did not enquire about the background of FSB members or the width of the membership.

In fact, the report gave figures that half the FSB members had been to public schools and half had been to Oxbridge. And the report conceded the absence of 'members of professions, such as law, medicine, architecture, engineering and accountancy'. Overall, the report defended the system of recruitment while calling for minor modifications. In particular it defended the system of subjective marking at Cizbee:

> Candidates are assessed on both potential and present performance and in the context of their opportunities as well as their achievements. This seems to us of fundamental importance to a selection system for the public service, which needs to be judged by its fairness as well as its effectiveness. The AT selection system meets that criterion of fairness; the system itself is a greater safeguard against the favoured treatment of an individual or a group than its substitution by an objectivity which, in the present state of knowledge, is likely to be spurious.

Just like the Davies Committee a decade earlier (see pp. 118-19), the evidence did not justify the conclusions. The figures given in the new report not only confirm the pattern reported in Chapter Six but underline the fact that bias does occur in the selection process, despite the report's observation that 'much of the apparent variation in the performance of candidates from different types of school reflected their university rather than their school background . . . Oxbridge candidates had in general a better class of degree: 14 per cent had first-class degrees compared with 5 per cent of candidates from other universities.'

In fact considerable biases still remain, as a detailed examination of the statistical appendices of the report shows. These give, for the first time, interrelated figures for degree class, degree subject, school and university. While there is no internal bias towards arts graduates (the apparent bias results from the fact that many more candidates, and therefore recruits, have arts degrees than any other kind), public school and Oxbridge candidates still have the best chances. Even among candidates with first-class degrees, the chance of success was almost twice as great in 1978 for public school/Oxbridge candidates as for maintained school/non-Oxbridge candidates (39 to 20 per cent). The figures for first-class graduates are, however, too small for precise calibration. More striking, and statistically safer, are the figures for second- and third-class graduates. Candidates with a public school and/or Oxbridge background, and preferably both, are preferred. These are the percentage mass rates (a) for all candidates, and (b) for candidates at the Cizbee stage (a 'pass' here includes obtaining a 'near miss' but still going forward to the Final Selection Board):

Education	Candidates with 2nd or 3rd class degrees: 1978	
	Percentage successful in passing all three stages	Percentage successful at Cizbee (including near misses)
Public school/Oxbridge	19	57
Maintained school/Oxbridge	12	53
Public school/Non-Oxbridge	6	42
Maintained school/Non-Oxbridge	4	38

Perhaps the last word for the time being should go to Robert Mays, a former statistician at the Civil Service Department and subsequently a research fellow at Nuffield College, Oxford. A week after the Civil Service Commission's report he told a conference of the British Psychological Society:

> Those subjective judgments [at Cizbee] cannot be viewed as valid measures of the candidates; indeed they may tell us more about the assessors than about the assessed. Among candidates of the same ability as measured by every test, exercise and subjective assessment of personality and intellect, those from Oxbridge have a better chance of selection in the final judgment.[23]

Whatever achievements or failures the Thatcher government eventually records, the role of Sir Robert Armstrong is likely to be significant. In October 1979 he succeeded Sir John Hunt as Cabinet Secretary. (Hunt promptly confirmed left-wing suspicions of mandarin attitudes by accepting a directorship with Unilever, and Prudential Life Assurance, and the chairmanship of the London-based subsidiary of the Banque Nationale de Paris.[24]) When Armstrong was appointed he was widely depicted as an identikit Permanent Secretary: Eton; Oxford; classics degree; Treasury career; Principal Private Secretary to two Prime Ministers. But in two respects he differs from most of his colleagues. First, surprisingly few Permanent Secretaries in recent times have been to Eton—or any of the other really posh schools, like Harrow and Winchester. Most went to the second-tier public schools: they are the socially upward-mobile who have finally arrived (see page 191).

Secondly, Armstrong is a few years younger than most other Permanent Secretaries. He joined the Civil Service in 1950, rather than just after the Second World War ended. The 'reconstruction' entrants (see page 182) were often inspired by the vision that a better Britain could and would be designed on the drawing-boards of Whitehall. Today many of them nurse their disappointments. Armstrong, on the other hand, joined when the problems had already started to overshadow the vision. He does not suffer illusions of grandeur—either about Britain or about himself.

But in one important sense Armstrong's character precisely reflects that of the modern mandarin class. He is vigorously *non-partisan*—he has worked closely with and gained remarkable respect from such diverse politicians as Edward Heath and Margaret Thatcher, Roy Jenkins and Harold Wilson—yet at the same time he is highly *political:* as Permanent Secretary at the Home Office from 1977 to 1979 he gained the reputation for acting more as a decision-making minister than as a deferential official. What is striking is that this role attracted admiration rather than disapproval from even the greatest critics of the Civil Service among James Callaghan's policy staff at Downing Street, when Labour was in power. 'He was certainly forceful,' recalls one of Callaghan's team, 'but he was honest and direct. It was a real pleasure to deal with him.'

Although Armstrong was the preferred candidate of the most senior Permanent Secretaries, it was significant that Thatcher chose him—not least because his rapport with Heath was far greater than is usual between Prime Ministers and their private secretaries. (Both men, for example, shared a passion for music, and this helped to cement the relationship.)

Civil servants like Armstrong do not fit into the constitutional myth that ministers have absolute control over their department. But neither do they help the simple criticism that ministers *should* have absolute control. It might be possible to devise a system of government in which all civil servants were wholly complaisant towards their political masters: but they could not be effective in either the routine administration of government work or the preparation of policy advice. Both tasks require skill, experience and a determination to do the job well. It is unreasonable for the public to expect, or for Whitehall to claim, that officials can or should be disinterested in the decisions ministers formally take.

Once it is accepted that civil servants do, *and properly should,* have a central role in deciding how Britain is governed, it is possible to leave the sterile world of constitutional mythology and examine more pressing issues, such as how to recruit future mandarins from a wider background of class and experience, how to achieve the kind of professionalism demanded by the Fulton Committee, how to reconcile sensibly the often complex conflicts between departmental wisdom and political strategy, and above all how to secure open and democratic supervision of the work the Civil Service does.

In this book we have examined the sorry record of how these matters have been handled in the last dozen years. The problems, however, do not just concern Whitehall; and their solutions, properly applied, cannot fail to have a very much wider impact. As Keith Middlemas, the biographer of Stanley Baldwin, and no militant left-winger, puts it in *Politics in Industrial Society:*

> Is it unreasonable to assume that, earlier than in any other industrial country, British governments began to make the avoidance of crises their first priority? That even before the era of full suffrage they had discovered how to exercise the arts of public management, extending the state's powers to assess, educate, bargain with, appease or constrain the demands of the electorate? . . . That they created in Britain a political *Gleichschaltung,* subtle and loose enough to be resented only by . . . deviants and minorities; in which . . . the challenges of Conservatism and Socialism were alike dispersed in a common reformist policy justified by an unreal assessment of historical tradition?[25]

Whitehall's mandarins have helped inflict, and now defend, this malaise and call it good government. To challenge the character and operation of the Civil Service is to assault the very citadel of Britain's closed corporate state. Possibly the biggest question facing the British political system in the 1980s is whether it has the will and the ammunition to mount that assault.

APPENDICES

THE FULTON
COMMITTEE

Biographical details of members at the date of their appointment (1966):

SIR PHILIP ALLEN. 53. Educated at King Edward VII School, Sheffield, and Queen's College, Cambridge. Career civil servant (Administrative Class), mainly in Home Office. Second Permanent Secretary in Pay and Management side of Treasury 1963-66 (the part then responsible for the Civil Service).

WALTER ANDERSON. 55. Bootle and Wigan Grammar Schools and Liverpool University. After some years as a solicitor in local government, became an official of the National Association of Local Government Officers; NALGO General Secretary from 1957.

EDWARD BOYLE. 42. Eton and Christ Church, Oxford. Conservative MP for Birmingham, Handsworth, from 1950. Minister of Education 1962-64.

SIR WILLIAM COOK. 60. Trowbridge High School and Bristol University. Career civil servant (Scientific Officer Class), mainly in government research establishments. Deputy Chief Scientific Adviser, Ministry of Defence, from 1964.

SIR JAMES DUNNETT. 52. Edinburgh Academy and University College, Oxford. Career civil servant (Administrative Class). Permanent Secretary at Ministry of Transport 1959-62, and at Ministry of Labour from 1962.

LORD FULTON. 63. Dundee High School, St Andrew's University, and Balliol College, Oxford. Tutor in Philosophy and Politics at Oxford 1928-47. Temporary civil servant (Assistant Secretary) in Ministry of Fuel and Power during the Second World War. Vicechancellor of Sussex University from 1959.

NORMAN HUNT. 45. Belle Vue High School, Bradford, and Sidney Sussex College, Cambridge. Fellow and Lecturer in Politics at Exeter College, Oxford, from 1952.

SIR NORMAN KIPPING. 65. University College School and Birkbeck College, London. Electrical engineer; wartime civil servant at Ministry of Production. Director General of Federation of British Industry 1946-65.

ROBERT NEILD. 41. Charterhouse School and Trinity College, Cambridge. Deputy Director of National Institute of Economic and Social Research 1958-64; Economic Adviser to Treasury from 1964.

ROBERT SHELDON. 43. Elementary and grammar schools; Stockport, Burnley and Salford Technical Colleges (engineering diploma). Director of textile company before becoming Labour MP for Ashton-under-Lyne in 1964.

PROFESSOR LORD SIMEY. 59. Balliol College, Oxford. Lecturer in Public Administration, Liverpool University, 1931-39; Professor of Social Science from 1939.

SIR JOHN WALL. 53. Wandsworth School and London School of Economics. Ministry of Food 1939-52. Executive with Unilever 1952-58; Managing Director of EMI from 1960.

THE QUARRY*

WHAT THE CIVIL SERVICE IS
Important to recognise what the Civil Service *is* and *does*
- is only a small part (10%) of the public sector work force not a mysterious mass of bureaucrats but real people doing jobs because the country wants them done
- providing services to firms (export credit guarantees), to farmers (drainage engineers), above all to the public generally (social security benefits, finding new jobs for the unemployed)
- thankless but necessary jobs (tax collectors; prison officers; driving test examiners; Customs Officers; Immigration Officers)
- backroom boys sometimes (research scientists – eg on road safety; the weathermen)
- about a quarter blue collar workers (printers, carpenters, welders); the Royal Ordnance Factories export more than half their annual sales of around £300m.
- not 'Head Office'; of non-industrial civil servants: 83% work outside Inner London, 73% outside head offices
- not a 'bowler brigade': 46% of non-industrial civil servants are women and about one-third are younger than 30.

PAY
1. Ministers, not civil servants, authorise Civil Service pay rates.
2. What essentially determines a particular rate is what is currently being paid outside the Civil Service for broadly comparable work.
3. The basic principle of fair comparison was recommended by the Priestley Royal Commission in 1956, and accepted by all Governments since, as the only principle which is both fair to the taxpayer and fair to civil servants.
4. Since then, detailed procedures have been developed to ensure that this principle works in practice. The facts are found by an

*June 1979 edition.

independent body, the Pay Research Unit, which for each grade undertakes a survey of similar jobs outside. A wide range of outside organisations is studied, including smaller firms. The Civil Service rate is pitched at the median of the outside rates, taking account of fringe benefits, pension arrangements, hours, leave and all other conditions of service.

5. The independence of the Pay Research Unit is safeguarded by an independent Board which makes sure the Unit is impartial. The Board has recently published its first annual report on the work of the Unit. The Unit's staff who undertake the surveys include people recruited or seconded from the private sector.

6. The 1 April 1979 settlement, based on the evidence provided by the Pay Research Unit, will be staged with the full pay research rates negotiated being implemented by 1 January 1980. Within the limits of the pay research rates the increases will be 9% from 1 April 1979 (plus £1 a week for those on salaries below £4,795), a further 5% from 1 August and any balance of the pay research rates from 1 January 1980.

7. Top salaries are based on rates recommended by the independent Top Salaries Review Body under Lord Boyle. TSRB take account of what is paid outside but do not try to match the highest private sector salaries.

8. In periods of pay restraint top salaries have often been held below the recommended TSRB rates. Last year the recommendations of TSRB Report No 10 were accepted, subject to staging: in 1978 10% was paid. This year the Government has accepted further recommendations for up-dating the 1979 stage of the TSRB 10 increases, but the full rates recommended as appropriate to 1979 will not be paid until 1980.

9. Pay of industrial civil servants is determined by different procedures, but on the same broad principles as the pay of non-industrial civil servants. This year a study is being undertaken into rates of pay for comparable work outside the Civil Service, and this will provide evidence for the negotiations leading to the settlement.

MANPOWER

Main Points

1. The size of the Civil Service depends principally on the tasks it is asked to perform. The Government are looking for a slimmer civil service, and are considering ways of achieving significant savings in the medium term. These can however only be secured through a commensurate reduction in functions.

2. Some 'fat' is an inevitable characteristic of all large organizations, including the Civil Service. The Government will continue to devote effort to identifying and eliminating waste and inefficiency.

3. Reduction in tasks means acceptance by the community of less Government involvement in social, industrial or economic activity. Conversely, if the community wishes central government to undertake new activities, additional civil servants will be required to do the work.

4. Civil Service numbers have fallen steadily for the past couple of years. By April 1979, there had been a net decrease of 15,300 civil servants compared with April 1976. This is partly due to high wastage rates and difficulties in recruitment, and partly to planned reductions in civil service manpower and related administrative costs. In the current year, Ministers have decided to reduce the pay component in existing cash limits by 3%. A temporary ban on recruitment has been introduced. Further reduction in numbers is to be expected.

5. Ministers and CSD officials subject all proposals requiring additional staff to the closest scrutiny and normally require priorities to be reviewed in order to accommodate them within existing numbers; and departments are constantly on the look-out for more efficient and economical ways of conducting their business.

6. There is a well developed system of staff inspection within the Civil Service which regularly examines the number and grading of individual non-industrial posts. This aims to cover the non-industrial civil service as a whole about every three years. Departmental staff inspection units are supplemented by CSD's central staff inspection resources. Similarly, each large department has its own management services unit and CSD's MS Divisions collaborate with other departments in their studies and provide a service to those who do not have MS units of their own. All these staff engage in a wide range of studies designed to improve the quality of management performance. More generally, a good deal of effort is being put into improving management accounting and information systems within the Service.

Facts and Figures

STAFF IN POST at 1 April 1979	732,300
Non-Industrials	565,800
Industrials	166,500
REDUCTION during the period 1/4/78-1/4/79	3,400

MAJOR DEPARTMENTS (STAFF IN POST AT 1 APRIL 1979)

Agriculture	13,956
CSD	5,043
Customs	28,771
Defence (including ROFs)	247,660
Education and Science	2,677
Employment Group	53,605
Energy	1,267
Environment (including PSA)	52,453
Foreign and Commonwealth Office	9,777

Health and Social Security	98,369
Home Office	33,490
Industry	9,514
Inland Revenue	84,645
Land Registry	5,531
Lord Chancellor	10,211
National Savings	10,808
Northern Ireland Office	216
Prices and Consumer Protection	319
Scottish Office	10,946
Stationery Office	6,689
Trade	7,308
Transport	13,908
Treasury	1,056
Welsh Office	2,607

Examples of Categories, Groups and Classes (All Departments)

Some examples of the distribution of staff at 1/1/79 are:

Under Secretary and above:	985*
Administration Group: (including 1203 Assistant Secretaries, 697 Senior Principals, 4534 Principals)	249,000
Local Officers:	46,000
Typing and Secretarial Group:	28,600
Office Keepers and Messengers:	9,300
Science Category:	16,400
Professional and Technology Category (including draughtsmen):	43,800
Accountants (Professional):	360
Legal Category:	870
Statistician Class:	530
Economist Group:	390
Medical Officers:	590

In addition about 600 other qualified accountants are employed on various aspects of accounting work in posts in the Administration Group and in Departmental Classes in District Audit, Exchequer and Audit Department, Inland Revenue and in the Insolvency Service in the Department of Trade.

*as at 1.4.79

PENSIONS

Main Points

1. *Civil Servants pay for their pensions.* In pay research, civil service salaries are reduced to take account of pension contributions by those outside; and a further adjustment is made, on professional actuarial advice, for the difference in benefits, including inflation-proofing, between the Civil Service and outside schemes. Men also pay direct contributions of $1\frac{1}{2}\%$ of salary for family benefits.

2. *Civil Service pensions are not high:* the average Civil Service pension (including those paid to widows and dependants) is about £21 a week. It was increased by less than £1.50 a week on 1 December 1978, an increase of 7.4%.

3. *Inflation-proofing is not unique to the Civil Service:*
   a. almost the entire public sector has inflation-proofing;
   b. inflation-proofing to some degree is very common in the private sector;
   c. the State retirement pension will in future be increased in line with prices;
   d. the new State Pension Scheme now gives all those in employment the chance to gain an earnings-related, index-linked pension, and Civil Service pensions will in future be increased by the same percentage and at the same time as these pensions.

4. Nearly all OECD countries index public service pensions. Some, like the UK, index to prices, and others go further and link them to salary.

5. The Pensions (Increase) Act 1971 was passed with the positive support of all Parties.

6. Pensions are inherently a long term business. Policies should not necessarily be changed in response to short term fluctuations in wage and price indices. Over long periods pay has consistently risen faster than prices.

Facts and Figures

Levels

Before 1 December 1978, the average pension in payment to former civil servants; widows and dependants; and both categories combined was £1230 per annum (£23.65 a week); £470 per annum (£9.04 a week); and £1030 (£19.81 a week) respectively. The increase on 1 December 1978 of 7.4% brought these to £25.40, £9.71 and £21.28 respectively. Before this increase two-thirds of Civil Service pensioners received pensions of less than £1000 per annum and 85% below £2000 per annum.

Cost

In a full year, the 1 December 1978 increase for the Civil Service will cost £25 million (total public services £115m). The continuing annual cost, including the December increase, for the Civil Service will be £362m (total public services £1,669m).

Coverage
The Pensions (Increase) Act 1971
covers directly
　Civil Service
　Teachers
　Local Government employees
　National Health Service employees
　Policemen
　Firemen
　Judges
　Members of Parliament and Ministers

and there follow by analogy:

　Armed Forces
　Universities
　Fringe Bodies

Equivalent increases:

The National Industries and Public Corporations generally have given increases equivalent to those under the 1971 Act, eg British Rail, British Steel, Post Office, British Broadcasting Corporation.

Numbers
The figures following have been derived from a variety of sources using various base rates and include estimates. They should therefore be used with care but can be taken to show relationships and orders of magnitude.

Group	Numbers Employed	In pension Scheme	Retired Public Servants	Dependants	Total Pensions
Armed Forces	318,000	318,000	238,000	34,000	273,000
Civil Service	736,000	736,000	257,000	82,000	339,000
Teachers	649,000	626,000	155,000	6,000	161,000
NHS	999,000	685,000	146,000	28,000	174,000
Police and Fire	156,000	156,000	63,000	30,000	93,000
Local Government	1,819,000	1,181,000	244,000	57,000	301,000
	4,677,000	3,702,000	1,103,000	237,000	1,341,000

Costs

Group	Cost of 1978 PI (in full year) £m	Annual Cost (with 1978 PI) £m
Overseas pensioners	5.8	84.3
Armed Forces	17.6	255.7
Civil Service	25.0	362.0
Teachers	21.5	309.6
NHS	12.5	181.5
Police and Fire	8.4	121.4
Local Government	24.5	354.5
	115.3	1669.0

Outside and Overseas Practice

Viewed overall, the pension arrangements for civil servants are on the level of those provided by good employers in the private sector. The range of benefits is below the maximum permitted by Inland Revenue. The Civil Service makes no distinction between grades when providing pensions, in contrast to many private sector schemes which often provide senior people with the maximum benefits permitted with, for example, full pensions (two-thirds of final pay) after only 10 years' service. Furthermore, full inflation proofing on a 1/80th pension (the public service pattern) costs no more than three-quarters inflation proofing on a 1/60th pension which is the private sector pattern (though often commuted). Outside schemes may also have pre-award dynamism, increasing their salaries by the Retail Price Index before award, under Inland Revenue Practice Note 6.14. In most OECD countries it is the practice to increase public sector pensions by at least price indexation, and in some countries salary indexation is used. The details are:

COUNTRY	METHOD OF INCREASE
Austria	Public Service salaries, ie parity
Belgium	Prices or parity
Canada	Prices

COUNTRY	METHOD OF INCREASE
Denmark	Prices
France	Parity
France	Parity
West Germany	Parity
Greece	Parity
Iceland	General earnings
Ireland	Parity
Italy	Prices
Japan	Parity
Luxembourg	Prices or parity
Netherlands	Parity
Norway	Prices or general earnings
Portugal	None
Spain	Parity
Sweden	Prices
Switzerland	Prices
Turkey	Prices
USA	Prices

We gave no evidence of any ceilings applying to these increases, but many public servants abroad do not receive any State pension in addition to their public service pension.

RECRUITMENT

Criticism of AT Recruitment

1. Accusations of Bias. Almost all the criticism of Civil Service recruitment is directed at CSSB/FSB. It is related, therefore, to an intake of 150-200 in an operation recruiting well over 70,000 people a year.

a. *Process gives advantage to Oxbridge candidates.* Graduates of Oxford and Cambridge certainly do better in AT selection but even the service's severest critics now acknowledge that 'if the Civil Service Commission is seeking to recruit the most able people' they are more likely to come from Oxbridge (Expenditure Committee, 11th Report). There is some evidence that Oxbridge graduates in the AT competition are better qualified academically.

b. *Procedure favours ex-independent school candidates.* More detailed examination shows that this statistical bias is more apparent than real. Ex-independent school candidates do better because more of them go on to Oxford or Cambridge so the statistical bias is largely a manifestation of the Oxbridge bias.

c. *Procedure is biased in favour of arts graduates.* This bias, if it exists, is very slight and probably reflects the fact that arts candidates have marginally better degrees. More detailed analysis shows that in all subject areas those with better degrees do better than those with less good degrees.

d. *Procedure favours the 'sons of privilege'.* The process is designed to select on merit irrespective of social background.

e. *We tend to pick people 'in our own image'.* There is no rational answer to the charge because it has no rational basis. The Civil Service uses outsiders in its selection work on a large scale, and one unparalleled by other organizations.

In response to the recommendations of the Expenditure Committee (11th Report) the Commissioners will be publishing in their Annual Reports, beginning with the 1978 Report, statistics on applicants for and recruits to AT according to the school and university attended and the class and subject area of their degree. Sub-paragraphs a, b and c above reflect the conclusions to be drawn from these more detailed statistics of AT candidates in 1978. The Government has also undertaken to appoint 2 part-time Commissioners from outside the Civil Service, the first of whom, Miss M P Downs, was appointed by an Order-in-Council made on and effective from 24 October 1978.

2. CSSB 'depends more on interviews than on written examinations'. The English Committee alone has made this a point of criticism. In fact, only about 15% of the candidate's time in the three-stage process (Qualifying Test/CSSB/FSB) is spent at interviews. The CSSB procedure blends these interviews with written work of different kinds. The whole AT system of selection is currently the subject of a review by the Civil Service Commissioners, including the newly-appointed Commissioner, who are being assisted by 2 outside members, one an academic and the other an occupational psychologist and consultant in selection.

Criticisms other than of AT recruitment
3. The Civil Service absorbs a disproportionate number of the nation's best graduates who could be more productively employed. There is no way to define whether the figures are 'disproportionate' or not. In 1977 under 4% of university first degree graduates entering permanent employment in the UK joined the Civil and Diplomatic Services compared with over 56% entering industry and commerce. In 1971, 6% entered the Service and 57% commerce and industry. Of those obtaining a first class honours degree in 1977, 5% entered the Civil and Diplomatic Services compared with 72% going into industry and commerce (the corresponding proportions in 1971 were 9% and 63%). Of those obtaining higher degrees in 1977, 340 or 7% entered the Civil and Diplomatic Services compared with 38% for industry and commerce.

4. The Commissioners are unfair to the disabled and to those who have suffered recent or severe mental illness. In requiring all those appointed to permanent posts to be capable of giving a regular and effective service for at least 5 years, the Commissioners maintain as fairly as possible a balance between the demands of the public service and the possibility of rehabilitation in the case of those about whom there are health doubts, physical or mental. In the last year the rate of rejection on health grounds was 0.14%. For the registered disabled, concessions are allowed in some competitions to make it easier for them to compete.

5. Age limits. Upper limits in particular are criticised for preventing people who are otherwise qualified from joining the Civil Service and (in an Industrial Tribunal case) specifically for discriminating against women. They are imposed to help in developing the career structure of a large, complex organisation, especially where the young direct entrant is one of the principal sources for filling middle and senior management posts in the future. They are used in a minority of competitions, with the active concurrence of the Staff Side with whom they are frequently reviewed. In accordance with the Industrial Tribunal's decision, management and the National Staff Side are currently considering what new upper age limit for EO recruitment should replace the present one which was found to discriminate against women.

6. Special Advisers and relaxation of the '5 year Rule'. The Commissioners have not abandoned the '5 year Rule' that no person can hold an appointment in the Civil Service for more than 5 years without their Certificate of Qualification. In fact, as announced by the then Minister of State in the House on 1 August 1978, a new Order-in-Council which came into effect on 1 December 1978 extended the Commissioners' powers so that they are now required to certificate all appointments (apart from a few specific exceptions including Special Advisers – see below) instead of only permanent (ie lasting more than 5 years) appointments. The Commissioners have also made General Regulations, effective from 1 December 1978 stating the circumstances in which, and the conditions on which, the Commissioners will authorise an appointment before certification.

Special Advisers are specifically excluded from the purview of the CSC because their appointments are made directly by a Minister of the Crown and are limited to the duration of the current administration. It clearly would be inappropriate for them to be recruited by open competition and the Commissioners could not therefore certificate them for employment in the Civil Service.

PERKS

1. There are virtually no perks in the Civil Service – people's rewards are the published and taxed salaries. Civil servants pay for their pensions.

2. Allowances or facilities are available only when essential for work purposes, and their use is governed by detailed regulations.

3. The payment of boarding school fees for children of diplomats, the armed forces and other civil servants posted abroad simply reflects the fact that boarding school education which is entailed by the absence on duty of their parents is not normally available in the state system. The rates allowed are strictly controlled.

4. There is no equivalent in the Civil Service of 'the company car'. No civil servant has a car provided for private or domestic use. The use of government pool cars for official purposes is strictly controlled.

5. There is no equivalent in the Civil Service of 'expense account

living'. The occasions on which hospitality is possible at official expense, and the levels of that entertainment, are strictly controlled.

HONOURS

Civil servants get too many honours. It is true that civil servants receive a large share of the honours, because honours have always been designed to give special recognition to servants of the Crown (whose achievements must otherwise be, for the most part, anonymous). It is fair enough to suggest that the system should be changed, but that is a different matter from criticising civil servants for receiving honours. Honours are, after all, simply public recognition, in a form involving virtually no cost to the taxpayer.

Moreover the main criticisms of Civil Service honours are misconceived:

Only a small proportion of honours go to civil servants. Their proportion of honours has deliberately been reduced from over 35% in the late 1950s and early 1960s to about 20% in the last few years, eg the number of civil servants holding knighthoods has declined between 1950 and 1978. In 1950, 115 Home Civil Servants and 63 members of the Diplomatic Service held knighthoods. In 1979, 38 Home Civil Servants and 33 members of the Diplomatic Service hold knighthoods.

Only a small proportion of civil servants receive honours. The proportion of civil servants who receive these honours is tiny. For example 148 out of some 726,000 home civil servants were so honoured in the 1979 New Year Honours List.

The small proportion honoured get their honours on merit, not automatically. While a very few civil servants – about 200 in the highest 2 ranks in the Civil Service – are almost bound to receive honours, there is nothing automatic about reaching this level in the Service, and the honours like the posts – go to those who have proved their ability in a full Civil Service career.

JOB SECURITY

In times of recession Civil Service jobs are no doubt more secure, by and large, than those in the private sector. But that is not the full story.

2. In times of full employment it is doubtful if there is much practical difference in security between jobs in the Civil Service and the great mass of jobs outside.

3. Where services cease to be required and those providing them cannot be redeployed, civil servants are as liable to redundancy as private sector people in the same position. But many civil servants are required to do whatever job they are given and to go wherever sent; and in recession the demand for their work increases (social security payments, unemployment benefits, finding new jobs, assistance to industry). These are the plain facts which make most civil

servants less subject to redundancy – just as they make others secure from redundancy where they apply.

4. Civil servants are not protected from dismissal for serious misconduct: standards of conduct are certainly as high as (and in some ways higher than) those in the private sector.

5. There is a separate question of weeding out inefficiency. The Civil Service has procedures for doing this as others have; it also has procedures to protect employees against unfair dismissal as others have. And civil servants are in fact dismissed under these procedures – perhaps not so many during periods of staff shortage as there might otherwise have been.

6. A major effort is put into avoiding problems in the first place, ie recruitment standards and strict probation for one or two years before appointment is confirmed.

7. In short, dismissals of various sorts are comparable with those of other organizations where similar circumstances apply. Indeed, if they were significantly higher we should want to know where our recruitment, probation, training and staff management were going wrong.

8. The minimum age at which most civil servants may retire is 60, but there is no common age at which it is customary for civil servants to retire. Civil servants may be retained beyond 60 at the discretion of the Head of their Department, provided they are fit and efficient and there are posts available. Those with short service have special claims to retention in order to earn a pension. Those who cannot be retained may be re-employed in a lower grade after retirement. Generally speaking, the higher the grade the lower the retiring age within the 60-65 age span. For example, staff in the Open Structure, ie those at Under Secretary level and above, are expected to retire at 60 unless there are strong management reasons to the contrary. With effect from 1 May 1977 all civil servants are required to retire not later than age 65 unless the overriding needs of the Service require their retention.

BUSINESS APPOINTMENTS

The Fulton Committee recognized that it is in the public interest that civil servants with experience of public administration should be able to move into business and industry.

Nevertheless it is proper to try and avoid the risk that a particular business appointment may shake public confidence in the integrity of the Civil Service. Consequently, there is a rule that whenever a more senior civil servant proposes to go within 2 years of leaving the Service to a firm with which he has had official dealings, or to a firm with a special relationship or extensive contractual dealings with the Government, he has to get permission. Cases are looked at to ensure propriety and fairness between competing companies.

The purpose of the business appointments rules is distinct from that of the Prevention of Corruption Acts. The law exists to deal with corruption. The business appointments rules exist to avoid public suspicion, however unjustified this may be, to the effect that firms could benefit improperly or unfairly by employing ex-civil servants. It is important to avoid the possibility that such suspicion might unduly interfere with the appointment in industry of able people from the public sector.

An Advisory Committee, chaired by Lord Diamond, advises the Prime Minister on business appointments of former Permanent Secretaries and Heads of Department.

Since 1973 about one-tenth of those leaving the Civil Service at Under Secretary level and above, including professional scientists and technologists, have applied to take up business appointments.

THE ROLLS-ROYCE
MINUTES

Reproduced below are the full minutes of the secret meeting called on 30 May 1977 by Sir Peter Carey, the Permanent Secretary at the Department of Industry, to discuss the possible transfer of Rolls-Royce Ltd, a publicly owned company, to GEC. Rolls-Royce had been nationalized in 1971 when the company faced bankruptcy – largely because of the financial burden of developing and producing the RB211 aero engine. Subsequently the motor car section of Rolls-Royce was separately sold back into the private sector, leaving the aero engine and gas turbine divisions – the lion's share of the original company in terms of sales – in public ownership. Following the establishment of the National Enterprise Board by the last Labour Government, the NEB was given overall control of Rolls-Royce. The day-to-day running of the company, however, was left to a board under the chairmanship of Sir Kenneth Keith, one of Britain's leading merchant bankers. (In 1972 he became Chairman and chief executive of Hill Samuel Ltd.)

GEC is one of Britain's largest manufacturing companies, making a wide range of products, from telephone exchanges to television sets. In some areas it competes with Rolls-Royce. As the minutes show, GEC's controversial Managing Director, Sir Arnold Weinstock, saw benefits in combining the two companies so that they need no longer undercut each other for export orders, and so that GEC could 'take advantage of RR's sophisticated selling organization overseas'. Weinstock also wanted to benefit from the prestige of the Rolls-Royce name. But he was unhappy about the financial risks still associated with the RB211 engine: he wanted the risks (and profits) to be taken by the Government.

Weinstock also made it clear that although the NEB could have a stake in the merged company, the stake would be small, as GEC would be taking over the running of a loss-making company: Rolls-Royce was then declaring a £20 million a year loss on a turnover of £600 million – though Weinstock maintained that the loss calculated by GEC's accounting standards was as high as £50 million. And, as Weinstock, according to the minutes, 'said that either he ran the new company or it would never be formed', there was no effective way in which the Government or the NEB would have any control over the new company.

Rolls-Royce's Chairman, Sir Kenneth Keith, also approved the merger: Rolls-Royce would be able to diversify more; and 'RR stood in need of restructuring anyhow'. A merger with GEC would facilitate both aims.

Subsequently Weinstock withdrew before ministers became involved. In addition, the NEB was not keen on losing Rolls-Royce. For some months the tensions between the NEB and Rolls-Royce remained private, but they surfaced in June 1979 when Keith described the NEB as 'a bureaucratic contraceptive'. Then, in October 1979, Murphy (by now knighted, and Ryder's successor as NEB chairman) responded by attacking Rolls-Royce's performance: it 'has not accomplished an adequate level of profits . . . Sooner or later there has to be a greater and more stringent application of commercial disciplines.' The arguments led to their well-publicized climax in November 1979. Keith resigned from Rolls-Royce earlier than expected. Rolls-Royce was taken from the NEB and put under the direct control of the Department of Industry. And the entire board of the NEB resigned in protest.

Two years earlier there was no public debate. Indeed not only did ministers not have to answer to Parliament – civil servants did not tell ministers all they were doing. As we have seen (p. 189), Eric Varley had an imperfect knowledge of the proposed deal with GEC.

According to one source closely involved with the events of 1977, the decision to label the minutes 'Secret' must be seen in that light. The CSD, in its evidence to the Franks Committee on the reform of the Official Secrets Act, stated that 'Secret' is the second highest security classification, after 'Top Secret'. It is supposed to apply to 'information and material the unauthorized disclosure of which would cause injury to the nation'. The kind of examples the CSD gives include: 'Papers which reveal highly embarrassing disagreement with a friendly Government', 'Vital military information . . . relating to important defences, establishments and installations', 'Emergency measures planned in case of strikes in essential industries', and 'Reference in one document to all the locations of Government in war'.

The Rolls-Royce minutes fall into no such, or remotely similar, category. The reason why they were labelled 'Secret' was not so much to stop them circulating *outside* the Government, as to limit the debate *inside* to civil servants – until they felt ready to tell ministers.

SECRETARY'S MEETING ON POSSIBLE RR/GEC MERGER: 3.45 PM MONDAY 30 MAY

Present:　　Sir Peter Carey　　　Sir Kenneth Keith – RR
　　　　　　Mr Rawlinson　　　　Sir Arnold Weinstock – GEC
　　　　　　Mr Lippitt　　　　　Sir Kenneth Bond – GEC
　　　　　　Mr Dearing　　　　　Lord Ryder – NEB
　　　　　　　　　　　　　　　　Mr Murphy – NEB

Sir Peter said that he had called the meeting in order to discuss in an exploratory fashion the possibility of an amalgamation between GEC and RR. He invited Sir Kenneth Keith to explain the background. Sir Kenneth said that Sir Arnold Weinstock had from time to time expressed an interest in part of RR's activities: RR had always refused and said that GEC would have to take the whole thing or nothing. Given that RR wanted a broader industrial base, the idea of an amalgamation with GEC had attractions, but both sides needed to know the Government's view of the merger before they proceeded any further. Otherwise they would be wasting their time – hence he had mentioned the idea to Sir Peter and hence the meeting.

Advantage to RR

2. Sir Peter said that he appreciated the merit in the amalgamation in that it would take RR out of the narrow field of aero engines, which was a field where, through a variety of reasons, future market growth was likely to be constrained. He asked what were the other advantages to RR. Sir Kenneth Keith explained that RR stood in need of financial restructuring anyhow. The amalgamation with GEC would provide the opportunity to separate out the work on the RB211 with the Government funding most of it. Sir Arnold said that everything hinged upon the Government being prepared to fund the aero engine side of RR's activities. GEC had looked at the figures and although they knew that the aero engine business was bad, they had not realized it was that bad! However, GEC would be prepared to take on this part of RR's operations also on the basis of no profit/no loss, i.e. with the Government taking out the risk element.

Advantage to GEC

3. Sir Arnold said that there were distinct advantages in the merger for GEC. At the moment RR competed with GEC in export markets and had tie-ups with various US competitors. It did not make sense for two British companies to undercut each other's prices and to compete in this way. He gave as an example of this the way in which RR had been forced to quote very low prices to win a recent large Russian contract. Moreover, neither GEC nor RR at present made a compressor. There were five compressor manufacturers in the world; GEC had tried to purchase all of them, but three were independently held and would not sell and the other two, held by holding companies, were also not up for sale. However, RR plus GEC could

manufacture a compressor: it was not a question of technical expertise but acceptability. The RR name would mean that the new compressor would be acceptable to customers, although as it was at present customers would always choose a proven design.

4. Sir Arnold also stressed the desirability of GEC being able to take advantage of RR's sophisticated selling organization overseas, especially in the US. He regarded RR's industrial and marine divisions as having good potential; but he emphasized that the aero engine side was a nightmare.

Advantage to Government

5. Sir Peter said that he could see the commercial benefits to both GEC and RR but asked what would be the advantage to Government. Sir Arnold said that anything which redounded to the advantage of RR and GEC was, speaking in broad terms, of advantage to Government. He and Sir Kenneth Keith argued that the Government was already committed to fund the future development of the RB211 indefinitely, so that the new separate funding arrangements which they sought would not change anything. As for loss of control of RR, which was a point that Sir Peter raised, Sir Arnold thought that in effect the Government's control of RR was pretty illusory anyway – at present the Government had the right to argue with RR and sack the management but little else.

6. Lord Ryder said that the only way that he could go along with the merger would be if the NEB had some form of participation in the top company resulting from the merger. Sir Arnold said that he had always been willing for the Government to take shares in GEC. However, based on the Government's present shareholding in RR – a company which was making a £20m loss, or by GEC's accounting standards, a £50m loss – the state shareholding in the new company would be fairly small.

7. During further discussion the following main points were made:
   i. *Management of New Company:* Sir Arnold said that either he ran the new company or it would never be formed. He said that this was a different situation from the GEC/Parsons merger on turbo-generation, however. There GEC was predominant. In this case RR would be able to go on without GEC and have a long-term future so that GEC would have to reach an 'accommodation' with RR. He mentioned briefly the possibility of setting up a separate board to manage the new company to circumscribe his own personal powers. Of course, the day-to-day running of the company wou d be left to a management team constructed out of the best of the two companies. Sir Kenneth Keith remarked that there would need to be a transitional period if and when the new company was set up. He mentioned in this connection that RR would need to be able to continue to sell their engines overseas, for instance with Cooper Bessemer in Canada: it had always been RR's practice to operate a policy of non-exclusivity on sale of

engines. Sir Arnold said that GEC would be happy for RR to sell engines to anyone they liked.

ii. *Funding of RB211:* Mr Rawlinson asked whether the Government would pay more or less if it funded the RB211 development separately. Sir Kenneth Keith said that the Government would not pay more. The fact was that Government was committed to the engine's future development. All aero engine work was non-commercial; in the US it was funded through the American military programme; the UK needed a different method. What he was suggesting was that the engine should receive launching aid and that the Government receive a return by means of a sales levy on engines sold. This made more sense than to fund the engine through the NEB using capital rather than income. If the Government were prepared to make separate funding in this way, then GEC would not be taking on an open-ended commitment in merging with RR. There would be benefit all round: RR brought a lot to the GEC table – their name and their relationship with Government; moreover, Marconi Elliot would benefit on the GEC side.

Mr Dearing pointed out that there were at present two elements in the funding of RR by Government: funding through the NEB and by launching aid. He asked whether the funding which Sir Arnold and Sir Kenneth Keith had in mind was for 100% separate launching aid funding. Sir Arnold said the latter was what he had in mind. Lord Ryder did not believe that the Government should fund the RB211 up to 100%. Sir Arnold said that he envisaged the aero engine side being run as a separate business for the account of Government, win or lose. However, he would be prepared for the new company to be set certain production targets and be penalized if these were not met, and rewarded conversely, thereby having a form of discipline imposed.

iii. *Relative Strength of GEC/RR Turbine Divisions:* Sir Arnold pointed out that GEC's gas turbines made a £5½m profit in the last financial year; the turnover next year was expected to be £65m giving an £8m profit. He did not think that RR's industrial turbine divisions matched this. In contrast Sir Kenneth Keith said that by coincidence RR happened to be at the bottom of both the trade and funding cycle of their operation. Sir Arnold did not accept this argument about cycles: he said that RR were holding out Indian cheesecloth and saying that it was silk; but even so, GEC were prepared to buy it! The RR name meant a lot; GEC's profits and RR's losses could in aggregate be turned to double GEC's profits in the future. GEC were paying for the removal of the threat that RR would combine with US companies and compete. They were prepared to pay a premium for the potential benefit of RR's business, as opposed to what it was actually worth. Whilst the turbine market might not look as rosy as it had done, since there was stiff competition from overseas, nonetheless there was still sufficient prospects to make a RR/GEC merger in this field worthwhile.

iv. *Parsons:* Sir Peter asked where Parsons would fit in to the new turbo generation side of the new company. Sir Arnold thought that there was no room for Parsons, although he did say that if the Government wanted GEC on a leash expressed through a share-holding in GEC, then the Government might buy Parsons before it was taken over by GEC. Sir Arnold did not seem keen on any Parsons involvement in the deal.

Conclusion

8. Sir Peter said he thought that the next step should be that the NEB should put down on a piece of paper an outline scheme of how the merger would work. This paper should be agreed by all parties. The paper should state the central proposition and the alternative variations from it. It would need to have some figures in it for the sake of example. Thereafter it would be appropriate to broach the subject with ministers. It was agreed that the note of the present meeting would be sent to Mr Murphy for his use in writing this paper.

9. Sir Arnold stressed the confidentiality of the proposition. He asked that no one else be consulted at this stage. His final remarks were that the Government would in no way be worse off if the merger went ahead, but might well be better off.

10. Sir Peter said that it went almost without saying that the respective workforces of RR and GEC would need to be consulted at some stage in the future and their agreement sought. Sir Arnold and Sir Kenneth agreed that unless the workforces could be carried, then the deal was off.

11. Sir Peter said that after the NEB had produced a paper agreed by all sides, then it would be appropriate to have another meeting.

R J HEYHOE   Distribution: Mr Rawlinson
PS/Sir Peter Carey   Mr Lippitt
815 V/S   Mr Dearing
215 5424   Mr Bullock

31 May 1977   Mr Murphy NEB

323

SIR DOUGLAS ALLEN'S

LETTER

CIVIL SERVICE DEPARTMENT

WHITEHALL LONDON SW1A 2AZ

Telephone Direct line 01 273 ....

Switchboard 01 273 3000

Sir Douglas Allen GCB

Head of the Home Civil Service

6 July 1977

Dear Head of Department

DISCLOSURE OF OFFICIAL INFORMATION

During the Debate on the Address on 24 November last, the Prime Minister announced that it would be the Government's policy in future to publish as much as possible of the factual and analytical material used as the background to major policy studies. A copy of the relevant part of the Prime Minister's speech is attached. I am writing in terms which the Prime Minister has specifically approved to let you know how his statement affects present practice and to ask you to ensure that your Department gives effect to it. You may wish to let your Minister see this guidance drawing particular attention to paragraph 10.

2. The change may seem simply to be one of degree and of timing. But it is intended to mark a real change of policy, even if the initial step is modest. In the past it has normally been assumed that background material relating to policy studies and reports would *not* be published unless the responsible Minister or Ministers decided otherwise. Henceforth the working assumption should be that such material *will* be published unless they decide that should *not* be. There is, of course, no intention to publish material which correctly bears a current security classification or privacy marking; at the same time, care should be taken to ensure that the publication of

unclassified material is not frustrated by including it in documents that also contain classified material.

3. In effect, what is proposed is an increase in the already considerable amount of material put out by Departments. The additional material will mainly consist of deliberate presentations in the later stages of discussion and development of new policy. Some of these will probably, as now, take the form of Green Papers. Some may have kindred form, like the recent Orange Paper on Transport. While most material will be released on the initiative of the Department, probably through HMSO, some of lesser importance, or of interest to a limited audience, may well be put out through other means such as publication in magazines or in response to specific requests in the same way that a good deal of unpublished material is already made available to bona fide researchers. In some cases it may be preferable simply to publicise the existence of certain material which would be made available to anyone who asked. Consideration should also be given to the issue of bibliographies or digests so that interested parties are advised what material is available.

4. In adopting the working assumption described in paragraph 2 above for policy studies, including PARs, the normal aim will be to publicise as much as possible of the background material subject to Ministerial decision once they have seen the study and reached their conclusions on it. When Ministers decide what announcement they wish to make, therefore, they will also wish to consider whether and in what form the factual and analytical material may be published, since there may, as the Prime Minister made clear in his statement, be circumstances in which Ministers will not wish to disclose such material.

5. It is not the intention to depart from the present practice of not disclosing PARs nor identifying them publicly; any question of releasing PAR material in circumstances not covered by a Ministerial decision should be referred to the Treasury.

6. In his November statement the Prime Minister said that it was the Government's wish to keep to a minimum the cost to public funds of the new initiative on disclosure. One inhibition to the publication of background material in the past has been that it has often been incorporated in submissions to Ministers which could not be published in their entirety. Re-writing material specially for publication is wasteful and expensive in staff time. Therefore when policy studies are being undertaken in future, the background material should as far as possible be written in a form which would permit it to be published separately, with the minimum of alteration, once a Ministerial decision to do so has been taken. It will generally assist Ministers to reach their decisions on publications if they can see an identifiable separate part of the report appropriately written for this purpose.

325

7. The form and way in which material is released will have to be considered on each occasion. The cost of any extra printing, or publishing, falls under present arrangements on the HMSO Vote, and HMSO is of course affected by the current restrictions on public expenditure in the same way as other Departments. HMSO is also responsible for deciding what prices should be charged for published material. You should ensure that discussions with HMSO are initiated at the earliest possible opportunity on any proposal which will add to expenditure. The following particular considerations should also be borne in mind:

i. Great care should be taken to keep costs to a minimum. If copies are to be run off in advance of demand, the quantity should be carefully and prudently assessed, to avoid waste rather than to offer instant response. (But, of course, there is a countervailing need to aim where appropriate for the economics of longer reproduction runs. The right balance here may be difficult and decisions should not be left to too low a level.)

ii. In general, double printing should be avoided, e.g. the published form of the material should be the same as that used internally (and the same print).

iii. There should be a charge for all material, at a price set by HMSO for each item, to include all aspects of reproduction and handling, but not of course any of the costs of the primary study itself.

iv. As regards Crown Copyright, attention is drawn to CSD General Notice GEN 75/76 dated 12 August 1975 (and corrigendum of 8 October 1976).

8. The Government's decision on this question is in a form which should not involve substantial additional work but which could all too easily be lost to view. There are many who would have wanted the Government to go much further (on the lines of the formidably burdensome Freedom of Information Act in the USA). Our prospects of being able to avoid such an expensive development here could well depend on whether we can show that the Prime Minister's statement had reality and results. So I ask all of you to keep this question of publicising material well on your check-list of action in any significant areas of policy formulation, even at Divisional level; and to encourage your Ministers to take an interest in the question.

9. Since the Prime Minister may well be asked what effect his announcement has had on the amount of information made available, I should be grateful if you could arrange to have some kind of record kept of the relevant items made available by your Department. Where the material is of an unusual kind, or of a variety not usually made available in the past, it would be useful if a copy could be sent to CSD. In cases where it has been decided not to publish material

which might be expected to be of considerable public interest, I suggest that the reasons should be briefly recorded.

10. The greater publicising of material can hardly fail to add to one cost – that of responding to the additional direct correspondence to which it may well give rise. In a Service operating under tight resource constraints, it may not always be possible to afford to give to such additional correspondence the kind of full and studied replies to which we have long been accustomed within the sort of timescale that has hitherto been customary. Nevertheless, Departments must do their best in these matters, and should inform a correspondent if the timescale for a reply is likely to be longer than normal.

11. I am copying this to Heads of Departments as on the attached list.

Yours sincerely
Douglas Allen

DEBATE ON THE ADDRESS – 24 NOVEMBER 1976
EXTRACT FROM THE PRIME MINISTER'S SPEECH

When the Government make major policy studies, it will be our policy in future to publish as much as possible of the factual and analytical material which is used as the background to these studies. This will include material used in the programme analysis reviews, unless – and I must make the condition – there is some good reason, of which I fear we must be the judge, to the contrary.

I am trying to help. I assure the House that we shall not endeavour to pull back the information. We shall look at every case to see whether we can make it available. The cost to public funds is a factor here, and we should like to keep that cost to a minimum. Therefore, arrangements will not be of a luxurious nature, but we shall make available what information we can to provide a basis for better informed public debate and analysis of ministerial policy conclusions.

FOOTNOTES

Chapter One: INTRODUCTION

1. Superannuation Act 1965, s. 98 (2).
2. ibid., s. 98 (1)
3. Tomlin Commission, quoted in the *Eleventh Report from the Expenditure Committee 1976-77*, vol. 1; HMSO, 1977, p. lxxvi.
4. *Expenditure Committee*, op. cit., pp. lxxvi-lxxvii.
5. ibid.
6. *Civil Service Statistics*, 1978, HMSO, 1978, table 1.
7. *The Civil Service: Government Observations on the Eleventh Report from the Expenditure Committee*, HMSO, 1978, paras 107, 108.
8. *The Quarry*, CSD, 1979, p.3; other statistics derived from *Civil Service Statistics 1977-1979*.
9. *The Times*, 5 December 1977.
10. *Eleventh Report from the Expenditure Committee, 1976-77*, vol 2, Part 1, HMSO, 1977, p. 302.
11. ibid., p. 304.
12. ibid., p. 319
13. *Sunday Express*, 25 July 1976.
14. *Sunday Times*, 19 December 1976.
15. Chapman, Leslie, *Your Disobedient Servant*, Chatto & Windus, 1978.
16. *Expenditure Committee*, op. cit., vol. 1, para 9.
17. *Hansard*, 15 January 1979, col. 1402.
18. Crossman, Richard, *The Diaries of a Cabinet Minister*, vol. 3, Hamish Hamilton & Jonathan Cape, 1977, p. 149.

Chapter Two: THE CULT OF THE GENERALIST

1. *The Civil Service: Government Observations on the Eleventh Report of the Expenditure Committee*, HMSO, 1978, para 2.
2. Reprinted in *Crisis in the Civil Service*, ed. Hugh .Thomas, Anthony Blond, 1968, pp. 25-6.
3. ibid., pp. 35-6.
4. ibid., p. 36.
5. *Sunday Times*, 5 September 1965.
6. ibid., p. xvi.
7. ibid., p. xxxv.
8. ibid., p. xxxv.
9. *The Civil Service*, vol. 1, HMSO, 1968, Appendix A.
10. *Hansard*, 8 February 1966, col. 210.
11. *The Civil Service,* vol. 1, Report of the Committee, (Cmnd 3638), HMSO, 1968, p. 107.
12. ibid., p. 11.
13. ibid., p. 11.
14. ibid., p. 9.
15. ibid., p. 11.

16. ibid., p. 16.
17. Evidence presented by the Association of First Division Civil Servants to the Fulton Committee, reproduced in *The Civil Service,* vol. 5 (1), HMSO, 1968, pp. 105-6.
18. ibid., p. 105.
19. Engholm, Sir Basil. Article in the *Guardian* dated 16 May 1977.
20. *The Civil Service,* vol. 2: Report of the Management Consultancy Group, HMSO, 1968, p. 20.
21. ibid., pp. 20-21. For good measure the Management Consultancy Group also pointed out that this frequent movement of Administrators between different jobs:

> wastes the time of specialists (e.g. engineers, planning officers) and supporting staff to have yet another administrator to introduce to the problems with which they are jointly concerned, particularly when the administrator is unfamiliar with the methods and terms of the specialists. A particularly flagrant example was in one area in which specialists were heavily involved, where there had been five different Under Secretaries and five different Assistant Secretaries to be briefed and introduced in the last two years.
>
> It discourages the development of expertise in areas that industry has long decided need long-term professionalism – e.g. personnel management, training, finance. It also tends to impede the development of individual aptitudes.

22. *The Civil Service*, vol. 1, p. 18.
23. *The Civil Service,* vol. 2, pp. 58-9.
24. *Public Expenditure 1968/9 until 1973/4*, Cmnd 4234, HMSO, 1969.
25. *The Civil Service,* vol. 1, p. 17.
26. ibid., p. 46.

Chapter Three: WHAT FULTON RECOMMENDED

1. *The Civil Service*, vol. 1. Report of the Committee 1966-68, (Cmnd. 3638, June 1968), p. 11.
2. ibid., p. 19.
3. ibid., p. 20.
4. ibid., p. 27.
5. ibid., p. 28.
6. ibid., p. 57.
7. ibid., p. 59.
8. ibid., p. 94.
9. ibid., p. 12.
10. ibid., p. 36.
11. ibid., p. 54.
12. See p. 33 et seq.
13. *The Civil Service*, vol. 1, op. cit., p. 177.
14. ibid., p. 64.
15. ibid., p. 71.

16. ibid., p. 74.
17. ibid., p. 74.
18. ibid., pp. 77-8.
19. ibid., p. 36.
20. ibid., p. 84.
21. ibid., p. 82.
22. Crossman, Richard, op. cit., pp. 98-107.

Chapter Four: HOW ARMSTRONG DEFEATED FULTON

1. Quoted in Garrett, John, *The Management of Government*, Pelican Books, 1972, p. 48.
2. *Hansard* (Lords), 24 July 1968, col. 1084.
3. ibid., col. 1105.
4. ibid., col. 1110.
5. ibid., col. 1086.
6. ibid., col. 1110.
7. *Hansard* (Commons), 21 November 1968, col. 1662.
8. *Hansard*, 26 June 1968, col. 456.
9. ibid.
10. Interview with author.
11. Interview with author.
12. ibid.
13. *Hansard*, op. cit., col. 456.
14. Interview with author.
15. *Developments on Fulton*, Civil Service National Whitley Council, February 1969, p. 24.
16. *The Removal of Class Barriers*, IPCS Internal Paper, December 1968, pp. 1-3.
17. Reproduced in *Management Services in Government*, May 1976, CSD, pp. 60-61.
18. Interview with author.
19. *The Study of Structure*, confidential CSD paper, April 1969, p. 2.
20. *The Civil Service*, vol. 1, op. cit., pp. 67-70.
21. *The Study of Structure*, op. cit., p. 2.
22. ibid., pp. 7-8.

Chapter Five: THE LOST REFORMS

1. *The Civil Service: Government Observations on the Eleventh Report from the Expenditure Committee*, HMSO, 1978, para 2.
2. *Eleventh Report from the Expenditure Committee, 1976-77*, vol. 2, Part 1, HMSO, 1977, p. 1.
3. ibid., p. 17.
4. *The Civil Service*, vol. 1, Report of the Committee, para 255.
5. *Expenditure Committee*. op. cit., vol. 2, part 1, p. 1.
6. *The Civil Service*, op. cit., recommendation 118.
7. *Expenditure Committee*, op. cit., vol. 2, part 1, p. 9.

8. *The Civil Service:* vol. 1, Report of the Committee, op. cit., para 124.
9. *Civil Service Commission Annual Report 1976*, table 2.
10. Interview with author.
11. *The Civil Service,* op. cit., vol. 1, para 128.
12. *Hansard,* 26 June 1968, col. 457.
13. *Expenditure Committee,* op. cit., vol. 2, part 1, p. 17.
14. ibid., p. 18.
15. ibid., vol. 3, p. 977.
16. ibid., vol. 2, part 1, p. 21.
17. ibid., vol. 2, part 2, p. 547 (1978 statistics from CSD).
18. ibid., p. 547.
19. *The Civil Service,* op. cit., vol. 1, para 37.
20. *Expenditure Committee,* op. cit., vol. 2, part 1, p. 29
21. *Observer,* 25 September 1977.
22. *Expenditure Committee,* op. cit., vol. 3, p. 630.
23. *Observer,* op. cit.
24. *The Civil Service,* op. cit., vol. 1, para 37.
25. *Civil Service Statistics 1979,* HMSO, 1979, table 4.
26. *Expenditure Committee,* op. cit., vol. 2, part 2, pp. 627-628.
27. *Civil Service Statistics 1979,* op. cit., table 4.
28. *Expenditure Committee,* op. cit., vol. 2, part 2, pp. 816-817.
29. Letter from Kenneth Sharp, 4 April 1978.
30. *Expenditure Committee,* op. cit., vol. 1, para 97.
31. *Hansard,* 21 November 1968, col. 1551.
32. *The Civil Service College 1970-71,* HMSO, 1972, p. 25.
33. ibid., pp. 27-28.
34. *The Civil Service College 1971-72,* HMSO, 1973, p. 3.
35. ibid., p. 34.
36. *The Civil Service College 1972-73,* HMSO, 1974, p. 14.
37. *Report on Civil Service Training,* CSD, 1974, para 5.3.
38. ibid.
39. *The Civil Service College 1974-75,* HMSO, 1976, pp. 3, 6.
40. *The Civil Service College 1975-76,* HMSO, 1977, pp. 10, 13.
41. *The Civil Service,* op. cit., vol. 1, para 164.
42. ibid.
43. *Expenditure Committee,* op. cit., vol. 2, part 1, pp. 22-24.
44. ibid., p. 51.
45. ibid.
46. ibid., pp. 77-78.
47. ibid., p. 115.
48. ibid., p. 121.
49. ibid., vol. 1, para 120.
50. ibid., para. 115.
51. *The Civil Service: Government Observations,* op. cit., para 45.
52. ibid., para 70.
53. *Expenditure Committee,* vol. 1, op. cit., para 1.
54. *The Civil Service: Government Observations on the 11th Report from the Expenditure Committee,* HMSO, 1978, para 2.

Chapter Six: RECRUITING AN ÉLITE

1. Figures supplied by Civil Service Department.
2. *Civil Service Statistics 1979,* op. cit., table 6.
3. Quoted in *The Civil Service,* op. cit., vol 1, p. 108.
4. ibid., p. 111.
5. Quoted in Cohen, Emmeline, *The Growth of the British Civil Service 1780-1939,* George Allen & Unwin, 1941, p. 106.
6. *Eleventh Report from the Expenditure Committee,* op. cit. vol. 1, para 13.
7. *Civil Service Statistics,* op. cit., table 8.
8. *Civil Service Careers 1978: GCE/CSE level,* Civil Service Commission, 1978, p. 4.
9. *Civil Service Statistics,* op. cit., table 8.
10. Sample test supplied by Civil Service Commission.
11. *Civil Service Statistics,* op. cit., table 10.
12. *Civil Service Careers,* op. cit., p. 6.
13. *The Times,* 30 January 1978.
14. CSC Executive and Clerical Division: Board Chairman's Newsletter no. 2, February 1977.
15. *Executive Officer Appointments 1977,* CSC, 1977, p. 24.
16. ibid., p. 25.
17. Ansky, Edgar, *An Introduction to Selection Interviewing,* CSC, 1977, p. 7.
18. ibid., p. 10.
19. ibid., p. 10.
20. ibid., p. 13.
21. ibid., pp. 14-15.
22. ibid., p. 23.
23. *Expenditure Committee,* op. cit., vol. 2, part 1, pp. 243, 245.
24. Interview with author.
25. *Application of Race Relations Policy in the Civil Service,* HMSO, 1978, p. 60.
26. ibid., p. 62.
27. Quoted in *New Statesman,* 24 November 1978.
28. *The Civil Service,* op. cit., para 76.
29. ibid., recommendation 28.
30. *The Method II System of Selection: Report of the Committee of Inquiry 1969,* HMSO, 1969, pp. 82, 84.
31. Quoted in Garrett, John, *The Management of Government,* op. cit., p. 52.
32. *Expenditure Committee,* op. cit., vol. 3, p. 1091.
33. ibid, para. 13.
35. Figures supplied by CSC.
36. *Civil Service Commission Annual Report 1978,* CSC, 1979, p. 50.
37. Note by CSC for Lord Crowther-Hunt, 1977, para 7.4.
38. ibid., para 5.1.

39. ibid., para 6.4.
40. *Expenditure Committee,* op. cit., vol. 2, part 1, p. 256.
41. Interview with author.
42. *Civil Service Commission Annual Report 1978,* op. cit., p. 50.
43. Sleigh, Jonathan, 'Civil Service Selection', *New Statesman,* 29 April 1977.
44. ibid.
45. Interview with author.
46. Cunningham, George, 'Myths and Mandarins', *New Statesman,* 23 September 1977.

Chapter Seven: HOW TO BECOME A MANDARIN

1. *Civil Service Statistics 1979,* HMSO, 1979, table 9.
2. *Expenditure Committee, 1976-77,* op. cit., vol. 3, p. 883.
3. Interview with author.
4. *Expenditure Committee,* op. cit., vol. 1, para 20.
5. *Report of the Administration Trainee Review Committee,* CSD, 1978, p. 23.
6. ibid., p. 34.
7. *Careers in Administration,* HMSO, 1977, pp. 6-7.
8. Interview with author.
9. ibid.
10. ibid.
11. *Careers in Administration,* op. cit., p. 9.
12. *The Times,* 3 October 1978.
13. *Expenditure Committee,* op. cit., vol. 2, part 1, p. 316.
14. Interview with author.
15. ibid.
16. ibid.
17. ibid.
18. *Careers in Administration,* op. cit., p. 10.
19. *The Civil Service,* op. cit., vol. 5, part 2, pp 930-931.
20. ibid., vol. 2, p. 19.
21. Interview with author.
22. Sheriff, Peta, *Career Patterns in the Higher Civil Service,* HMSO, 1976, table 25.
23. Interview with author.
24. *Careers in Administration,* op. cit., pp. 12-13.
25. Interview with author.
26. ibid.
27. ibid.
28. *Newsweek,* BBC TV, 9 November 1978.
29. CSD standards quoted in *IPCS Handbook 1977,* pp. 505-509.
30. *Civil Service Yearbook 1978,* HMSO, 1978, cols. 437-445.
31. Interview with author.
32. ibid.
33. Interview with author.
34. *Hansard,* 7 November 1978, col. 142.
35. ibid., col. 139.

36. Interview with author.
37. ibid.
38. *Hansard,* 15 January 1979, cols. 1303-1304.
39. Wilson, Harold, 'The Governance of Britain', *Sphere,* 1977, p. 164.
40. *Expenditure Committee,* op. cit., vol. 2, part 2, p. 659.
41. ibid., vol. 2, part 1, p. 316.
42. ibid.
43. ibid., vol. 2, part 2, p. 547.
44. Interview with author.
45. *Hansard,* 7 November 1978, cols. 797-799.
46. Interview with author.
47. ibid.

Chapter Eight: THE PERMANENT SECRETARIES

1. Interview with author.
2. ibid.
3. *The Civil Service,* op. cit., vol. 1, para 260.
4. *Expenditure Committee,* op. cit., p. 2.
5. Interview with author.
6. Crossman, Richard, op. cit., vol. 1, p. 122.
7. *Talking Politics,* BBC Radio 4, 4 June 1977.
8. 'Ministers and their Mandarins', lecture at London School of Economics.
9. *Tonight,* BBC TV, 13 November 1975.
10. Letter to Heads of Departments, 6 January 1976.
11. Interview with author.
12. *Sunday Times,* 4 December 1977.
13. Interview with author.
14. ibid.
15. ibid.
16. Civil Service Department; Who's Who.
17. Kelsall, R.K., *Higher Civil Servants in Britain,* Routledge & Kegan Paul, 1955, table 20.
18. Sheriff, Peta, op. cit., pp. 37, 47.
19. *Hansard,* 14 July 1977, written answers cols. 203-268.
20. Sheriff, op. cit., p. 51.
21. *Hansard,* 15 January 1979, cols. 1407-1408.
22. Civil Service Department; Who's Who; Directory of Directors.
23. *Royal Commission on the Standards of Conduct in Government,* HMSO, 1976: annex 13.
24. Civil Service Department.
25. *Guardian,* 23 January 1979.
26. Crossman, op. cit., vol. 3, p. 732.
27. ibid., p. 755.
28. Interview with author.

Chapter Nine: MANDARINS AND MINISTERS

1. *Expenditure Committee,* op. cit., vol. 2, p. 764 (my italics)
2. ibid., vol. 3, p. 785.
3. Chapters 4 and 5 above.
4. *The Response to the Fulton Report,* CSD, 1975, para 2.
5. *The Civil Service,* op. cit., vol. 1, p. 57.
6. *Response to the Fulton Report,* op. cit., paras 131 and 132.
7. OECD Report.
8. *Guardian,* 11 February 1978.
9. Headey, Bruce, *British Cabinet Ministers,* George Allen and Unwin, 1975.
10. *Expenditure Committee,* op. cit., vol. 1, p. lxiii.
11. ibid.
12. ibid., pp. lxiii and lxiv.
13. ibid., pp. lxiii and lxiv.
14. ibid., p. lxvi.
15. ibid., pp. lxxix and lxxx.
16. Interview with one of the authors.
17. Interview with one of the authors.
18. *Hansard,* 7 November 1978, col. 798.
19. Interview with one of the authors.
20. *The Civil Service,* op. cit., vol. 4, p. 38.
21. Crossman, Richard, op. cit., vol. 1, p. 168.
22. ibid., p. 385.
23. op. cit., vol. 2, pp. 753-4.
24. op. cit., vol. 2, p. 753.
25. Haines, J., *The Politics of Power,* Jonathan Cape, 1977.
26. Williams, Marcia, *Inside Number 10,* Weidenfeld and Nicolson, 1972.
27. *Hansard,* 7 November 1978.
28. Pages 169-70 above.

Chapter Ten: CIVIL SERVANTS AND PARLIAMENT

1. Bagehot, Walter, *The English Constitution,* Fontana edition, 1963, p. 168.
2. ibid., p 43.
3. *First Report from the Select Committee on Procedure 1977-78,* vol 3, HMSO, 1978, p. 5.
4. ibid., vol 2, p. 142.
5. *Hansard,* 16 February 1972, cols. 531-532.
6. *Sunday Times,* 22 January 1978.
7. *The State of the Nation,* Granada TV, 24 July 1973.
8. Ridley, Nicholas, *Industry and the Civil Service,* Aims of Industry, 1973, p. 4.
9. Bagehot, op. cit., p. 177.
10. Mainly arising from *Sunday Times* inquiries; quoted by Harold

Evans, speech to the Company of Stationers and Newspaper Makers, 14 February 1979.

11. *Fourth Report from the Expenditure Committee, 1975-76*, HMSO, 1976, pp. 4, 6, 10.
12. ibid., p. 22.
13. ibid., p. 25.
14. ibid., p. 30.
15. ibid., p. 30.
16. ibid., p. 32.
17. ibid., p. 34.
18. ibid., p. 55.
19. *Procedure Committee*, op. cit., vol. 1, p. 39.
20. ibid., p. 40.
21. ibid., p. 40.
22. ibid., p. 41.
23. ibid., p. 42.
24. ibid., p. 43.
25. ibid., pp. 43-44.
26. ibid., p. 44.
27. ibid., p. 45.
28. ibid., p. 45.
29. ibid., p. 45.
30. ibid., para 7.15.
31. ibid., para 5.24.
32. ibid., para 6.36.
33. ibid., para 6.37.
34. ibid., paras 6.39, 6.40.
35. *Sunday Times*, 22 January 1978.
36. *The State of the Nation*, op. cit., 25 July 1973.
37. *Hansard*, 20 February 1979, cols. 291-292.
38. *The State of the Nation*, op. cit.
39. *Procedure Committee*, op. cit., para 6.33.
40. Normanton, E.L., *The Accountability and Audit of Governments*, Manchester University Press, 1966.
41. *Procedure Committee*, op. cit., vol. 2, p. 133.
42. *Eleventh Report from the Expenditure Committee, 1976-77*, op. cit., vol. 2, part 2, p. 651.
43. *Procedure Committee*, op. cit., p. 135.
44. ibid., p. 134.
45. ibid., p. 135.
46. ibid., p. 135.
47. ibid., p. 136.
48. *Third Special Report from the Expenditure Committee 1977-78: Observations by the Comptroller and Auditor General*, HMSO, 1978, para 10.
49. *Report by the Committee of Inquiry on the Crown Agents*, HMSO, 1977, para 417.
50. ibid., paras 418, 419.
51. *Fourth Report from the Committee of Public Accounts, 1974-75,*

HMSO, 1975, p. 245.
52. *Sunday Times,* 19 December 1976.
53. *World in Action,* Granada TV, 8 May 1978.
54. Memorandum by the Comptroller and Auditor General to the Public Accounts Committee, 5 June 1978.

Chapter Eleven: CIVIL SERVANTS AND SECRECY

1. *Departmental Committee on Section 2 of the Official Secrets Act 1911,* HMSO, 1972, vol. 1, para 275.
2. ibid., vol. 4, pp. 188-189.
3. *Sunday Times,* 23 July 1978.
4. *New Society,* 17 June 1976.
5. *Hansard,* 22 November 1976, col. 1887.
6. *Hansard,* 22 November 1976, cols. 26-27.
7. Briefing by Lord Peart, Lord Privy Seal.
8. *The Times,* 20 July 1978.
9. *Reform of Section 2 of the Official Secrets Act 1911,* HMSO, 1978, para 13.
10. ibid., paras 46, 47.
11. *Newsweek,* BBC TV, 9 November 1978.
12. ibid.
13. *New Statesman,* 10 November 1978.
14. Interview with author.
15. ibid.
16. *Newsweek,* op. cit.
17. *Hansard,* 7 November 1978, cols. 743, 748.
18. *Sunday Times,* 20 June 1976.
19. Quoted in *Eleventh Report from the Expenditure Committee,* op. cit., vol. 3, p. 111.
20. ibid.
21. *Newsweek,* op. cit.

Chapter Twelve: POSTSCRIPT: 'THE BIGGEST PRESSURE GROUP'

1. Richard Crossman: *The Diaries of a Cabinet Minister,* vol. 1, p.30; Hamish Hamilton & Jonathan Cape, 1975.
2. *Management Services in Government,* November 1979, p.184, CSD.
3. *Sunday Times,* 16 December 1979.
4. Letter from Sir Keith Joseph, 5 April 1977.
5. Letter from Leslie Chapman, 25 July 1977.
6. Letter from Sir Keith Joseph, 15 May 1978.
7. Letter from Sir Keith Joseph, 3 August 1978.
8. Letter from Leslie Chapman, 20 July 1979.
9. Letter from Richard Wilding to Establishment Officers, 12

June 1979.

10. Institution of Professional Civil Servants circular to officers, July 1979.
11. Civil Service Department Press Release, 6 December 1979.
12. *Sunday Times*, 9 December 1979.
13. CSD press release op. cit.
14. *Times*, 27 November 1979.
15. *Times*, 18. December 1979.
16. *Hansard*, 24 May 1979, written answers col. 179.
17. *Times*, 30 November 1979.
18. Protection of Official Information Bill S.1(1).
19. Op. cit. S.8(1).
20. Op. cit. S.9.
21. *Times*, 14 November 1979.
22. *Report of the Committee on the Selection Procedure for the Recruitment of Administration Trainees*, Civil Service Commission, 1979.
23. *Times*, 18 December 1979.
24. *Financial Times*, 4 December 1979; *Sunday Times*, 6 January 1980.
25. Keith Middlemas, *Politics in Industrial Society*, pp. 18-19, Deutsch 1979.

INDEX